Science Adventures

Indoor and Outdoor Experiences for Young Children

by Elizabeth A. Sherwood, Robert A. Williams, and Robert E. Rockwell

Thanks to

- our editors, Kathy Charner and Charlie Clark, for their support, encouragement, and expertise
- Keith Mitchell, Ph.D., photographer and coordinator for Technology Initiatives, Texas Regional Collaboratives for Excellence in Science Teaching, University of Texas, Austin, TX
- Shawn Quinn, photographer and Bob Williams' son-in-law from Titusville, FL
- the students in Elizabeth's graduate curriculum class for reviewing many of our ideas
- Bill Brinson, photographer at Southern Illinois University, Edwardsville, IL
- Roxy Rodriguez, teacher at Generations Child Development Center 1, 8203 Sam Rayburn Drive, Austin, TX
- Stephanie Henschen, teacher at Southern Illinois University Early Childhood Center, Edwardsville, IL
- Generations Child Development Center 1, 8203 Sam Rayburn Drive, Austin, TX, where children helped us gather ideas and where pictures were taken
- Southern Illinois University Early Childhood Center, Edwardsville, IL, where children helped us gather ideas and where pictures were taken

Dedication

To my grandchildren, Phillip and Anna, my favorite companions for playing in the rain and digging in the dirt.
—Elizabeth A. Sherwood

I would like to dedicate this book to my grandchildren, Jeffrey, Julianna, and Katerina, who will move forward in this world with so much more to learn and experience. I know that the world of nature is adding its sanity to their lives.
—Robert A. Williams

To my great-grandchildren, Tyler, Megan, Ethan, and Mya, may you learn to know and love the natural world.
—Robert E. Rockwell

GH19436
A Gryphon House Book

Early Childhood Education

Elizabeth A. Sherwood
Robert A. Williams
Robert E. Rockwell

Science Adventures

Nature Activities for Young Children

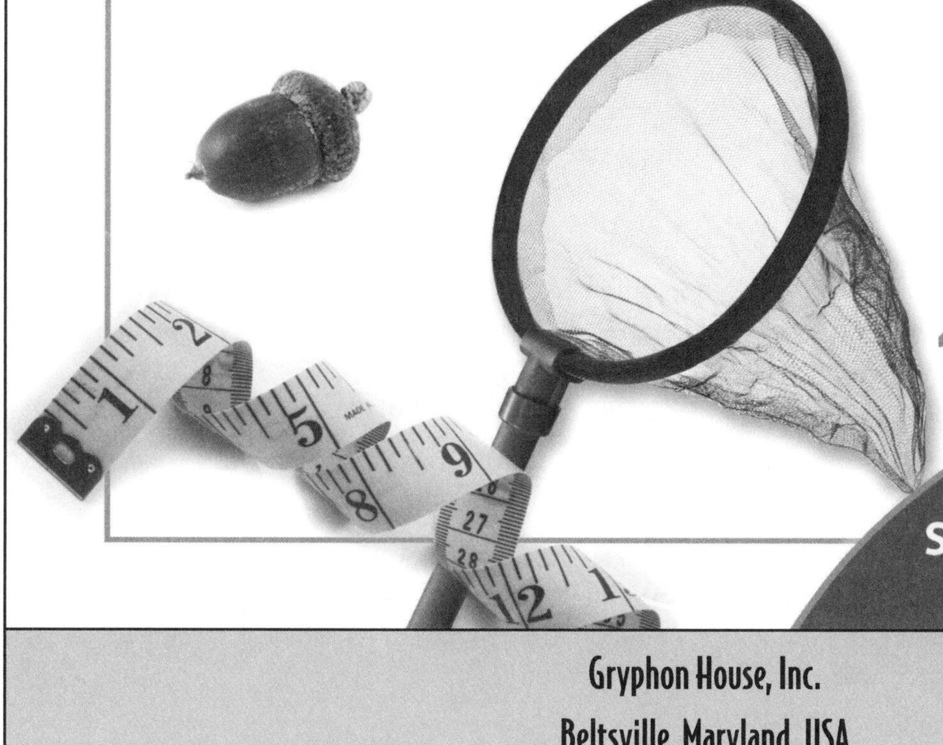

Science Content Standards Included

Gryphon House, Inc.
Beltsville, Maryland, USA

Published by Gryphon House, Inc.
10726 Tucker Street, Beltsville, MD 20705
800.638.0928; 301.595.9500; 301.595.0051 (fax)

Visit us on the web at www.gryphonhouse.com

Illustrations by Kathi Whelan Dery
Cover Art: © 2007 Straight Shots Product Photography, www.we-get-it-shot.com, for Gryphon House, Inc.

Library of Congress Cataloging-in-Publication Information

Sherwood, Elizabeth.
  Science adventures : indoor and outdoor experiences for young children /by Elizabeth A. Sherwood, Robert A. Williams, Robert E. Rockwell.
      p. cm.
  Includes index.
  ISBN: 978-0-87659-015-7
  1. Science—Study and teaching (Early childhood)—Activity programs. I. Sherwood, Elizabeth A. II. Williams, Robert A. III. Title.
  LB1139.5.S35R63 2008
  372.35'044--dc22

                          2007027504

Bulk purchase

Gryphon House books are available for special premiums and sales promotions as well as for fund-raising use. Special editions or book excerpts also can be created to specification. For details, contact the Director of Marketing at Gryphon House.

Disclaimer

Gryphon House, Inc. and the authors cannot be held responsible for damage, mishap, or injury incurred during the use of or because of activities in this book. Appropriate and reasonable caution and adult supervision of children involved in activities and corresponding to the age and capability of each child involved, is recommended at all times. Do not leave children unattended at any time. Observe safety and caution at all times.

Gryphon House is a member of the Green Press Initiative, a nonprofit program dedicated to supporting publishers in their efforts to reduce their use of fiber-sourced forests. This book is made of 30% post-consumer waste. For further information, visit www.greenpressinitiative.org.

Table of Contents

5+ Activities

Appendix 255

Index 264

Introduction

Science and Young Children

Whether children live in an urban, suburban, or rural setting, they need experiences with nature. Nature provides a multitude of resources for children to learn about themselves, about others, and about their world. Most adults say that their bond with nature began with experiences in their own neighborhoods, with whatever natural space and materials they had within walking distance. Simply playing outside as children sets the stage for lifelong connections (Stephens, 2002). By using materials from nature to introduce children to the basic concepts of scientific inquiry, we are providing them with the opportunity to develop a bond with nature and the outdoors. It is important that we provide children with opportunities to learn about and interact with nature because, for many reasons, children are not always able to spend time outdoors when they are at home (White, 2004). You do not need access to a wildlife preserve to provide wonderful natural experiences for children. Every setting—urban, suburban, and rural—has the resources to explore weather and the changing seasons. Every teacher can find ways for children to observe growing plants, whether they are dandelions in a crack in the blacktop, grass growing in a paper cup on the windowsill, tomato plants in a community garden, or the sycamore tree on the corner up the street. These encounters, large and small, can have an impact that lasts a lifetime, and each time you take children outside and share an appreciation of the natural world, you will help to reinforce that impact.

Using natural materials to conduct science activities, or bringing the children outdoors as they learn about science, opens up a never-ending world of exploration. Children want to be active learners and explorers; they continually seek to learn about their world and how to function within it. This process involves curiosity, trust, and a desire to learn. Your role is to supply the materials they need to explore. For example, not many young children have experience with a pulley. If you provide the materials, children can explore this complex physics tool and develop a basic understanding of how it works. Additionally, setting up the pulley outdoors means that interested children can continue their explorations any time they are outside. Teachers will have fewer concerns about the noise and activity level created when children are busy hauling blocks or rocks outside instead of in the classroom!

Benefits of Outdoor Activities

The activities in this book encourage children to learn in all settings, but stress the importance of their being able to experience science and nature outdoors. The benefits of spending time outdoors with children go beyond developing an appreciation of nature and an understanding of science concepts. Spending time outdoors

◆ creates a more optimistic outlook in both children and adults (Kuo and Taylor, 2004) and may reduce symptoms of hyperactivity and attention deficit disorder (Louv, 2005; Taylor, Kuo, and Sullivan, 2001). While the overall effect on young children of spending time outdoors is not entirely understood, it is clear that it has a positive impact.

◆ enables children to practice and develop physical skills and improves motor development. Time spent outdoors strongly correlates with increased physical activity in children (Sallis et al., 2003). This is a key factor in addressing the challenge of childhood obesity. It is also has a positive impact on self-esteem and confidence.

◆ supports creativity and resourcefulness as children create their own materials for play and learning. Children realize they can have fun with objects they find or make themselves.

◆ stimulates children's brain development and learning (Rivkin, 1995 & 1997). In addition, active play, the kind we stress in many of our activities, improves brain function and releases chemicals in the brain that improve both the storage and retrieval of knowledge (Jensen, 2000).

◆ develops children's social skills in an environment that differs from a classroom and seems to give some children more confidence. Time and time again, we have observed a quiet child come alive when sharing a discovery with other children. We have seen challenging children become focused and engaged as they gently hand a living creature to a friend. Research is beginning to support our observations (Louv, 2005).

◆ provides opportunities for children to explore, question, and develop theories about how things work. We control things in our classrooms, at least to some degree. In contrast, nature provides a constantly changing view of our world that can be seen over and over, day after day. Through experiences with nature, children can develop a sense that they are connected to something larger than themselves (Bohling-Philippi, 2006). They begin to be aware that the sun comes out every day and that seeds that seem like little bits of nothing grow into interesting plants.

◆ enhances children's understanding of the environment. The importance of outdoor learning and the lasting influence that it has on attitudes in adulthood is well documented. Outdoor activities provide opportunities for children to develop attitudes and skills that will enable them to become environmentally responsible adults. This is especially important because the relationship between children and

their environmental experiences has changed dramatically over the last decade or more. Many children are uncomfortable outside and show a marked preference for indoor play and electronic entertainment (Nelson, 2006). We hope to counter that trend by providing positive outdoor experiences for children.

While it is crucial that children have the opportunity to experience the outdoors as much as possible, sometimes this can be difficult. Whenever possible, let the children explore and experience the activities outside, but modify the activities if your location, weather, or time of year makes it impossible to bring children outside.

This book is for anyone who wants to help children develop a relationship with the environment. The activities are simple to do and are designed to introduce children to the outdoors and to how scientists work.

How to Use This Book

We designed the sections of this book to give you, briefly and simply, all the information needed to carry out the activities successfully.

The short introduction to each activity provides enough information to help you decide if it will be appropriate for the children you teach. A quick glance at **What to Do** and **Observing and Assessing the Children** should confirm this.

The **3+, 4+,** and **5+** boxes appearing at the beginning of each activity indicate the age appropriateness for each activity. These age ranges are approximate and based on our experience with children engaged in these and similar activities.

Remember, children have individual knowledge that will influence their responses during a particular activity. Use your judgment to determine whether the children are ready to participate in each activity. Consider changing the direction of an activity to suit your children's abilities. For older children, consider using some of the activities as introductions for more advanced learning experiences.

Each chapter begins with the simplest activities and ends with the most challenging ones.

Standards are increasingly crucial in current education practices; therefore, we identified the **Science Content Standards** and **Science Process Skills** addressed in each of the activities. The science content standards and science processes in this book are a combination of national standards and various state early learning standards. You may need to modify these skills and standards to meet your educational program's own standards or guidelines. A more in-depth discussion of standards is on page 12.

Things You Can Use lists materials needed for the activity. In most cases, these are readily available and often are free or inexpensive. If you do not have the materials needed, substitute other appropriate items. Read through the activity and use what is available.

Words You Can Use contains vocabulary appropriate for each activity. Some words may sound too advanced for young children, but keep in mind that the words are not to be memorized by the children. Exposure to the vocabulary words is what is important. Children, and all of us, learn new words by hearing them used frequently in a meaningful context. Young children are no exception. You will be amazed at how quickly young children learn to use many of the terms. Even those words the children do not learn can become familiar through your use of them, and may eventually enter the children's vocabulary. Knowing the name of a creature or plant is fun and it is a means of communicating about and focusing in on observations.

Things to think about with **Words You Can Use** are:

- The best way to introduce words is while conducting an activity. Repeat the words in context as many times as appropriate during the activity.
- Listen for the children to use the words to describe their actions during the activity.

- Listen for the children to use the words during another activity.
- Several days later review the words in the same or a similar context.
- Repeat or extend the activity, again using the words in context.

Before the Activity provides directions for any preparation that is necessary.

What to Do consists of the simple directions that make up the core of the activity. To determine the appropriateness of the activities given the skills and interests of the children, read the activity from start to finish and then ask yourself:

- Do the children have the skills to do this activity, or should they do other activities first? (For example, children need to be able to sort things into groups before they can do some of the more complex classifying activities.)
- What is the best place to do the activity?
- How many children should participate at one time?
- Is this something all the children will enjoy?

Want to Do More? provides suggestions for building on and expanding the initial activities. Most of these ideas are at the same skill level as the original activity, although a few are more complex. You may find that the **Want to Do More?** activities are more suitable for the children you teach than the actual activities. Always use what works best for the children. Reading the ideas and activities in **Want to Do More?** before beginning the main activity will give you numerous possibilities for extending or adapting the experience while it is in progress rather than waiting for another opportunity.

Learning in Other Curricular Areas shows how the activity meets standards for other curricular areas, such as mathematics and literacy.

Observing and Assessing Children includes an assessment component, which is essential to each activity. While the children are involved in the activity, make and record observations to document their learning. To check for understanding, talk with individual children as they work. Can the child talk about the activity and use some or all of the related vocabulary words? Some children will have better language skills and be able to share their knowledge verbally, while other children may be better at showing you what they have learned. These conversations and observations will tell you whether a child has learned key concepts or skills. For assessment purposes, base your observations on the behavior of each child and not on the children as a group.

If a child does not master a skill, repeat the activity with the child. Children at this age often want and need to repeat activities again and again to gain a sense of mastery. Do not be too quick to move on to something new. You can also provide a similar activity with the same concept. Keeping continuous records of your observations of each child's progress will enable you to document learning and determine how best to support the development of learning.

Sidebars provide special information or connections to support or help you teach the children in your class. Some sidebars provide content information that might be helpful or safety information that will protect you or the children.

Science Content Standards

The National Science Teachers Association (NSTA) and the American Association for the Advancement of Science (AAAS) began developing national standards for science in the early 1990s. In 1996, the National Research Council (NRC) developed the National Science Education Standards. Although these content standards have not been adopted nationally, they serve as models for each state. These standards were initially developed for K–12 students.

More recently, individual states and the federal Head Start program have developed early learning standards or guidelines that define expected outcomes for children prior to kindergarten. The website of the Early Childhood Assessment

Consortium of the Council of Chief State School Board Officers provides links to the early learning standards of each state at **www.ccsso.org/content/PDFs/ECstandards.pdf.** Simply scroll through the list to find your own state. The Head Start Child Outcomes Framework is online at **www.headstartinfo.org/pdf/ hsoutcomespath28ppREV.pdf.** Most local childcare resource and referral agencies also provide information and professional development about early learning standards. Many states have combined the national science standards to create fewer standards overall.

The National Academy of Sciences developed science content standard categories for grades K–12. We adapted portions of these content standard categories to meet the educational needs of children ages 3–6. We used five of the eight content standard categories from the National Academy of Sciences to organize the chapters of this book. The standards that we used to organize the chapters are: Science as Inquiry; Physical Science; Life Science; Earth and Space Science; and Science and Technology. We also incorporated the content found in the National Academy of Sciences' final two categories—Science in Personal and Social Perspectives, and History and the Nature of Science—in activities throughout the book.

Below is a list of the descriptions we used to explain how each activity relates to science content standards. Because we designed the activities in this book for children younger than those for which the National Academy of Sciences designed its standards, we modified our descriptions so they also align with state and Head Start standards for children ages 3–6, in order to make these descriptions more effective educational tools for teachers of children in that age group.

Standard A—Science as Inquiry
Ages 3–4:
- Uses senses for observation
- Asks questions and uses active exploration to find answers
- Explores through trial and error

Ages 4–5:

◆ Describes and records observations (drawings, dictation)
◆ Makes predictions based on prior experiences
◆ Makes comparisons among different observations
◆ Explores in response to teacher's questions

Ages 5–6:

◆ Collects, describes, and records observations (charts, photographs, drawings, journals)
◆ Uses resources for acquiring information
◆ Initiates different approaches to solve a problem or answer a question

Standard B—Physical Science

Ages 3–4:

◆ Observes and interacts with physical science tools such as magnets and ramps
◆ Matches like objects

Ages 4–5:

◆ Uses descriptive language when making observations of objects (rough, cool, bumpy)
◆ Begins to sort and categorize objects by physical characteristics

Ages 5–6:

◆ Uses more than one sense in making observations
◆ Uses more complex descriptive language
◆ Discusses predictions and explanations about experiences

Standard C—Life Science

Ages 3–4:

◆ Begins to use simple, descriptive language about living things
◆ Begins to understand the differences between living and nonliving things

Ages 4–5:

◆ Notes similarities and differences among living things and can describe them
◆ Begins to understand the needs of living things

Ages 5–6:

◆ Describes and documents different environments (urban, rural, forest)
◆ Begins to understand the effects of people on environments (littering, recycling)

Standard D—Earth and Space Science

Ages 3–4:

◆ Explores the characteristics of soil, rocks, and water
◆ Makes simple observations of the movement of sun and shadows
◆ Uses weather vocabulary (cloudy, snowy, hot)

Ages 4–5:

◆ Describes changes in seasons and observable weather patterns
◆ Select appropriate clothing and activities for different weather or seasons

Ages 5–6:

◆ Describes and documents different environments (urban, rural, forest)
◆ Begins to understand the effects of people on environments (littering, recycling)

Standard E—Science and Technology

Ages 3–4:

◆ Begins to explore with tools of sciences (magnifiers, levers)

Ages 4–5:

◆ Uses scientific tools for investigation (balance, measuring cups, thermometers)
◆ Begins to distinguish between natural and manufactured objects

Ages 5–6:

◆ Becomes increasingly accurate in the use of scientific tools
◆ Describes how people use tools to do work

Note: The authors chose not to include activities directly related to the following two areas as they address concepts that are beyond the capabilities of most young children.

Standard F—Science in Personal and Social Perspective

Standard G—History and the Nature of Science

Complete information on the national standards is available on the National Academy Press website at www.nap.edu/readingroom/books/nses/.

Science Process Skills

Scientists use science processes every day to accomplish their work. They use the processes to acquire information and to understand how the world works. With three- to six-year-old children, it is best to focus primarily on the processes of observing, classifying, communicating, and measuring. These processes are the foundation of exploration and learning. With your support, as children develop and gain more experience, they will begin to use more complex processes, such as predicting, inferring, and making models. Both predictions and inferences require having some experience with the materials and the procedure. Young children also need your direct guidance. For example, if you give children unfamiliar objects and ask whether they will sink or float, the children will likely just guess, having no empirical evidence on which to base an answer. Your support helps children think about what they know and have observed with other objects sinking and floating. This way, they can learn to predict. Simply saying, "That car is made of wood. What happened to the other wooden objects we put in the water?" can help children pause and think. This thought process changes their answer from a guess to a prediction.

The most basic science process skill is observation. At the preschool level, it is acceptable to introduce the other basic processes together or in no particular order. The secondary process skills use the basic ones to complete more-advanced skills and assume higher-level functioning. Some advanced processes require skills that are too difficult for young children. These skills are best for the children to explore when they are older.

The activities in the book develop the following:

Basic Science Process Skills (young children can engage in these processes independently)
- Observing
- Classifying
- Communicating
- Measuring

Secondary Science Process Skills (young children can engage in these processes with a teacher's help)
- Predicting
- Inferring
- Interpreting data
- Constructing models

Advanced Science Process Skills (young children cannot meaningfully engage in these processes)
- Identifying and controlling variables
- Defining operationally
- Experimenting

The content standards and science process skills provide broad guidelines for children's learning. The following chart offers additional guidance about appropriate experiences for young children by providing examples of what you might expect children to achieve from the ages of three to six. It is important to remember that the descriptions provided are loosely related to age, as the development of young children varies widely even among children the same age.

Each pair of sample activities listed addresses similar content or processes, with the second activity building on the experiences provided in the first activity. You may choose to select activities in this way. What is most important in planning is your knowledge of individual children and their prior experiences, your professional judgment, and your familiarity with your early learning standards. This will guide you in choosing appropriate activities for use with your children.

SCIENCE CONTENT AREA	AGES 3–4	AGES 4–5	AGES 5–6
Science as Inquiry (Chapter 1)	Uses senses for observation Asks questions and uses active exploration to find answers Explores through trial and error Examples of Activities: Outdoor Collage (page 24) Pair Them Up Two By Two (page 28)	Describes and records observations (drawings, dictation) Makes predictions based on prior experiences Makes comparisons among different observations Explores in response to teacher's questions Examples of Activities: Can You Find It? (page 32) Can't Peek (page 50)	Collects, describes, and records observations (charts, photographs, drawings, journals) Uses resources for acquiring information Initiates different approaches to solve a problem or answer a question Examples of Activities: A Picnic Basket Full (page 66) Name It and Label It (page 72) **Physical Science (Chapter 2)**
Observes and interacts with physical science tools such as magnets and ramps	Can match like objects Examples of Activities: Clear Containers and a Sunny Day (page 80) Iron and Sand in a Bottle (page 86) Uses descriptive language when making observations of objects (rough, cool, bumpy)	Begins to sort and categorize objects by physical characteristics Examples of Activities: Acorns That Sink or Float (page 102) Pulley on a Limb (page 108) Uses more than one sense in making observations Uses more complex descriptive language	Can discuss predictions and explanations about experiences Examples of Activities: Moving Sunlight (page 120) Mirror Play Outside (page 128) **Life Science (Chapter 3)**
Begins to use simple descriptive language about living things Begins to understand the differences between	living and nonliving things Examples of Activities: Leaf Banners (page 130) Leaf Match (page 132) Notes similarities and differences among living things and can describe them Begins to understand the needs of living things	Examples of Activities: Ant Restaurant (page 144) Counting Leaves (page 148) Make comparisons and contrasts the different characteristics of living things with increased accuracy Can describe what some living	things need to survive Examples of Activities: A Tree Through Time (page 166) Go Fish for Plants (page 170) **SCIENCE CONTENT AREA** Earth and Space (Chapter 4)

	(cloudy, snowy, hot)	weather or seasons	recycling)
AGES 3–4 Explores the characteristics of soil, rocks, and water Makes simple observations of the movement of sun and shadows Uses weather vocabulary	Examples of Activities: A Settling Experience (page 176) Rocks That Write (page 178) **AGES 4–5** Can describe changes in seasons and observable weather patterns Selects appropriate clothing and activities for different	Examples of Activities: Dirt Detectives (page 188) Coloring and Mixing Sand (page 192) **AGES 5–6** Can describe and document different environments (urban, rural, forest) Begins to understand the effects of people on environments (littering,	Examples of Activities: Sifting Soil (page 206) Drifting Snow (page 208) Science and Technology (Chapter 5)
Begins to explore with tools of sciences (magnifiers, levers) Examples of Activities: Can You Make a House? (page 210)	Elf House (page 212) Uses scientific tools for investigation (balance, measuring cups, thermometers) Begins to distinguish between natural and manufactured objects	Examples of Activities: Balancing Collections (page 216) How to Measure: How Hot or Cold? (page 232) Becomes increasingly accurate in the use of scientific tools Can describe how people use tools to do work Examples of Activities:	Meet the Meter Stick (page 248) Outdoor Temperatures (page 250) **Safety Outdoors** There are a number of key safety factors to consider when doing science

Safety Outdoors

There are a number of key safety factors to consider when doing science outdoors with young children.

Rules: Talk about any rules and precautions about which the children need to be aware. Do this in a non-threatening way so the children understand the rule is for their safety and protection. Children are more likely to follow rules when they understand the reasons behind them. You may have general rules that apply to most settings and special safety guidelines for specific locations, such as an area with water, fire ants, or a patch of poison ivy.

Supervision: Outdoor activities, just like indoor activities, require close and alert supervision. It is important to explain the activity, model how to do it, and then step back so the children can discover for themselves as they put their own skills and ideas into play.

Clothing: Clothing for outdoor activities will vary with the weather and climate conditions. Children should wear clothing that minimizes their exposure to the sun's ultraviolet rays (UV). Children under the age of six have skin that is sensitive to these rays and tends to burn easily. Protect their skin as well as yours by applying sunscreen with a minimum of 20 SPF (sun protection factor) 30 minutes before going outside, and reapply the sunscreen again every two hours.

Allergies: It is a school's responsibility to be aware of any allergies the children enrolled in their program may have. Outdoor activities may expose them to substances that might trigger an allergic response. Talk with the families and record any allergic reactions the children have in order to ensure the children avoid those substances when doing science activities outdoors. It is important that all staff members are aware of identifiers of allergic reactions, such as swelling, hives, sneezing, asthma, coughing, or difficulty breathing. Maintain updated medical information and emergency contact information for all children.

Animals: Establish safety procedures to protect the children from any animal hazards as well as to ensure the humane treatment of the animals. Many children have a natural impulse to touch animals. Teach them that they need to check with an adult before getting close to or touching any living creature. Because children can unintentionally be rough in handling things, it is often wise to place animals in a container of some kind, rather than allowing them to hold the animal. This may be the time to encourage the children to observe the animal rather than squash it.

Field trips: Field trips provide a way for the children to experience the environment in a setting beyond the classroom or playground. Before taking a field trip, visit the site, establish emergency procedures, and obtain parental or guardian permission. Field trip cost and safety are issues for many early childhood programs, as budgets are tight and providing insurance often make such ventures prohibitive. One solution to this problem is to invite people into the classroom to share their experiences or expertise with the children.

Poisonous plants and substances to avoid: Some plants and trees pose potential problems for outdoor activities. Being aware of these will help you to avoid potential problems. Most school playgrounds are plant and tree safe; however, field trips to parks or other areas in the community may unnecessarily expose the children to common and seemingly innocuous plants and trees that can cause serious problems. Be aware of these so you and the children can avoid them. Contact your local nursery or state-university extension office to find what plants in your locale are poisonous or hazardous to children. A comprehensive listing with photographs is available on line at www.ansci.cornell.edu/plants/comlist.html.

Family Meetings

"Educating children has become a shared responsibility among families, childcare programs, and schools. Early childhood educators recognize the need for communication and collaboration with the children's families. The family meeting format has proven to be an excellent strategy for establishing a reciprocal relationship between home and school. This relationship, once established, enhances a program's positive impact on child development and develops and strengthens home-school connections" (Rockwell & Kniepkamp, 2003).

The hands-on meetings in this book (pages 259–263) invite the entire family to be a part of science activities. Family gatherings at the childcare center offer a way to educate children's guardians and siblings about the importance of environmental education. The meetings give families an opportunity to interact with science activities and materials in the same way that their children do at school. After attending the meetings, families will likely be more adept at supporting, modeling, and discussing environmental science with their children. Family meetings that focus on environmental science education provide a natural avenue for children, families, and teachers to work together to help children develop lifelong positive attitudes toward science and the outdoors.

References

Bohling-Philippi, V. 2006. The power of nature to help children heal. *Exchange,* September/October.

Carson, R. 1965. *A sense of wonder.* New York: HarperCollins.

Jensen, E. 2000. Moving with the brain in mind. *Education Leadership,* November, 34–38.

Kuo, F. & A. Taylor. 2004. A potential natural treatment for attention deficit disorder: Evidence from a national study. *American Journal of Public Health,* 84, 1580–86.

Louv, R. 2005. Nature deficit, *Orion Magazine.* July/August.

Louv, R. 2005. *Last child in the woods: Saving our children from nature-deficit disorder.* Chapel Hill, NC: Algonquin Books.

Nelson, E. 2006. The outdoor classroom: No child left inside. *Exchange.* September/October.

Sallis, J., et al. 2003. Environmental and policy interventions to promote physical activity. *American Journal of Preventative Medicine.*

Stephens, K. 2002. Nature connections for kids in cities and suburbs. *Parenting Exchange,* Nature Connection Library #10.

Rivkin, M. 1995. *The great outdoors: Restoring children's right to play outside.* Washington, DC: National Association for the Education of Young Children. (ERIC Document Reproduction Service No. ED 388 414).

Rivkin, M. 1997. The schoolyard habitat movement: What it is and why children need it. *Early Childhood Education Journal,* 25(1), 61–66.

Rockwell, R. & J. Kniepkamp. 2003. *Partnering with parents: Easy programs to involve parents in the early learning process.* Beltsville, MD, Gryphon House, Inc.

Taylor, A., F. Kuo, & W. Sullivan. 2001. Coping with ADD: The surprising connection to green play settings. *Environment and Behavior,* 33 (1) 3–27.

White, R. 2004. Young children's relationship with nature: Its importance to children's development and the Earth's future. www.whitehutchinson.com/children/articles/childrennature.shtml

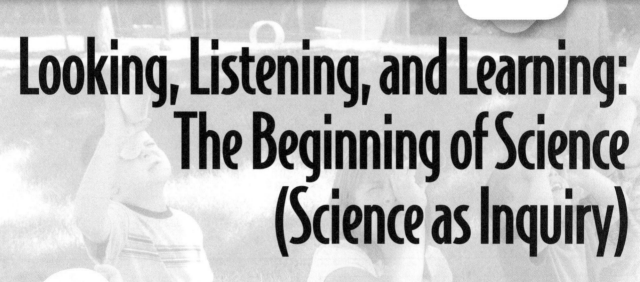

CHAPTER 1

Looking, Listening, and Learning: The Beginning of Science (Science as Inquiry)

3+ Tell Me What Your Senses Sense

This activity helps develop a skill that is very important for scientists. The abilities to observe and describe are highly regarded scientific skills, as all scientific endeavors include a clear description of the activity or object that scientists choose to research.

Science Content Standard—uses senses for observation (Science as Inquiry)
Science Process Skill—observing

Words You Can Use

Descriptive words for the objects

Feel	Pair
Identify	Same
Match	Similar

Things You Can Use

5–10 identical items from outdoors, such as black rocks of the same size, leaves or twigs that are about the same size and come from the same kind of tree, acorn caps, the same-sized pinecones (one of each item for each child in your class)
Paper bags
Chart paper and marker

Before the Activity

Make a set of objects—one of each outdoor item—for each of the children. Place the sets of objects in paper bags large enough that the children can reach into them.

What to Do

1. Start with sets of four or five objects and add more as the children's skills develop. Initially, choose items that are very different from each other.
2. Give each child a bag with a set of objects in it. Tell the children to take the objects out of their bags and explore them. Feel each item. Encourage the children to use a variety of words to describe how the items feel. They might use words like cool, smooth, bumpy, or scratchy. Make a list of the children's texture-descriptive words on chart paper.
3. Ask the children to look at the objects and describe how they look. List the children's visual-descriptive words on chart paper.
4. Ask the children, "Do the objects smell?" If so, list the words that the children use to describe how the objects smell. Ask, "Do the objects make a sound of any kind?" List what the children say. Review all the words that the children use to describe each object by using their senses.
5. Tell the children to put their items back into their bags. Ask one child at a time to reach into her bag, find an item, choose a sense to use, and then, without taking the object out of the bag, describe it using only that sense.
6. Challenge the other children to use the same single sense to find the same object in their own bags. After the children find the item in their bags have the children put the objects back into their bags, then choose another child to reach into her bag and describe another item using a different sense.

Observing and Assessing the Children

Can the child accurately match the given items to those found in the paper bag?

Learning in Other Curricular Areas

Language and literacy
- describing the appearance of the objects (expressive language)

Motor development
- grasping and touching the objects (small motor)

How Do We Get from Here to There?

3+

If you have interesting places within safe walking distance from your school, you have a wonderful opportunity to develop children's observation skills. Choosing one route to go to a destination and another route for the return trip gives the children the opportunity to compare their observations of the two routes.

Science Content Standard—uses senses for observation (Science as Inquiry)
Science Process Skills—observing; communicating

Words You Can Use

Destination
Different
Directions
Fastest
Map
Relationship words
   (around, far, under,
   over, and so on)
Shortest

Things You Can Use

Crayons, pencils
Paper
Clipboards

Before the Activity

Choose a destination that is within walking distance. You do not need to stop and visit the place; it will simply serve as a landmark for the children to see at the end of their walk. It could be a tree or the blue house that is a block away.

What to Do

1. Talk with the children about how there can be different ways to get to one location. If you have done other mapping activities with the children, talk about those activities.
2. Walk with the children to the site, taking one route to go there and a different one to return. As you walk with the children, encourage them to talk about what they see.
3. Stop from time to time so the children can look around, notice, and talk about what they see. If desired, give the children clipboards, paper, and crayons and pencils to draw some of the things they see.
4. Compare the two routes. Were there things they saw on one route that they did not see on the other route? Was there anything special they would like to see again?
5. Make a list of all the things that the children noticed. With the children's help, draw a map of the two routes, indicating where the children saw the different special things.

INCORPORATING TECHNOLOGY

Use a digital camera to record landmarks and unusual sightings along the route. Ask the children to sequence the pictures as they recall the walk. They can place them in order on a long piece of mural paper or put them in a book. Suggest that they dictate captions for the photographs.

INVOLVING FAMILIES

Share with families the route maps that the children helped make. If you took photographs and made them into a book as described above, put the book in your lending library for families to check out.

Want to Do More?

◆ Take the children to other places, using one route to go and another to return.
◆ Take walks during different seasons and compare what children notice.

Observing and Assessing the Children

Can the child identify differences between the two routes?

Learning in Other Curricular Areas

Language and literacy
◆ describing the route followed (expressive language)
◆ following directions (receptive language)

Math
◆ comparing distances (measurement—nonstandard)

Motor development
◆ walking various routes (large motor)
◆ drawing (small motor)

Social Studies
◆ creating maps (geography)

Getting There One Way or Another

Children often know how to get to a place close to school or their homes, but may have trouble verbalizing the directions. This activity gives the children an opportunity to describe how to go from one place to another and to analyze the routes by choosing a destination outside and comparing their ideas of the fastest or longest ways to reach it.

Science Content Standard—explores through trial and error (Science as Inquiry)
Science Process Skills—observing; communicating

Words You Can Use

Different   Map
Destination   Quickest
Direction   Shorter
End   Shortest
Identify   Time
Longest   Travel
Longer

Things You Can Use

Crayons
Paper
Pencil
Stopwatch

Before the Activity

Choose an outdoor area large enough for children to move from one point to another by several different routes. Use a big star, a flag, or two signs, one with "Start" written on it and one with "End" written on it, to designate the starting and ending spots.

What to Do

1. Take the children outside and show them the "Start" and "End" signs or symbols.
2. Go to the Start sign and ask the children, "How many ways are there to get to the End from here? What is the shortest way? What is the longest way? How can we find out?"
3. Use a stopwatch to time the various routes the children try.
4. Let the children decide whether they should walk, run, jump, or crawl the distance.
5. After all the children finish going from Start to End, ask them questions. For instance, "Which route is the easiest to travel? What makes it the easiest? Is one way more fun than another? What is the trickiest way?"

Want to Do More?

◆ Help the children draw maps of the shortest and longest routes.
◆ Bring out a map of the city and compare it to the maps that the children made.

Observing and Assessing the Children

Can the child identify differences between any of the routes?

Learning in Other Curricular Areas

Language and literacy
◆ verbalizing the various ways to get to given destinations (expressive language)
◆ listening and following directions (receptive language)

Math
◆ estimating the time (faster or slower) it will take to reach a specific destination (measurement—non-standard)

Motor development
◆ using various movement patterns to reach specific destinations (large motor)

3+ Outdoor Collage

Positional words, such as on top of, beside, and under, help children understand written and oral language, as well as mathematics. Children practice using positional words while making this group collage.

Science Content Standard—explores through trial and error (Science as Inquiry)
Science Process Skill—communicating

Words You Can Use

Behind
Beside
Bottom
Counting words
Next to
Over
Position
Side
Top
Under

Things You Can Use

Materials collected on a walk, such as rocks of various sizes, a branch, a brick, a log, a bottle, a tire, leaves, a board, or anything else the children find (each child needs 1 or 2 objects)
Chalk or stick
Digital camera (optional)

Before the Activity

Select a spot outside where you can draw shapes on the sand, pavement, or soil.

What to Do

1. Go on a collecting walk with the children. Have the children carry what they collect to the spot you selected.
2. On the dirt or on the pavement, draw a square using a stick or chalk. Ask the children to hold their objects and sit on the ground along one side of the square.
3. Talk with the children about collages they have made in the past using glue, paper, and other materials. Tell the children that they are going to make a giant outdoor collage.
4. Begin to direct the construction. For example, tell the children that you are going to place a brick you found in the middle of the square. Ask "Jake" to place a little rock on top of the brick. Ask "Yasha" and "Kyle" to put the board they found at the bottom of the square. Ask "Manuel" to put his bottle cap in a corner of the square. Provide the children with help, as needed. Adjust your choice of words to meet the abilities of individual children.
5. Continue until all of the children have had the chance to place at least one object in the collage.
6. Talk about the outdoor collage. If you like, take a photo of your group collage, and then ask the children to remove all the objects from the square.
7. Repeat the activity, but let each child decide where she wants to put her object. Encourage the children to say where they are going to put their objects before they do so.
   Note: Some children will not be able to articulate this information yet. For these children, ask them where they put their objects only after they placed them in the square. With some children, you may want to narrate their action, "Jake put his rock at the top of our square."
8. As before, when the collage is complete, invite the children to admire their work.

CONNECTING TO CHILDREN WITH SPECIAL NEEDS

Keep the instructions simple and make the collage in a reasonable time to keep the activity going. If it takes too long, children with attention deficit disorder may lose interest.

Chalk lines or lines drawn in the sand help some children who have large or fine motor issues to place the objects in the correct location by giving them a more contained target. For other children, this can make placing the objects more difficult. Observe your children and adjust accordingly.

INCORPORATING TECHNOLOGY

Take digital photographs of the collages different small groups create. Challenge the children to identify the collages they helped construct.

Want to Do More?

◆ To make the activity more physical, create an "action" collage. Ask the children to stand up, and then hop or run to pick up an item that is in another location, and carry out a task while carrying that item.

◆ Challenge the children to build three-dimensional collages. Talk to the children as they do so, using a broader range of position words.

◆ On a card, write the words that you and the children use to describe the outdoor collages. This will help you target words you know the children need to practice.

◆ Ask the children to count the number of objects they place in the collage.

Observing and Assessing the Children

Can the child use positional words to place objects in a requested location?

Learning in Other Curricular Areas

Arts

◆ creating a group collage (visual arts)

Language and literacy

◆ placing the objects as directed (receptive language)

Math

◆ creating patterns (algebra)

Motor development

◆ placing the items on the directed location (small motor)

The Order Activity

This activity introduces the children to the concept of seriation, or putting things in order. Use a collection of natural things because nature seldom produces all things of the same kind at the same size. While observing that pinecones come in a variety of lengths, the children can line up the cones in order from longest to shortest and from shortest to longest.

Science Content Standard—begins to use simple, descriptive language about living things (Life Science)
Science Process Skills—classifying (ordering); measuring (non-standard linear)

Words You Can Use

Long
Longest
Order
Short
Shortest

Things You Can Use

Found objects such as pinecones, leaves, twigs (long and short), and weeds
Masking tape

What to Do

1. Count with the children or have them count out an appropriate number of the same kind of objects. With children who are beginning to understand comparative relationships, you may want to begin with three items that have very different lengths. Children with more advanced skills may want to work with a greater number of objects or with objects that have similar lengths.
2. Using masking tape, make one line on the ground for each child.
3. Show the children how to line up the objects you set out for them, using the tape as a baseline.
4. Ask the children to place the objects on the line, putting the shortest one on the left and the longest on the right.
5. Give each child a different set of objects and challenge them to arrange the objects in order of length.
6. As the children's skills increase, give them larger groups of items to seriate.
7. Mix up two or more sets of objects and challenge the children to place them on the line from the longest to the shortest.

Want to Do More?

◆ Challenge the children to find another way to order the objects you gave them. One way would be to put the largest item in the middle and challenge the children to order the rest of the objects in an alternating pattern on either side of the first object.

◆ Set out interlocking cubes or a ruler with which the children can measure the lengths of the various objects.

◆ Make labels with the words "long" and "short." As the children make collections of objects they consider short or long, they can place them by the appropriate label.

◆ Give each child one object and keep one for yourself. Put your object down and then choose a child to go next. Say, "If your object is shorter than mine, place it on this side (gesturing to the left). If it is longer, place it here (gesturing to the right)." Help the child place the object on the appropriate side of your object and then invite that child to choose another child to place her object on the appropriate side. Encourage the children to continue taking turns until all the objects are in order.

ADDRESSING THE NEEDS OF ENGLISH LANGUAGE LEARNERS

This activity provides a good opportunity for English language learners to become familiar with comparative language through meaningful interaction with real objects as the words are being used.

Observing and Assessing the Children

Can the child accurately use the terms "long" and "short"?
Can the child order the objects from shortest to longest or longest to shortest?

Learning in Other Curricular Areas

Math

◆ placing objects in order by length (measurement)

Motor development

◆ manipulating objects (small motor)

3+ Pair Them Up Two by Two

Many young children enjoy creating order. They like sorting, matching, and lining things up. During this activity, you may hear the children say they are "helping each shell find its friend" as they spontaneously make pairs of similar shells.

Science Content Standards—uses senses for observation (Science as Inquiry); explores through trial and error (Science as Inquiry)
Science Process Skill—classifying

Words You Can Use

Count
Match
Object names
Pairs
Remainder
Two

Things You Can Use

A collection of 5–20 different natural objects, such as acorns, pinecones, shells, small twigs, or seeds (Make sure you have at least one pair of every item and multiple pairs of many items.)

What to Do

1. Show the collection of objects to a small group of children and invite them to explore the objects. Talk with the children about where you found the objects. Perhaps they remember collecting some of the items themselves.

2. As the children explore the objects, ask them to show you how to sort the objects into piles of objects that are alike. Point out that in nature things are very similar, but not exactly alike. A handful of acorns, shells, or small pinecones are all very similar, but each one is minutely different from the others. Encourage the children to point out some of the differences they see.

ACORNS   SHELLS

3. Using the objects in one of the piles, show the children how to pair the most-similar objects together in a long line. You might say, "When we put two things together like this, it is called a pair. Look at all the pairs in this line." If it is appropriate for your group, you may want to have them count the pairs with you.

4. Encourage the children to form pairs with the various objects in the piles. Challenge the children to create a line of different pairs; for example, challenge the children to make a line of one pair of pinecones, then one pair of shells, then three pairs of small sticks.

   Note: If you add teddy bear counters or other familiar objects, you can talk about the differences between natural and manufactured objects.

Want to Do More?

◆ Repeat the activity with socks, shoes, or gloves.

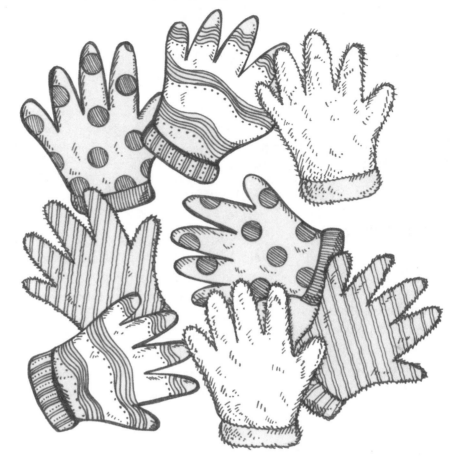

CONNECTING TO CHILDREN WITH SPECIAL NEEDS
Children with limited motor skills may have difficulty placing objects in a specific designated spot. Provide containers in which to place the pairs of objects. If the items are small, the children could place pairs in a compartment of an egg carton.

◆ Line up the pairs from each pile to count and compare the amounts. Graph the results.
◆ With children who are ready, use the pairs to count by twos.
◆ Making pairs is common in games for young children. Examples include Memory and Go Fish. With the children, find and make a list of "Games that use pairs."

Observing and Assessing the Children

Can the child make pairs, realizing that a pair is two objects that go together?

Learning in Other Curricular Areas

Math
◆ counting pairs (number operations)
◆ sorting and classifying objects by a variety of properties (algebra)
◆ ordering objects in series or rows (measurement)

Motor development
◆ placing objects in pairs and in a line (small motor)

3+ Is This Half?

Once children understand the concepts empty and full, try introducing them to the simplest fraction, half. This favorite water play activity is a great way for children to begin to understand what half means.

Science Content Standard—uses senses for observation (Science as Inquiry)
Science Process Skill—classifying

Words You Can Use
Half
Whole

Things You Can Use
4–6 matching, clear plastic cups
Water play materials, such as plastic cups and containers of various sizes
Water Table or large pan full of water

Before the Activity
Set up an area for outdoor water play.

What to Do

Note: In this activity, the children will be learning to estimate how to fill containers half full, just as adults typically do when they only need to have an approximate amount of something. Learning to measure exact amounts will come as they get older.

1. Water play provides the perfect opportunity to explore the concept of half. Join the children in their play. As you do, describe what you see. Point out when someone's cup is full or empty. Join in the children's play, filling and emptying a container, describing the action as you do so. It can be fun to play "1, 2, 3, everybody empty your container!" and "1, 2, 3, everybody fill up your container!" Enjoy the splashes of dumping and filling.

2. Pick up one of the matching cups, fill it, and pour half the water into another cup. Place the two cups side by side. Ask the children, "Are these full? No? Are they empty? No?" Explain that each cup is half full. The empty space in the cup is about the same size as the space filled with water. Invite the children to use their thumbs and forefingers to compare the amount of water and empty space.

3. Hold a full cup of water and ask who has an empty cup they want to be half-full. When a child holds out her cup, say, "Watch. I'll share half my water with you. Now we both have a cup that is half full."

4. Encourage the children to find matching cups and make them each half full. Encourage them to place their cups beside your half-full cups to check. Remember that they are only estimating, so it is okay if their measurement is close but not exact.

5. When the children understand the concept half full, encourage them to fill containers of all sizes half full.

6. While you are outside, the children might enjoy pouring half-full cups of water on any plants in the vicinity.

Want to Do More?

◆ Bring in a variety of containers and ask the children to fill all of the containers halfway with water. Ask the children if some of the containers take longer to fill.

◆ Ask the children to fill a container and then pour out half of the water. This may take some practice while the children learn about what half means. They are also developing the motor skills and self-control to stop at the halfway point.

◆ Teach the children about the concepts a quarter ($\frac{1}{4}$) or a third ($\frac{1}{3}$) by challenging them to pour water evenly among three or four cups.

◆ Offer the children more experience with measuring by providing measuring cups and pint, quart, liter, and two-liter containers.

Observing and Assessing the Children

Given a container, can the child fill it half full of water?

Connection to Other Curricular Areas

Language and literacy

◆ listening with understanding and responding to directions (receptive language)

Math

◆ recognizing patterns (algebra)

◆ counting (number operations)

Motor development

◆ picking up and pouring water in and out of containers (large and small motor)

4+

Can You Find It?

An outdoor scavenger hunt can be a fun challenge for children because there are so many objects that can meet a specific characteristic. For example, if they are looking for a round object, they may find a rock, a twig, or even a shiny piece of aluminum foil. Give older children a list of things to find. For younger children, name one item on the list at a time, and ask everyone to search for it.

Science Content Standard—explores through trial and error (Science as Inquiry)
Science Process Skills—observing; classifying

Words You Can Use

Alike
Collect
Different
Descriptive words
    (round, long, green,
    rough, fuzzy, bumpy,
    sharp, crinkly)
Find
Match
Scavenger Hunt

Things You Can Use

Bags for collecting things
Index cards and markers

Before the Activity

Prepare several Can You Find It? cards by writing one descriptive word on each index card. Use words that describe objects that the children are likely to find outside. Examples of words to use include such words as shape words (round, square), color words, size words (length or weight), and descriptive words (sharp, rough, crinkly).

What to Do

1. Take the children outside to the playground or for a walk to a nearby location where they are likely to find many natural or manufactured objects.
2. Have 6–10 Can You Find It? cards ready. Select one card, such as the card with the descriptive word "round" written on it, for example. Show the card to the children and challenge them to look around for another round object. Mark off a special spot where the children can put the objects they find. When each child finds an object, ask her to bring it back and place it with the round objects everyone else found. If appropriate, have the children work in pairs. Examples of round objects the children might find include a round rock, a sweet gum ball, a ball, or a bottle cap. Accept all the items the children bring as long as they can show that it does in some way resemble the description. If an object does not fit the description, talk with the children about why it does not match.
3. Go through several Can You Find It? cards with the children. Encourage the children to race back with their finds to keep the pace of the game exciting. Safety note: If the children are carrying sticks or large objects that could be potentially dangerous, warn them to walk carefully to avoid injury.
4. Finish the hunt once everyone finds an object that matches each descriptor on the Can You Find It? cards. As the children become adept at the game, consider increasing the number and complexity of the cards.

Want to Do More?

- Encourage the children to continue searching for objects on their own.
- Challenge the children to find objects that match two or more descriptors at once. For example, ask the children to find something that is both brown and round, or something that is rough, green, and long.
- Repeat the activity in another location. With the children, compare the objects found in the different locations.
- Introduce the children to the names of the objects that the children found, such as acorns or dandelion flowers.

Observing and Assessing the Children

Can the child find items that match the meaning of the different descriptor words?

Learning in Other Curricular Areas

Language and literacy
- listening with understanding and responding to directions (receptive language)

Math
- classifying, sorting, and matching objects (algebra)

Social Studies
- recognizing the reason for rules in games (social interaction)

CONNECTING TO CHILDREN WITH SPECIAL NEEDS
Children with sensory integration issues may need to look at the array of items and select those materials they are comfortable touching.

4+ Senses Walk

The children "turn on" their senses of hearing, touching, smelling, and seeing in this activity, and become aware of how frequently they use their senses.

Science Content Standards—uses senses for observation (Science as Inquiry); begins to use simple, descriptive language about living things (Life Science)
Science Process Skills—observing; communicating

Words You Can Use

Hearing words
Senses
Sensory
Sight words
Smell words
Touch words

Things You Can Use

A notebook for listing the children's observations

Before the Activity

Look for a location outdoors where you can do this activity.

What to Do

1. Divide the children into four groups. Explain to the children that each group will be in charge of making observations using one particular sense. Challenge each group to find at least five things using only their designated sense.

2. One group of children is in charge of using their sense of sight to observe things that are different, special, or unusual. The other groups are responsible for observing things that are different, special and unusual by using their senses of hearing, smell, and touch.

3. Remind each group to remember where they made their observations. Help them by making notes and looking at what the groups find.

4. When all the groups are finished using their designated sense to make their five special observations, ask each group to share their five different, special, or unusual sensory observations with the rest of the children. Some observations, such as a police siren, birdcall, or the aroma of lunch cooking, may not linger for others to experience them. The group that saw a butterfly may have to describe it rather than show it to their friends.

Want to Do More?

◆ Make a list of the things the children find for each sense, adding each new discovery to the list.

◆ Make a sensory trail for other groups to follow. Wherever the children discover a particular sense observation, place a picture of a nose, ear, eye, or finger, depending on which sense the children used to make the observation.

◆ Grow an herb garden (use pots if you are growing it inside). Talk with the children about the various scents that develop as the plants grow.

CONNECTING TO CHILDREN WITH SPECIAL NEEDS

Children with developmental delays or other learning challenges may benefit by limiting their focus to one sense at a time. Using the sense of smell or touch may be difficult for children who have sensory integration dysfunction.

CHIVES

SPEARMINT

BASIL

ROSEMARY

SAGE

◆ Tape the children talking, and then play it back to see if the children can identify one another's voices.

Observing and Assessing the Children

Can the child work with others to observe and find special sensory items? Can the child share the observations in some way?

Learning in Other Curricular Areas

Language and literacy

◆ listening with understanding and responding to directions (receptive language)

◆ communicating observations, ideas, and thoughts (expressive language)

4+ What Can Your Fingers Find?

Whether walking along a city street, exploring a wooded path, or taking a new look at your own playground, interesting textures are everywhere. Encourage the children to be scientists and use their senses to make observations about the textures they see.

Science Content Standard—uses sense for observation (Science as Inquiry)
Science Process Skill—observing

Words You Can Use

Bumpy	Smooth
Feel	Soft
Hard	Texture
Rough	Touch

Things You Can Use

Box with a lid, such as a shoebox
Collecting bags
Glue and glue sticks
Large index cards for gluing items on
Index cards labeled with individual texture words
Specimens of texture
Tape

Before the Activity

Obtain a box large enough to hold several of the texture cards. Into the side of the box, cut an opening large enough for a child to reach inside. Print several texture words on 3" x 5" cards and set them aside. These are the texture-word cards.

What to Do

1. Talk with the children about the meaning of the word "texture." You might have them explore the textures of their own clothes and bodies to begin the conversation. Ask them whether they are wearing something soft. Ask them what the bottoms of their shoes feel like. What about earlobes, eyebrows, and fingernails?

2. Show the children the texture words written on the cards, and talk with them about how people use these words to describe how things feel.

3. Take the children on a collecting walk. Explain to them that the object of the walk is to give the children the chance to gather several objects that have a wide range of different textures. Remind the children that the objects they bring back should be small enough that they can fit on the texture cards.

4. When you return from the walk, help the children glue and tape their objects to a separate set of index cards. Ask the children to describe the different textures of the objects on the cards, and write the texture words on those cards.

Note: Be sure the words the children use to describe the textures match those on the texture word cards you made prior to the activity.

5. Place three or four of the textured cards in the box and put the box lid on the top. Next, choose one card from the stack of texture-word cards you made before the activity, and read the texture word with the children.

6. Choose one child to reach inside the box and feel the different textures until they find a texture that matches the one on the texture-word card. When the child selects the texture card out of the box, ask, "Is it rough, soft, smooth?"

7. Ask the child to pull out the texture card and check the selection against the texture-word card. Pass the texture card around to the other children, inviting them to feel the texture and decide if they agree with the selection. As they do, talk about the item on the card and ask them to describe how it feels. "Are there other words you can think of that describe it?"

Safety note: Be sure the children wash their hands after the collecting walk and after the activity.

Want to Do More?

◆ Make a texture lotto game using rubbings made from the texture cards.
◆ Repeat the activity, using materials from the recycling bin.
◆ Select a texture word and see how many items the children can find that have that texture.

Observing and Assessing the Children

Can the child match a texture to the word that describes that texture? Can the child use words to describe the various textures?

Learning in Other Curricular Areas

Language and literacy
◆ understanding that symbols have meaning and that print carries a message (early literacy)
◆ communicating to others how different textures feel (descriptive language)

Motor development
◆ walking and collecting textured objects (large motor)
◆ gluing objects to the texture card; touching objects (fine motor)

INVOLVING FAMILIES

Ask families to send in small items or pieces of fabric with various textures.

USING MUSEUMS AND OTHER COMMUNITY RESOURCES

Some museums have materials with interesting textures available for you to borrow, such as a collection of fabrics or furs.

4+ Count with Nature

In this activity, the children count the number of a certain kind of object, like rocks or seashells, as they put them into containers. This activity teaches the children to count as well as helps them learn the names of the objects they count.

Science Content Standard—describes and records observations (Science as Inquiry)
Science Process Skills—observing; classifying (sorting, grouping)

Words You Can Use

Names of objects
Number words

Things You Can Use

Objects to count: seeds, such as acorns, pinecones, eucalyptus seeds, sweet gum balls, or hickory nuts; seashells of various kinds; rocks of various kinds (landscaping companies often allow teachers to collect a bucket of assorted small landscaping rocks at little or no charge); other available collections of small objects
10–15 containers (reused aluminum pie pans or plastic food tubs work well)
Permanent markers

Before the Activity

Use permanent markers to write one of the numbers 0–5 (or 10, or 15, depending on the children's skill levels) on the bottom of each container.

What to Do

1. The children can do this activity individually or in pairs. Show the children the numbers on the bottoms of the containers, and explain to them that the goal of this activity is to put the correct number of objects in each container.
2. Challenge the children not to mix items when they put them in each container. If a child has a container with "3" written on it, for instance, the child should put three acorns in the container, not one acorn and two pinecones. If the child only has two acorns, then she should use them to fill the container with "2" written on it.
3. When finished, encourage each child to check another's container; double-check them yourself, too.
4. When the children finish checking each other's containers, ask them to empty the containers so they are ready for other children to use.
   Note: To make this an independent, self-correcting activity, provide only the correct total number of items. When the children correctly fill all the containers, there should be no leftovers.
5. Consider having the children who just completed the activity draw from a hat or container the names of the next two children to do the activity.

Want to Do More?

◆ Challenge the children by writing larger numbers on the containers.

Observing and Assessing the Children

Can the children put the correct number of objects in a numbered container?

CONNECTING TO CHILDREN WITH SPECIAL NEEDS

For children with autism spectrum disorder, this activity encourages active participation and interaction with other children in the class in a predictable way.

INVOLVING FAMILIES

For variety, ask families if they have a collection of sturdy objects the children could count, such as shells, old keys, or buttons.

Learning in Other Curricular Activities

Language and literacy
◆ listening with understanding and responding to directions and conversation (receptive language)

Math
◆ counting (number operations)
◆ recognizing patterns (algebra)

Motor development
◆ picking up and placing objects in containers (small motor)

4+ Leaf Coverage

This enjoyable activity is easy to do in the fall when plenty of leaves are everywhere, and they are free! With leaves and old newspapers, children can begin to explore the concept of area. At the same time, the children will experience a basic concept of nature—that leaves from the same plant have a consistent size and shape.

Science Content Standard—makes comparisons among different observations (Science as Inquiry)
Science Process Skill—observing

Words You Can Use

Area
Collect
Compare
Cover
Leaves
Same
Size

Things You Can Use

Leaves from the same tree (Because the leaves will be about the same size, this allows you to compare the numbers needed to cover pieces of paper of different sizes. A mixture of large and small leaves may be confusing.)

Pieces of newspaper in various sizes, such as full pages, half pages, ads, and magazine pages

What to Do

1. Explain to the children that the objective of this activity is to find enough of the same kind of leaves to cover newspaper pages of various sizes. Explain that this does not need to be exact, and that the leaves only need to cover most of the paper.

2. Bring the children outside and help them collect a pile of leaves from one kind of tree. Choose the most abundant species of tree, so there are several leaves available. Encourage the children to check with each other to be sure they have the right leaves.
   Note: If you do not have a set of trees nearby where the children can pick up the leaves themselves, pick up a number of leaves before school and bring them in for the children to use.

3. Place a piece of paper on the ground and cover it with the leaves. Point out to the children how many leaves it takes to cover the paper. Ask the children to count them aloud together. When they finish counting, write the number on the piece of newspaper.
   Note: If it is a bit breezy, you may need blocks or rocks to hold the paper and leaves in place.

4. Choose a different-sized piece of paper. Ask the children whether they think they will we need more or fewer leaves to cover the new piece of paper. Invite the children to cover the paper with leaves, then count them and compare the new number of leaves with the old number. Were they right? Again, write the number on the piece of newspaper.

5. Talk with the children about the relationship between the size of the paper and the number of leaves. Ask what they think would happen if they used a different kind of leaf.

MAPLE
LEAF

Want to Do More?

- ◆ Give pairs or small groups of children the same-sized piece of paper and ask each group to count the number of leaves it takes to cover the paper. Compare the groups' results. Are they the same? Ask the children why they think the numbers are different. Explain that the numbers vary because the leaves are about the same size, but not exactly the same size, while the pieces of paper are exactly the same size.
- ◆ Challenge the children to time how fast it takes them to cover a piece of paper with leaves. Give them different sizes of paper, and encourage them to compare the different times.
- ◆ Show the children how to make a graph of the leaves to compare how many leaves it takes to cover different-sized sheets of paper.
- ◆ Graph the number of leaves used to cover each page. Let the children discover that the numbers are different if they use different leaves. Encourage them to try different sizes of the same species of leaf or different species or a mixture of both.

CONNECTING TO CHILDREN WITH SPECIAL NEEDS

Children who have visual impairments may not be able to see or place the collected leaves in the various size categories. Emphasize the use of touch to help these children assess the sizes and shapes of the leaves.

MAPLE LEAF

OAK LEAF

SWEET GUM

Observing and Assessing the Children

Can the child tell that it requires more leaves to cover a larger sheet of paper?

Learning in Other Curricular Areas

Language and literacy
- ◆ listening and responding to directions (receptive language)

Math
- ◆ identifying shapes and their properties; identifying spatial relationships (geometry)
- ◆ counting (number operations)

Motor development
- ◆ walking and collecting leaves (large motor)
- ◆ placing leaves on the shapes (fine motor)

4+ Pick-Up Sticks

After the children enjoy counting the sticks they collect in the park or playground, they can use their imaginations to make things from them. If you do not have plentiful twigs, use the materials do you have!

Science Content Standard—explores through trial and error (Science as Inquiry)
Science Process Skills—observing, communicating

Words You Can Use

Counting words
Bundles

Things You Can Use

Cards numbered in ranges appropriate for the children (1–5 or 1–20 depending on their age and experience. Also, consider using a zero card.)

Sticks the children collect, or any other available items the children can count

Before the Activity

Prepare the number cards by writing one numeral, the number word, and that number of lines or dots on each card.

What to Do

1. Bring the children outside and invite them to collect several sticks.
   Safety note: Supervise carefully, ensuring that the children do not wave the sticks around or hit one another with them.
2. Help the children break the larger sticks so they are all about the same size.
3. Mix up the number cards, and then pick one.
4. Show a child or pair of children the card and challenge them make a pile of sticks equal to that number. Encourage the children to count with each other and perhaps work in pairs. Provide counting support as needed.
5. Show other children different number cards and challenge them to repeat the activity until each child or pair of children has a pile of sticks for at least one number card.

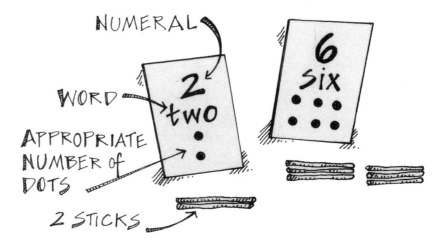

NUMERAL

WORD

APPROPRIATE NUMBER of DOTS

2 STICKS

Want to Do More?

◆ Have each child choose a collection number; five, for example. Explain to the child that it is her job to make several collections of five objects—five acorns, five blocks, five teddy bear counters, and five buttons. Help the children to choose numbers that are appropriate for their developmental level.

Observing and Assessing the Children

Given a pile of sticks, can the child count to a specific number appropriate for her developmental level?

Learning in Other Curricular Areas

Language and literacy

◆ listening with understanding; responding to directions (receptive language)

◆ understanding that symbols have meaning and that print carries a message (early literacy)

Math

◆ counting (number operations)

Motor development

◆ picking up and placing sticks on the number cards (small motor)

4+ Hit the Bucket

Adults know that skills improve with practice, but young children may not grasp this important idea. By participating in this tossing activity, the children can learn how practice improves a particular skill.

Science Content Standard—explores through trial and error (Science as Inquiry)
Science Process Skills—observing; communicating

Words You Can Use

Accurate
Counting words
Estimate
Improve

Things You Can Use

Plastic bucket or
    wastepaper basket
Pinecones, crumpled
    wads of newspaper, or
    other "tossables" in
    groups of 10, at least
    four different types of
    items

Before the Activity

Select a site for this
activity. Set the bucket
against a wall or fence
and out of the way
enough that no other
children will notice it.

What to Do

1. Bring the children outside. Show them the bucket and the objects they will be tossing. Demonstrate how to make an underhand toss, and explain to the children that for this activity, they should make all their tosses underhand.
    Note: We strongly recommend letting each child choose how far she wants to stand from the target. Standing right next to the target so she hits it every time can be boring. Children will naturally begin to challenge themselves by moving farther away as their skills improve.

2. Divide the class into groups of two or three. Give each child 5–10 of one particular object, depending on the child's counting skills. Invite the children to work together as they take turns tossing the objects at the bucket.
    Note: Have each child use a different set of items so she can identify her objects from those of the other children in her group.

3. When the children finish, ask them to count how many objects made it into the bucket.

4. Encourage the children to practice the bucket toss as often as they like. Suggest that they count how many items get in the bucket each time, and compare the numbers with past results. Help them by recording the results on paper. This way they can see their numbers improve with practice.

5. Ask questions. How many rounds of tosses does it take a child to consistently get her items in the bucket? Do the children's results improve each time they play, or do their results fluctuate?

6. If a child is having a hard time improving her tosses, talk to her about ways she might alter her tosses to improve her success. Invite her to try tossing a different set of items. Talk with the child about how the change affects her accuracy.

Want to Do More?

◆ As children become more adept, challenge them to move farther away from the bucket and try the toss again.

◆ Talk with the children about how different people toss things in different ways. Invite the children to demonstrate their "best ways" to toss.

- Show the children how to record the results of their tosses as fractions. For instance, five out of ten tosses would be $\frac{5}{10}$.
- Older children may enjoy keeping track of their progress either on individual scorecards or on a chart like the one below.

NAME	First try	Second try	Third try	Fourth try	Fifth try	Sixth try	Seventh try	Eighth try

Observing and Assessing the Children
Can the child attempt the object toss and record the results?

Learning in Other Curricular Areas
Math
- counting; recording data (number operations)

Motor development
- tossing objects at the target (large motor)
- picking up the objects to toss (fine motor)

4+

How Many Rocks in My Hand?

Use this simple activity any time. Pick up a few rocks and play counting, addition, and subtraction with the children.

Science Content Standard—makes comparisons among different observations (Science as Inquiry)
Science Process Skill—observing

Words You Can Use
Number words
How many?

Things You Can Use
5–10 acorns, rocks, or seeds
Collecting bag

Before the Activity
Gather several acorns, rocks, or seeds small enough that you can hold a number of them in your hand at once.

What to Do
1. Show the children the rocks or other objects that you gathered.
2. Pick up each item one at a time, counting them with the children. Count out three to five rocks, depending on the children's counting skills.
3. Put the rocks in your hand, and wave your hand in the air. Drop one or several of the rocks and say, "Rocks fall, isn't that grand? Now, how many rocks are in my hand?"
4. Let the children look at the rocks that fell out of your hand and encourage them to determine how many rocks are still in your hand.
5. Demonstrate the activity once or twice more for the children, then let them take turns dropping the rocks for each other.
    Safety note: Supervise carefully to ensure the children do not put items—that present a possible choking hazard—into their mouths.

Want to Do More?
◆ Suggest that the children try splitting up the rocks between two hands and counting how many are in each hand.

Observing and Assessing the Children
If the child knows the total number of rocks in a set, can she look at the number that fall out of your hand and determine how many remain in your hand?

Learning in Other Curricular Areas
Language and literacy
◆ listening with understanding and responding to directions (receptive language)
◆ communicating information with others (expressive language)
Math
◆ exploring quantity and number (number operations)
Motor development
◆ holding small objects; dropping objects and picking them up (small motor)

Color Scramble

Take the children outside, pick a color, and then shout "Scramble!" to send the children running to find the color. The children will have fun with this fast-paced activity. If the children find lots of colorful litter, help the environment by encouraging them to pick it up.

Science Content Standard—uses senses for observation (Science as Inquiry)
Science Process Skills—observing; classifying

Words You Can Use
Color words
Estimate
Less
More
Same

Things You Can Use
Coffee can or sack
Crayons in different
    colors

Before the Activity
Familiarize yourself with the area where you will do the activity, and be sure there are lots of colorful objects the children can find.

What to Do
1. Take the children outside. Show them the crayons. Review the colors' names, if necessary. Explain to the children that for this activity, when you say the name of a color, "red," for instance, then shout "Scramble!," everyone should run around and find something red. Tell them it is okay if more than one person finds the same thing. As the children get better at the activity, challenge them to find an object no one else has seen.
2. Place all the crayons in the can, shake it, and then, with a bit of drama, reach in and pull out a crayon. Say, "I have a brown crayon. Scramble! Find something that is brown and stand by it."
   Hint: The first few times choose a crayon color that is easy to find.
3. After the children find several brown objects, look at all the different things together. Continue to "Scramble!" for other colors.
4. As you try different colors, the children will realize that some colors, like green or brown, are much easier to find than other colors, such as pink.

Want to Do More
♦ With older children or for an additional challenge, repeat the activity, adding the rule that each child has to find a different object.

Observing and Assessing the Children
Can the child find an object of a given color in a specified area?

Learning in Other Curricular Areas
Arts
   ♦ recognizing colors, including their various shades (visual arts/creativity)
Math
   ♦ estimating (number operations)
Motor development
   ♦ scrambling to find a color (large motor)

Follow the Directions

Want to have the children follow directions, use position words, and run or walk a bit? Grab a pile of objects, pick the position words that you want to review, and out you go!

Science Content Standard—explores in response to teachers' questions (Science as Inquiry)
Science Process Skill—communicating

Words You Can Use

Behind	Position
Beside	Run
Bottom	Skip
Counting	Side
words	Top
Hop	Under
Jump	Walk
Over	

Things You Can Use

Materials, such as acorns, leaves, flowers, a board, rocks, shells, plastic trash, and aluminum cans, to name a few

Before the Activity

Select an open area with a number of landmarks. A playground works as well as a field. Place a pile of objects at each landmark and have a pile at the starting point. Review the positional words that you want the children to use and learn.

What to Do

1. Bring the children outside and show them the first collection of objects piled on the ground. Tell them this is the starting point.
2. Explain to the children that there are similar collections in containers on the ground beside some landmarks, such as the swing, the slide, a tree, and a gate.
3. Tell the children that, for this activity, you will ask each child to perform two or three tricky tasks. Explain that they will need to listen carefully and move quickly to see how fast they can perform these tasks and get back to the starting point. Point out that because the children will all have different tasks, they will be challenging themselves, not competing to be "the winner."
4. One at a time, give each child a different set of tasks. For example, say, "Aaron, pick up an acorn and walk to the swing. Put the acorn on the swing seat. Pick up a can and put it under the climber, then run back to me as fast as you can." Remember to suit your instructions to the abilities of the children. For children that need a simpler set of tasks, say something like, "Take this pinecone, put it next to the gate, and run back to me." Staying enthusiastic as you give the children tasks, and encouraging them to maintain a quick pace will generate the excitement needed to make this fun!
   Note: Help children that have poor senses of direction by adding clues or markers to your instructions.

Want to Do More?

◆ As the children become more adept at the activity, increase the difficulty of the directions.

◆ Challenge the children to pick up specific numbers of the different objects.

Observing and Assessing the Children

Can the child use the position words to locate the objects and their containers? Can the child follow multiple directions properly?

Learning in Other Curricular Areas

Language and literacy

◆ listening and following directions (receptive language)

Motor development

◆ repeatedly picking up objects (small motor)

◆ moving objects to different locations (large motor)

Can't Peek

Young children can often identify objects that they collect, but few have the vocabulary necessary to describe those objects. This variation of a traditional game gives children an opportunity to practice their descriptive language skills.

Science Content Standard—describes and records observations (Science as Inquiry)
Science Process Skills—observing; communicating

Words You Can Use

Descriptive words of the objects in your collection, such as color words, shape words, and texture words that will vary with the object
Names of things you have collected from the outdoors

Things You Can Use

Two resealable, identical bags
Various items, such as rocks, leaves, or shells

Before the Activity

With young or inexperienced children, begin by putting two or three very different objects in each bag. More experienced children will enjoy the challenge of working with a larger collection. Prepare several matching bags by putting identical objects in each.

What to Do

1. Divide the children into pairs. Have each pair sit back to back, and give each child a bag. Designate one child in each pair as "IT." Ask the children who are IT to take an object from their bags.

2. In each pair, IT describes the object she pulled from the bag while the other child looks at the items in her own bag to find the matching object. Initially, the children may need help with descriptive terms. You might provide prompts, such as, "Does it bend?," "Is it smaller than your hand?," or "Is it smooth or bumpy?"

Note: By creating bags with varying degrees of difficulty, all the children can play the same game and experience success at their own levels.

3. Once the child correctly guesses which item It holds, the two children switch roles and repeat the activity.
4. Once the children understand the activity, encourage them to continue playing it on their own.

Want to Do More?

◆ Write down the words that the children use to describe the objects and discuss them with the children later. Bring in a new item and see if the children can identify the new object using either the same descriptive words they used before, or by using new descriptive words.

◆ Set out several pairs of objects and bags so the children can make their own pairs of bags.

Observing and Assessing the Children

Can the child describe an object using enough descriptive words that another child to identify the object?

Learning in Other Curricular Areas

Language and literacy

◆ communicating information to others using descriptive language (expressive language)

◆ listening with understanding and responding to directions and conversations (receptive language)

4+ Looking Through the Spyglass

Looking through a cylinder limits the scope of the eye and forces the observer to focus on specific rather than general aspects of the environment. In this activity, children take long and close-up looks at their world, and discover new things to see through these special windows.

Science Content Standard—describes and records observations (Science as Inquiry)
Science Process Skill—observing

Words You Can Use
Binoculars
Cylinder
Field of vision
Focus
Telescope
View

Things You Can Use
Cardboard rolls (paper towel, foil, or wrapping paper rolls)
Paper and pen or tape recorder and cassette tape
Sheets of paper with large circles drawn on them
Crayons and markers

Before the Activity
Locate a variety of observation points at or near your school.

What to Do
1. Bring the children to the observation site. It can be a familiar place or a new place.
2. Once you reach the destination, give each child a viewer (cardboard rolls, in a variety of lengths and sizes).
3. Invite the children to look for a specific natural object to observe, like a large tree or nearby building. Ask the children to move close enough to the object they are viewing that they can only see a portion of it through their spyglasses.
4. Ask one child to focus on a particular spot on the object and describe what she sees. Challenge the other children to find the same spot.
   Note: This limiting of perspective can reveal beauty hidden by the overwhelming visual stimuli in an environment. Focusing on one flower in a field of many helps children become aware of the little things that go together to make a whole.
5. Record the children's observations on paper or tape for later comparison, discussion, and reconstruction of the observation.
6. Put out paper with large circles drawn on them, as well as crayons and markers, and ask the children to draw what they see through their spyglasses in the circles on the sheets of paper.
7. After the children finish drawing what they see, invite them to move closer or farther away from the object, look at it again, and describe the changes they see, then to draw the object again from their new vantage points.
8. When the children finish with their drawings of the object, return to the classroom and help the children put the drawings together to form a mural.
   Safety note: Do not let the children walk while looking through viewers, as they are likely to stumble and fall.

Want to Do More?
◆ Bring the children to a different observation site and repeat the activity.

Observing and Assessing the Children

Does the child describe the differences she observes in objects from up close, and then from farther away?

Learning in Other Curricular Areas

Language and literacy

◆ describing what is visible through the viewer (expressive language)

Motor development

◆ walking to find various observation points (large motor)

Make a Pattern, Make It Again

All you need to explore patterns is a chalk line on the sidewalk or blacktop and a few objects from nature, such as acorns, leaves, sticks, or pinecones.

Science Content Standard—makes comparisons among different observations (Science as Inquiry)
Science Process Skill—classifying

Words You Can Use
Line
Next
Object names, such as
    acorn, pinecone, leaf,
    and so on
Pattern

Things You Can Use
Small stones, acorns,
    pinecones, seashells,
    small sticks, sweet
    gum balls, and other
    natural objects, in
    groups of 5–10 each
Chalk

Before the Activity
Make sure you have
enough of the natural
objects for the children
to make several patterns.
Ask the children to help
you sort the objects into
separate piles.

What to Do
1. Place the objects in front of you, and ask the children to gather around you. Use the chalk to draw a line on the ground.
2. Tell the children that you are going to use the objects in front of you to make a pattern along the line you drew on the ground.
3. Along the line, make a pattern, using an acorn, a pinecone, another acorn, and then another pinecone. Be sure the children can all see the line where you are making the pattern.
4. Ask one child to pick the two items that will continue the pattern, and then place the items on the line in the correct order. Then ask another child to continue the pattern further. Explain to the children that this is an AB pattern.

5. When the children understand the AB pattern, try another pattern. If the children have a lot of experience with patterning, they may be able to make complex patterns. If they are just starting to learn about patterning, be sure to do several basic demonstrations on the chalk line before they begin making their own patterns. For example, demonstrate AABB patterns, ABC patterns, and AABBC patterns.

6. Once the children show they understand the basic concept of patterning, draw several additional chalk lines on the ground and invite the children to create their own patterns. As you observe the children creating patterns, you can add the next sections to the patterns, showing the children that you understand their patterns.

Want to Do More?

◆ Give the children string and blunt needles and challenge them to create patterns from leaves, seeds, and other thin natural objects.

◆ Glue patterns on tag board, leaving room for the children to continue extending the patterns along the board, or set out blank tag boards and help the children make new pattern boards.

Observing and Assessing the Children

Can the child assemble a pattern on a chalk line, using two or more sets of objects?

Connecting to Other Curricular Areas

Mathematics

◆ recognizing and creating patterns (algebra)

4+ Probably Will Catch One!

This activity explores the concept of probability. In it, children grab a handful of items and search through them to find the one or two that are different from the rest. The possibility of picking a dissimilar item corresponds to the ratio of these dissimilar items to the similar items in the entire collection. This is probability and, probably, the children will grasp the concept!

Science Content Standard—makes comparisons among different observations (Science as Inquiry)
Science Process Skill—interpreting data

Words You Can Use

Chance   Probability
Handful   Probable
Least   Same
Most

Things You Can Use

Several of one kind of natural object—suggestions include acorns, pinecones, small rocks or pebbles, sweet gum balls, alder cones, and maple seeds (Plastic bottle caps, old keys, or plastic counters can also be used.)

Note: Ask the children to help you collect the objects.

White, red, and blue paint and a small paintbrush

Container, such as a bag or box

Before the Activity

Collect a set of one kind of object, such as acorns. Select eight of them and paint a white spot on one, a red spot on two, and a blue spot on five. Allow them to dry before returning them to the set.

What to Do

1. Show the children the entire set of one kind of object, such as acorns. Explain that while most of the acorns are the same, eight have spots painted on them. Show the children the acorn with the white spot, the two with red spots, and the five with blue spots.
2. Mix all the acorns together in the container (bag or box).
3. Ask the group if they think it will be easy for them to close their eyes, reach into the container, and pull out one of the dotted acorns. Ask, "Which kind of acorn is the easiest to find? Which kind of acorn is the hardest to find?"
4. Choose one child and ask her to grab a handful of acorns from the container, then ask her to show each acorn to everyone as she orders them based on type.
5. Give the child a chart like the one below, and, depending on her ability, help her or let her record how many of each type of acorn she pulled from the container.
6. Ask the child to return the first handful of acorns to the container, mix them up, and then repeat the process another four times.
7. Talk with the children about what happened. Ask, "Which kind of acorn was most common? The plain acorns? Which color of acorn was most common? Blue? How often did she find the acorn with a white dot? How about red ones?"
8. Repeat the activity with another child, recording the data in the same way.
9. After all the children complete the activity, compare the charts. Ask the children what kind of acorn was the most common for them to grab.

The number of acorns collected in five different handfuls

Handfuls	Plain #	White dot #	Red dot #	Blue dot #
First				
Second				
Third				
Fourth				
Fifth				

Want to Do More?

◆ Repeat the process using measuring cups. Ask the children to describe the differences between what they get when they scoop with a ½- and 1-cup size measuring cups.

◆ Repeat the activity, using Lego blocks. When a child grabs a handful of blocks, which color is most common? Which color block is the rarest?

Observing and Accessing the Children

Given a set of objects, such as acorns, in which a small portion is marked with dots of various colors, will the child be able to say which kind she is most likely to find in a handful?

Learning in Other Curricular Areas

Language and literacy
◆ communicating information with others (expressive language)

Math
◆ collecting and organizing data and applying probability (data analysis and probability)

Motor development
◆ grabbing handfuls of objects (small motor)

4+ Photo Finder

To help children differentiate between real objects and graphic representations, take digital photographs of familiar outdoor items. Have the children look at the photos, and then challenge them to find and collect the real objects. This is a great activity for children who have a wide range of skills. One child can go in search of two particular items, while another child seeks out five of something else. This is a fun challenge for the entire class.

Science Content Standard—explores through trial and error (Science as Inquiry)
Science Process Skills—observing; classifying

Words You Can Use

Collecting   Pair
Duplicate   Search
Environment   Sound
Explore   Texture
Find   Touch
Match

Things You Can Use

Outdoor objects, such
    as small twigs,
    pebbles, leaves, sweet
    gum balls, or anything
    that is plentiful and
    common to your
    location
Collecting bags, such as
    grocery bags or paper
    sacks
Shoebox

Before the Activity

Take pictures of items commonly found in an accessible outdoor area, such as the playground or the area around the building. Print the photos.

What to Do

1. Show the children the photographs of the various objects, asking them to identify the items they know. Explain to the children that the objects in the photographs are all from the area around the school. Talk about any items the children find unfamiliar.

2. Give the children collecting bags. Ask each child to choose one or two photos to look at carefully and then search for and collect the items in the photos they chose.

3. Bring the children to the area where you took the photos, and invite them to collect the items in their bags. After all the children think they have the objects in the photographs, return to the classroom to confirm their finds.

4. As the children become more adept at this activity, increase the number of items they are to find.
   Note: This activity is especially helpful for children who need to strengthen their visual memory skills. They can place the photographs of the objects they are looking for inside their bags, so that if they forget, they can check in the bag for a reminder.

Want to Do More?

◆ Make this activity more challenging by including photographs that show just part of an object. For example, show the children a photograph of a spigot on the corner of a building, the step on a climber, or a colored mark on the pavement. Challenge the children to find the place, then come back and describe the location to everyone.

Observing and Assessing the Children

Can the child find the item in her picture? How does the child respond to the challenge of a harder task?

Learning in Other Curricular Areas

Language and literacy
- ◆ listening with understanding and responding to directions (receptive language)

Math
- ◆ identifying shapes and patterns (geometry)
- ◆ counting (number operations)

Motor development
- ◆ collecting objects and placing them in the collecting bag (large and small motor)

4+ ABC Walk

An alphabet walk helps children focus their observations as they explore the outdoors. On each walk, focus on finding things that begin with the sound of a specific letter—dandelions, dogs, dirt, dragonflies, doors, and dump trucks. Ask what letters the children see on signs. Try going on a walk to find every letter of the alphabet. Find out which letters are the hardest to find. Focus on "F" when flowers are in bloom.

Science Content Standard—describes and records observations (Science as Inquiry)
Science Process Skill—classifying

Words You Can Use
Alphabet letters
Object names

Things You Can Use
Alphabet letter cards
Index card and markers
Masking tape
Clipboard, paper, and
  pen

Before the Activity
Take a brief walk to find the best route to take with the children.

What to Do

1. Prepare to take an ABC Walk with the children. Ask the children to choose a letter, or select one for them, "G," for instance. Make copies of the letter on cards. Show the children the letter and review the sound(s) the letter makes.

2. Go on the walk, telling the children to keep an eye out for objects whose names start with "G." When a child finds an object that begins with "G," ask that child to introduce it to all the other children.

3. Place a card with the letter on the ground near the object. Use tape or a rock to hold it in place, as needed. On a "B" walk, for instance, the children might find a beetle, something brown, a butterfly, a bottle, a branch, a bee, or a blossom. On an "M" walk, the children might find mud, metal, a maple tree, a machine, moss, a mess somebody made, or a moth. On an "I" walk, the children might find insects, irises, the color indigo in a flower, or icicles. Think about what is in your area as you choose which letter to use.

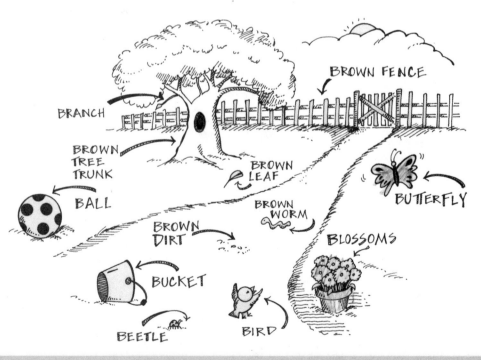

4. Write down the name of each item the children find.
5. Continue on the walk, always placing a card where the children find objects whose names begin with the appropriate letter.
6. After the children find several items, return to school using the same path. When the children discover a letter card, ask them what they saw there. Give them hints, if necessary. When the children name the item, choose a child to pick up the card.
7. After finishing the walk, tell the children how many items they found by adding the number of items on your list. Encourage the children to count along with you.
8. On another day, repeat the walk, focusing on another letter. Afterwards, ask the children if they found more or fewer items than on the previous walk? It will become apparent to the children that it is easier to find things that begin with some letters than with others.

Want to Do More?

◆ Set out magazines and newspapers and invite the children to find pictures of the objects they saw on the walk, and then use them to create a letter scrapbook.

◆ Do an ABC Walk inside and compare the things the children see to the things they found outside. Ask, "Are inside and outside vocabularies the same?"

◆ Choose several letters and tally how many things the children can find whose names start with each letter. Ask the children which letter is the most common and which is the least common.

Observing and Assessing the Children

Can the child remember some of the names of the objects the children found on the ABC Walk?

Learning in Other Curricular Areas

Language and literacy

◆ identifying letters and making letter sound matches (reading readiness)

Math

◆ counting or tallying the items found for each letter (number operations)

Motor development

◆ walking to find and record the items (large motor)

"Official" Outdoor Scientists

4+

Children are used to going outside to play. How can we help them become observers instead? Special Outdoor Scientist Badges and simple science tools help focus their attention on all the interesting things there are to see when they become Outdoor Scientists.

Science Content Standard—uses senses for observation (Science as Inquiry)
Science Process Skill—observing

Words You Can Use
Equipment
Observation
Observe

Things You Can Use
Outdoor Scientist Badges made from tag board with the children's names
Magnifiers
Resealable plastic bags (collecting bags)
Cardboard tubes (rolls from paper towels, wax paper, wrapping paper)
Clipboard, paper, and marker or pen

Before the Activity
Prepare an Outdoor Scientist Badge for each child. (See illustration)

What to Do

1. Tell the children that you are taking them to a special place to observe things in nature. (In science, this means looking at nature.)
2. Bring a set of science equipment (such as magnifiers and collecting bags) with you to help the children make observations.
3. Hang an Outdoor Scientist Badge around each child's neck. As you do so, say, "This Outdoor Scientist Badge means that you are a good observer and can discover special things in nature."
4. Pick out a tree, shrub, or other area to observe. As they stand at some distance from the tree, give the children the cardboard spyglasses, and invite them to observe it.
   Safety note: Be aware that some children may have allergic reactions to certain plants in the exploration area.
5. Ask the children what they see in the tree with their spyglasses. Have them start by looking at the bottom of the tree, then move up, observing all of its parts. Encourage the children to talk about what they see. Ask, "What parts of the tree do you see? Do you see any animals?"
6. Ask the children to lower their spyglasses, move a little closer, and then look again. Ask what else they can see.

BADGE

7. Bring the children closer to the tree and encourage them to take turns using magnifiers to observe a leaf, bark, or small animals crawling on the tree. Again, encourage them to describe what they see.

   Note: Young children may have a hard time using magnifiers. Some children are more successful if they hold one hand over the eye they are not using, and look through the magnifier with the other. Even when children are unable to use magnifiers well, they enjoy playing with them. It also reminds them to look for little things they might otherwise not notice.

8. Explain to the children that to be an Outdoor Scientist, they must use their eyes to discover things about nature. Ask the children to sit together facing the tree and talk about all the things they notice.

Want to Do More?

- Challenge each child to make a drawing based on his or her observations.
- Invite the children to observe another tree and compare it to the first tree they observed.
- Encourage the children to observe another object in nature, like a patch of grass or puddle, or a manmade object, such as a sidewalk or a fire hydrant. Ask them to describe the differences between this and the tree they originally observed.
- Bring in real binoculars for the children to explore.

Observing and Assessing the Children

Can the child make a set of observations using the materials given?

Learning in Other Curricular Areas

Language and literacy
- communicating observations with others (expressive language)
- listening with understanding and responding to directions (receptive language)

Motor development
- walking to and around the observation area (large motor)

4+ Our Outside Book—All Year Long

Photograph albums and vacation scrapbooks are wonderful visual records of family events. An Outside Book is a record that helps children document the changes that occur in particular part of the outdoor world. This activity helps children strengthen their ability to organize and communicate about their observations. It also tells children that outside spaces, wherever they are, are interesting and important.

Science Content Standard—describes and records observations (Science as Inquiry)
Science Process Skills—observing; measuring; communicating

Words You Can Use

Animal names
Count
Measure
Plant names
Record

Things You Can Use

Brads
Camera (optional)
Crayons and other drawing materials
Drawing paper
Glue or tape
Scrapbook (ready made), a loose-leaf notebook, or your own book made of heavy construction paper or drawing paper

Before the Activity

Select a site that you can visit easily and where children can observe signs of life and seasonal changes. In the city, there are often places along sidewalks set aside for a tree or plants. Areas with many shrubs or plants are likely homes of insects and small animals.

What to Do

1. Take the children for a walk to the selected site. Talk with the children about what they see. Ask, "What here comes from nature? What is man-made? Does anyone see any leaves or plants?" Point out anything else worth noticing, an anthill in the crack in the blacktop or a puddle from a recent rain, for example.

2. Talk with the children about how different things happen each day. Some are exciting and easy to notice, such as getting a new haircut, while others are harder to notice, like growing taller. Engage the children in a discussion about how the outside world is an interesting place full of constant changes. Ask the children if they notice anything in nature changing around them.

3. Tell the children they will be making a book about what they see outside. Give the children crayons, markers, drawing paper, and so on. Encourage them to look at the objects, plants, and animals they see in the area, and make a drawing of whatever intrigues them. Talk with the children about their drawings. Some children might draw the sky. If so, ask if it is a cloudy day or whether the sky is blue? Other children may draw themselves. Ask, are they wearing T-shirts, or coats and mittens? Ask if anyone can find dry dirt or mud or sand? Is anything flying by? Help the children find the many "signs of nature" unique to the setting. Encourage the children to collect small objects from the area that they can tape or glue on a page in the book, or make texture rubbings of tree bark or a brick.

4. If possible, use a digital camera to take a group photo of the children and close-up pictures of the different items the children find interesting.
   Note: A digital camera is an asset to this activity but not absolutely necessary, as the children will be making their own individual drawings.

USING MUSEUMS AND OTHER COMMUNITY RESOURCES

Invite a local representative of the department of natural resources to visit you at your outdoor site. Urban areas often have people who are experts at finding signs of nature in unlikely places.

5. Help the children label the drawings and photos and then help them write descriptions based on the children's narratives. Be sure to date them.

6. Come back to the classroom, set out a large folder, and ask the children to place the drawings and photos in it.

7. Bring the children back to the same site from time to time throughout the year, encouraging them to observe the big changes that occur there, such as snowfall, along with the subtle little changes that occur, like a plant growing another set of leaves or a flower bud. Remind the children to look carefully each time they come, and to observe these changes closely. Encourage the children to make new drawings of the changed scenery, and take photos of various items as well.

8. Return to the classroom with the children and together compare their new drawings to the earlier drawings and photographs. Add the new illustrations and photographs to the Outside Book.

9. Occasionally bring out the Outside Book and look through it with the children. Invite the children to talk about the significant events and changes that took place at the location, as well as how the children's appearances changed over time.

Want to Do More?

◆ Provide measuring tools, such as interlocking cubes, for the children and encourage them to measure different objects in the outdoor area and document the growth and changes.

Observing and Assessing the Children

Can the child describe how "her spot" changed over time?

Learning in Other Curricular Areas

Arts
◆ describing and responding to their own work and the creative work of others (visual art/creativity)
◆ making drawings of their observations (visual art/creativity)

Language and literacy
◆ understanding that different text forms are used for different purposes (early literacy)
◆ observing and describing changes over a period of time (descriptive language)
◆ relating prior knowledge to new information and communicating information with others (expressive language)
◆ understanding that pictures and symbols have meaning and that print carries a message (early literacy)

Math
◆ observing the passage of time (measurement)

Motor development
◆ going to the observation site and exploring the area to pick a location for repeated observation (large motor)

A Picnic Basket Full

This activity gives children the opportunity to explore the concept of volume while pretending to create a picnic for an animal friend. They will quickly discover how the sizes of objects have an impact on how they fit in a container. Volume is yet another way scientists measure things.

Science Content Standard—explores in response to teacher's questions (Science as Inquiry)
Science Process Skill—measuring (volume)

Words You Can Use

A lot	Much
Big	Many
Bigger	More
Few	Same
Full	Small
Less	Smaller
Little	

Things You Can Use

Objects of various sizes, such as small pebbles, acorns, pinecones, seashells, big rocks, little rocks, corncobs from field corn, bark nugget mulch, or whatever is common in your local environment

Containers to hold the objects—gallon ice-cream tubs, dish pans, or plastic tubs

Plastic berry baskets

Before the Activity

Collect a pail-full of each object you plan to use in this activity.

What to Do

1. Either outside or in the classroom, set the containers of pinecones, seashells, and other objects in front of the children. Tell the children these various containers hold the favorite "food" items of several imaginary animal friends.

2. Give the children berry baskets and ask them to put in their baskets the various "foods" they want to feed the imaginary animal friends. As they do so, ask the children to name the pretend animals they might want to feed. A squirrel? A rabbit? A whale?

3. When the children's baskets are all full, ask them to count how many items they each have in their baskets. Record these numbers for the children. Ask the children who had the largest number of items. Ask who had the smallest number, and if anyone had the same amount.

4. Ask the children to group the items in their baskets based on physical similarities. For instance, group pinecones together, then group sea shells together.

5. Once the children have their own items in groups, split the children into pairs and encourage them to compare their piles with one another by making simple line graphs out of the objects. (If you are outside, use the lines on the sidewalk, or make a line with chalk or in the dirt to make a baseline. If you are inside, use tape or paper.) Model for the children how to line their objects up in lines beside one another. For example, if "Tia" lines up her pinecones, then "Sam" places his

BERRY BASKET

BASELINE

in a line beside hers. "Tia" might have one pinecone while "Sam" has three (see illustration). Have them continue lining up the remaining sets of objects.

6. Ask the children questions about the simple graphs they are making. Ask each child to share at least one observation with the children. For instance, "Tia" might say, "Sam has more pinecones than me," and "Sam" might say, "I have the most rocks. I got 17."

7. Look at the graphs with the children, and ask them to indicate who had the smallest or largest overall number of items. If "Jason" has the largest number of items, say, "Jason had the most things in his basket and Lea had the fewest. Let's put their things side by side and see what we notice. Who had more big things? Who had the more small things?" Point out that the more large objects a child had, the smaller the number of total objects the child could put in her basket. Encourage the children to discuss this idea. The smaller the object, the more of them it will take to fill a container. Or, the larger the object, the fewer it will take to fill a container.

Want to Do More?

◆ With children who are not yet able to count reliably, compare acorns to pinecones by asking the children to make a row of 10 pinecones, and then place one acorn next to each pinecone. Invite the children to continue adding to the row of acorns until it is the same length as the row of pinecones. Even without counting, it will become clear to the children that it takes more acorns than pinecones to cover the same distance.

◆ Set out several large containers and several piles of various natural objects. Ask the children to predict how many of each object it will take to fill the containers, and then have the children fill the containers to verify their estimates.

Observing and Assessing the Children

Given a container and two sets of objects of various sizes, can the child tell it will take more of the smaller objects to fill the container?

Learning in Other Curricular Areas

Language and literacy
◆ listening with understanding and responding to directions (receptive language)
◆ communicating ideas and thoughts with others (expressive language)

Math
◆ counting and estimating numbers of objects to put into containers (number operations)
◆ exploring and discovering volume concepts (measurement)

Motor development
◆ picking up and filling container with objects (small motor)

5+ Snatch a Rock

This activity is a variation on an old Scottish game. Though the activity is deceptively simple, as the children play it, they will begin to develop strategies for winning. In this way, the activity encourages the children to develop their mental subtraction skills.

Science Content Standard—uses senses for observation (Science as Inquiry)
Science Process Skills—observing; classifying; measuring

Words You Can Use

Alternate	Row
Different	Same
Estimate	Set
Identical	Subtract
Line	Take away

Things You Can Use

Small rocks, acorns, shells, or other similar plentiful objects
Plastic bags

Before the Activity

Place several sets of small stones in different bags and label them for this activity. You will have these in case the children become very involved in this activity.

What to Do

1. To start the activity, tell the children they will be going outside to collect various stones, acorns, or other objects about the size of a penny. If you do not have access to a location where the children can gather such objects, fill a bag of them yourself at another location on a previous day, and present the objects to the children.
   Safety note: Supervise the children carefully throughout this activity.
2. Ask the children to group the stones in sets of six, nine, 12 or more, depending on their counting abilities. Help the children place the sets in plastic bags and bring them into the classroom.
3. Play a practice round of the game with one child, explaining the game to the children as you go. Once the children are comfortable with the game, create pairs of children to play together. The rules of the game are as follows:
   ◆ Divide the stones into three equal piles, and then line them up in equal rows. (Children just beginning to learn about numbers will be more successful if they have only a few objects in each line.)
   ◆ Count the stones in each row to be sure they each have the same number.

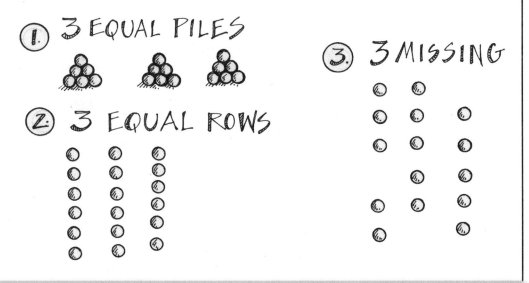

- Next, one child in the pair hides her eyes while the second child takes stones from any or all of the three lines, taking only as many as she can hold in her hands, then tells the first child to open her eyes.
- The first child opens her eyes, looks at the remaining stones, and then guesses how many stones the second person is holding in her hands.
- If the guess is correct, the child guessing gets to keep the stones. If the guess is wrong, the rocks go to the child who picked them up.
- The children alternate turns until all rocks are gone. The child with the most rocks goes first in the next game.

Want to Do More?

- Challenge the children to try playing the game in groups of four. This might require a greater number of stones in the set.
- Compare the number of large stones to the number of small stones the children can fit in their hands.
- Set out dry cereal, or prepare carrots or grapes as a snack, and invite the children to play Snatch a Snack.
- Show children who like this game how to play Tic-Tac-Toe.

Observing and Assessing the Children

After finishing several games, can the child begin to determine the number of rocks her opponent removes with each turn?

Learning in Other Curricular Areas

Language and literacy
- listening with understanding and responding to directions (receptive language)

Math
- counting and problem solving (number operations)
- using non-standard measurement tools to determine size of stones they are collecting (measurement)

Motor development
- picking up stones and holding them (small motor)

Social/emotional development
- engaging in cooperative play, sharing materials, and taking turns (social interaction)

Using the Sidewalk as a Measuring Place

Children use comparisons every day. They begin to notice who in the room is tallest, shortest, or about the same as they are. While they can compare themselves to other individuals, they may not have a complete sense of how their heights relate to everyone else's. This activity gives the children a chance to measure and compare themselves to one another.

Science Content Standard—collects, describes, and records observations (Science as Inquiry)
Science Process Skills—observing; predicting

Words You Can Use

Big
Bigger
Biggest
Longest
Measure
Same
Shortest
Tallest
Other appropriate
    comparative terms

Things You Can Use

A collection of sticks, plants, or other objects in a variety of sizes
Chalk or masking tape

Before the Activity

Collect several sets of objects to order and measure.

What to Do

1. Bring the children outside. Hold up two sticks (or two of any object). Ask the children which of the two is bigger, longer, or smaller. Show the children how to compare things by placing them side by side. Ask each of the children to gather a stick. If there are no sticks available, consider bringing several sticks from another location.
   Safety note: Supervise the children closely.
2. Use chalk to draw a line on the playground or sidewalk. Ask the children to line their sticks on the line.
3. After the children line up their sticks ask, "Latisha, can you tell which stick is the longest? Point to the stick. Which is the shortest? Do you see two that are about the same length? Which two?"
4. Once the children become adept at this, ask, "I wonder, who is the tallest child in the room? Shall we use the sidewalk and find out?"
5. Ask the children to lie down with their feet along one edge of the sidewalk. When the children are in place, use the chalk to outline the tops of their heads on the sidewalk.

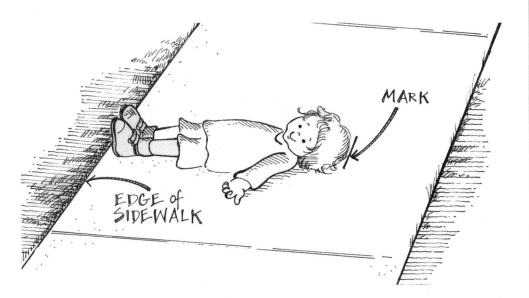

MARK

EDGE of SIDEWALK

6. After the children get up, help them use chalk to write their names under their lines.

7. Look at the lines and determine which is the tallest, which is the shortest, and which children are about the same height. Ask the children, "Is it easy to look at the marks and tell who is tallest or shortest? How can we figure out the order of all the children in between?" Tell the children that scientists use the word "data" to talk about information they collect. Explain that the marks on the ground represent data about everyone's heights, but because it is all mixed up, it is hard to use it to determine the order of the children's heights.

8. Help the children look at the marks on the pavement and begin to group themselves. Say, "Look at Anna's mark. Now look at your own. Do any of you have marks that are about the same length as hers? If you do, go stand by Anna. Let's see what other groups we can make." Help the children make three or four clusters, and then place the clusters in order.

9. Ask the children to stay in their groups and then lie down. Use a new color of chalk to make another set of marks around the children's heads. When the children get up, talk with them about what they notice: It is easier to find similarities and differences when data is more organized.

10. If they are interested, help the children organize the data even more completely. It should not take long for the children to figure out that it is much easier to organize themselves according to height while they are standing up!
    Note: Children can be just as sensitive about their size and shape as adults. Be sure to talk about this with the children. Remind them that the activity is about collecting data rather than finding out who is tallest or shortest.

Want to Do More?
- Set out a ruler and invite the children to measure one another.
- Cut lengths of string that match the children's heights and use them to make a wall chart.

Observing and Assessing the Children
Given a set of objects, can the child determine which is the longest, the shortest, and which are the same size?

Learning in Other Curricular Areas
Language and literacy
- listening with understanding and responding to questions (receptive language)
- understanding that print carries a message (early literacy)

Math
- recording data using non-standard units of measurement (measurement)

Motor development
- lying down and getting up from the sidewalk (large motor)

5+

Name It and Label It

Connecting names and words to objects is how children learn new vocabulary. In this activity, the children gather natural objects and label them. By adding names and printed words, miscellaneous "stuff" can become a collection.

Science Content Standard—uses resources for acquiring information (Science as Inquiry)
Science Process Skills—observing; communicating

Words You Can Use
Object names

Things You Can Use
Natural objects
Cards (5" x 5")
Markers
Glue or paste
Pens

Before the Activity
Conduct several collecting walks with the children in the days leading up to this activity, or ask the children to bring in objects that they find in their neighborhoods.

What to Do

1. Bring out the objects that you and the children gathered. Go through the objects with the children, asking if they can name some of them. Select the objects the children can name as the first to label.

2. One at a time, help the children print the names of the objects on cards and then glue or paste the objects next to their names. Spell out the names with the children as you help them write the names down, and then say the word. The children may or may not want to be very specific as they name the items. For instance, if there are three different pinecones, the children may choose to name them all "pinecones," or to name them "white pine pinecone," "pinecone from school," or "pinecone from Nick's house."

3. After the children finish naming and labeling the objects they are familiar with, move on to the unknown items and introduce the children to these objects.

4. Give each object a blank label until you find the answer. This shows the children that sometimes the answers are not readily available, and that it is okay if they do not yet know the answer.

5. Ask the children if they can guess where the various items originate. Give them clues as they guess. Once the children guess, or you tell them what a particular object is—a coconut, for instance—tell the children a few things about coconuts, or encourage them to search books in the classroom or use the Internet to find information about coconuts.

6. With all the interest that this activity will generate, your collection of natural objects is sure to increase. Try storing these items in plastic tubs or trays, and put them in the Science Center where the children can handle and name them.

Want to Do More?

- Have the children pick an object they want to focus on for a day or week. It can be something unusually attractive, such as a beautiful flower, shell, or feather. It could also be something mysterious, such as an unfamiliar fruit or vegetable, a snakeskin, a cicada shell, or a bone found in a field. Invite the children to speculate about the mystery for a while before providing more information.
- For children who are adept at organizing the various natural objects, challenge them to classify them based on different characteristics.
- Invite an employee of a museum or nature center to come in and verify the collection for the children.

Observing and Assessing the Children

Can the child name some of the natural objects in the collection?

Learning in Other Curricular Areas

Language and literacy
- understanding that pictures and symbols have meaning and that print carries a message (early literacy)
- identifying labels and signs in the environment (early literacy)
- listening with understanding and responding to directions (receptive language)
- explaining what the objects are and naming them (expressive language)

INCORPORATING TECHNOLOGY

If there are various items you know the children will find in the area when they go on their collection walks, download pictures of these items and collect them in a field guide. Mount the images on index cards, label them, and laminate them. Punch a hole in the top left corner and use a metal ring or yarn to hold them together. Let the children use the guide to identify their finds.

Following Written Directions: By Yourself

This activity challenges children to follow directions by giving them a series of steps (made of drawings or simple words) they will need to follow in consecutive order. Children love to work in pairs to puzzle out and follow the directions.

Science Content Standard—explores through trial and error (Science as Inquiry)
Science Process Skills—communicating

Words You Can Use

Direction and position words such as, to, toward, left, right, and away
Map
Names of major locations on the playground, such as the climber, yellow slide, and so on
Names of objects the children use
Position words such as under, over, on, next to, beside, and near

Things You Can Use

Collection of small objects that fit into a child's hand
Multiple copies of a simple map of your outdoor space that shows the basic shape of the space with a sketch of major "landmarks," such as a climber, a tree, the fence, and so on

Before the Activity

Place a collection of small objects throughout the outdoor area. Using the copies of the map of your outdoor space, create several simple drawings of a set of actions for each pair of children to follow. For instance, include a drawing indicating that the pair is to start at the climber, go to the slide, put a rock next to it, then come back to the climber and put a leaf under it.

Note: Each map should have a different set of directions. You will need one map for each pair of children.

What to Do

1. Divide the children into pairs and give each pair a map with various objects marked throughout the area.

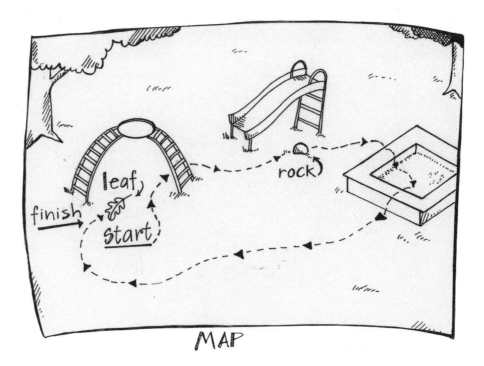

MAP

2. Explain to the children that they will need to use the maps to find the different objects and locations. Encourage the children to bring the objects they find to you for confirmation. Before they go, explain to the children any symbols you use on the maps. For instance, explain that an arrow pointing down means the children should put something down at that location.

3. Send the children off to follow the directions on their maps. Wander around the area as they do so, encouraging and helping the different pairs.

4. When all the pairs finish following the directions on their maps, ask them to find you. Retrace the children's steps with them, encouraging them to show you where they put various objects.

5. Once the children finish retracing their steps with you, challenge them to collect their objects, return to the starting point, trade maps with someone, and try a new set of directions.

Want to Do More?

◆ Prepare a Treasure Hunt. Make a list of steps the children must follow, and put a reward at the end of the hunt.

◆ Invite the children to make their own maps and give them to other children to follow.

◆ Help the children draw a large map of the play area. Encourage them to add as many details as they can. If appropriate, make a map of the surrounding area, beginning with the buildings immediately around your school.

Observing and Assessing the Children

Can the child follow the directions on a map by placing the objects in their proper places as the map specifies?

Learning in Other Curricular Areas

Language and literacy

◆ listening with understanding and following directions and conversations (receptive language)

◆ understanding that pictures and symbols have meaning and that print carries a message (print awareness, writing, and comprehension)

Math

◆ following directions as they determine where to place the objects (problem solving)

5+ The Group Must Decide

Some college campuses have a large rock that the students paint as they wish. This activity is similar. In it, the children must all decide together how they are going to paint the rock.

Science Content Standard—initiates different approaches to solve a problem or answer a question (Science as Inquiry)
Science Process Skill—classifying

Words You Can Use

Bottom
Center
Color names
Decide
Half
Paint
Quarter
Top
Whole

Things You Can Use

Tempera paints
Paintbrushes
Camera, digital or film

Before the Activity

Find a rock that is about 15"–20" (30–50 cm) and move into an appropriate open area outside. The area around the rock will have paint seeping and chipping off over time, so it should be some distance from where the children most frequently gather and run.

What to Do

1. Bring the rock into the schoolyard. When the children ask you why it is there, tell them that it is the Painting Rock, and that you put it in the schoolyard for the children to paint.

2. Explain to the children that they must work as a group to decide the following things before painting the rock:
   - what colors to use
   - when to paint the rock
   - who will paint the rock

3. Moderate as the children make these decisions. It might help them if you take notes on poster board.

4. Once the children decide how to proceed with painting the rock, set out the materials and watch as they paint.

5. After they finish, take a picture of the Painting Rock. Each time the children repaint the rock, take another photograph to remember the event.
   Note: Be sure to take a picture of the Painting Rock before the first painting, so the children can see what it looked like before the first painting.

6. After the children have painted the rock several times, gather the photographs of it together into a book. Ask the children to describe each photograph, and what they remember about the process of painting it, and add these descriptions to the book.

USING MUSEUMS AND OTHER COMMUNITY RESOURCES

Take a field trip to a local university to visit its painted rock.

Want to Do More?

◆ Occasionally look at the rock with the children to see if the paint is chipping off or seeping to expose the bare rock.

◆ After the children paint the rock several times, help the children chip off some of the layers and discuss the different levels.

Observing and Assessing the Children

Does the child work with the group to decide how to paint the rock?

Learning in Other Curricular Areas

Language and literacy

◆ listening with understanding and responding to directions (receptive language)

◆ communicating information to others (expressive language)

Motor development

◆ painting the rock (small motor)

Squares Add Up

This is a very simple competitive game. In it, the children add items to squares that have predetermined values, trying to force their opponents to make a move. This activity helps children develop their strategic thinking skills.

Science Content Standard—initiates different approaches to solve a problem or answer a question (Science as Inquiry)

Science Process Skills—observing, communicating

Words You Can Use

Add
Number words

Things You Can Use

Leaves, small stones, small sticks, or any other natural items
Cards with numbers written on them for each square set
Chalk

Before the Activity

Using chalk, draw sets of 10 equal-size squares on the sidewalk or blacktop. Two to four children will use each set of 10 squares. Prepare number cards from 1–10, or whatever range is appropriate for your children.

What to Do

1. Randomly place a number card in each of the 10 squares. Show the children the set of squares with cards placed on them at random.
2. Ask each child to take a handful of leaves or some other natural object. Explain to the children that each set of 10 squares represents a game board, and that between two and four children will use each board. Explain the following rules to the children:
   - The children in each group take turns placing one leaf at a time in each square until there are as many leaves in the square as the number on that square's card. When a child puts the fifth leaf in the square with the 5 card in it, for instance, that child gets to pick up the card, and the children do not use that square for the rest of the game.
   - The object of the game is to get as many cards as possible.
   - Play until the children pick up the last card from the game board. The child with the most cards at the end of a round gets to go first in the following round.
3. As the children begin to play, they will start to develop strategies to avoid letting the other children in their group pick up cards. For instance, children will try to avoid putting the first leaf in the square with the 2 card, as the next child can close out that square and get the 2 card.

Want to Do More?

- Change the number of objects the children place at one time to two or three.

Observing and Assessing the Children

Can the child place the appropriate number of leaves in a square before picking up the card?

Learning in Other Curricular Areas

Math
- counting and adding (number operations)

CHAPTER 2

Ramps, Wheels, and Wings: Learning About the Physical World (Physical Science)

Clear Containers and a Sunny Day

Sunlight shining through a water-filled, clear plastic or glass container produces different shapes and patterns of light, which vary depending on the volume and shape of the container. Some containers produce the color spectrum. Handling the containers themselves helps to teach the children about the effects of light passing through water. Try it and see what happens!

Science Content Standard—observes and interacts with physical science tools (Physical Science)
Science Process Skills—observing; classifying

Words You Can Use

Light
Rays
Reflect
Sun
Water

Things You Can Use

Clear plastic containers
   or bottles in different
   shapes and sizes with
   lids
Water

What to Do

1. On a clear day, select a sunny spot and ask the children to help you fill a few clear plastic containers or bottles with water, making sure to reattach the lids securely.
2. Line up the clear water-filled containers so the sun will hit them all at the same time.
    Note: You can do this activity outside or inside, provided there is a sun-filled window in your classroom.
3. Point out to the children the shapes and colors the sun makes when its light passes through the water-filled containers.

4. Encourage the children to pick up the containers and move them to see how the sunlight passing through makes different shapes as they move the container.
5. Ask the children to describe what they see when the sunlight hits the containers. Ask them to pick which containers they think generate the best light patterns. Ask, "Do all the containers show shapes and patterns?" Encourage the children to describe the different ways the various containers affect the light.

Want to Do More?

◆ Fill several colored containers and bottles with water and set them out for the children to look through. Ask the children to describe the differences between how these containers affect the light, as opposed to the clear containers.

◆ Bring in plastic or glass prisms for the children to use and compare.

Observing and Assessing the Children

Given a bottle filled with water, can the child produce light patterns and talk about the light shining through the containers?

Learning in Other Curricular Areas

Language and literacy

◆ listening with understanding and responding to directions (receptive Language)

Math

◆ recognizing patterns (algebra)

Motor development

◆ picking up the containers and manipulating them to make different patterns (small motor)

Floater or Faller

What goes up must come down. In this activity, the children use the force of gravity to classify objects as either floaters or fallers. How does one tell? Well, the floaters linger as they descend to the ground, that's how!

Science Content Standard—matches like objects (Physical Science)
Science Process Skills—observing; classifying

Words You Can Use

Classify
Fall
Float
Gravity

Things You Can Use

Buckets to hold objects
Objects that will float a bit in the air, such as a feather, a leaf, or a small scarf
Objects that will fall quickly, such as a rock, acorn, or pinecone

What to Do

1. Talk with the children about how the force of gravity causes all objects to fall to the ground. Then explain how some objects, like leaves, fall more slowly than other objects because their flat shapes enable them to catch the wind's currents, rather than falling through them. As an example, explain that a parachute is a real big floater!

2. Put an assortment of leaves and other objects in a bucket and set the bucket out for the children. Ask one of the children to take the items from the bucket and drop them one at a time.

3. Challenge the children to classify each object, as either a "faller" or a "floater." It may take a few rounds of dropping each object before the children agree on which objects go in the two classification groups. Dropping a few non-floaters before a floater can help to clarify the differences between the two and help the children make knowledgeable comparisons.

4. Once the children have a clear sense of the differences between the two categories, invite them to collect various objects, test them, and then place the objects in the correctly labeled "floaters" or "fallers" bucket.

Want to Do More?

◆ Show the children how to make a parachute by tying strings to the four corners of a handkerchief and tying the strings to a small block or other object as a weight. Toss it in the air and watch it float down to the ground.

Observing and Assessing the Children

Given a set of natural objects, can the child predict which objects will float or fall when the child drops them?

Learning in Other Curricular Areas

Language and literacy
◆ listening with understanding and following directions (receptive language)

Motor development
◆ picking up and dropping objects to the ground (small motor)

Sound Containers

In this simple activity, the children make their own sound apparatus by using items found on the playground or other outdoor spaces. They will find an endless variety of objects to place in plastic containers, each with its own particular sound.

Science Content Standard—begins to sort and categorize objects by physical characteristics (Physical Science)
Science Process Skill—observing

Words You Can Use

Noises
Sound
Sound words, such as hard, soft, loud

Things You Can Use

Opaque margarine or butter containers with lids
Plastic bag (large enough to hold the many containers)

Before the Activity

Collect the containers and the large bag the children will use to hold the items they find.

What to Do

1. Go for a walk with the children.
2. Tell each child to select the two containers he wants to use to collect various objects. Encourage the children to find objects on the ground that will make interesting sounds when the children put them in their containers.
3. Provide an example for the children. For instance, say, "I am going to put one rock in this butter container and put the lid back on it. Then I am going to take three rocks and put them in another container."
4. Shake the containers and compare the sounds. Ask, "Do they make the same sounds?" Explain how different numbers of objects will make different sounds when put together in one container.
5. Set your two containers aside for later and ask the children to fill their containers with different objects so that each makes a different set of sounds. When everyone has two sound containers, invite the children to take turns shaking one another's, to compare the sounds they make, and to guess what is inside each.

Want to Do More?

◆ Challenge the children to classify the containers by types of sounds.
◆ Repeat with metal containers. Compare the differences in sounds.

Observing and Assessing the Children

Given a set of containers, can the child make a set of different sounds?

Learning in Other Curricular Areas

Language and literacy
◆ making and communicating ideas and thoughts about sound matches (expressive language)
Motor development
◆ collecting items to place in the containers (small motor)

How Far Can You Squeeze a Squirt?

Children love experimenting to see which squeeze bottles make the best "squirters"! In the process, the children learn how scientists compare the performances of similar objects.

Science Content Standard—begins to sort and categorize objects by physical characteristics (Physical Science)

Science Process Skill—measuring (non-linear)

Words You Can Use

Farther
Farthest
Force
Full
How far
Squirt
Water
Work
Words that describe the size of holes: small, big, and so on

Things You Can Use

Plastic squeeze bottles such as containers that hold mustard, ketchup, and shampoo, in a variety of sizes (the bottles should have holes of various sizes)
Chalk

Before the Activity

Send a note home asking families to collect as many squeeze bottles as possible. Make sure they are all clean.

What to Do

1. Fill a squeeze bottle with water and show it to the children. Tell them that you are going to use the bottle to water the plants in the classroom. Hold the squeeze bottle near the plants, squeeze the bottle, and water the plants. Continue squeezing until the bottle is empty.

2. Ask the children if they think that some bottles are better than other bottles for watering plants. Explain that when you hold most bottles upside down, they will leak water, and that the bigger the hole, the more water comes out. Explain that you force water out of a bottle by pushing on its sides, and that the harder you push, the more water comes out. Hands supply the force that pushes water through the holes.

3. Ask each child to choose a bottle that he thinks will squirt water the farthest, then bring the children outside and encourage them to practice squeezing the bottles.
   Note: Caution the children to be respectful of one another, and to squirt water only at the ground.

4. Once the children are comfortable with the process, start the great bottle squeeze-off! Use chalk to make a line on the sidewalk. Have the children

line up at the chalk line to stand at the edge of the sidewalk. Ask the children to take turns squeezing their bottles onto the sidewalk. Use the splash lines each squirt makes to see which bottle squirts water the farthest.

5. When the bottles are empty, review the results with the children, and select the bottle that squirts water the farthest.

6. Encourage the children to discuss whether other factors might have affected the results. For example, does each child's varying hand strength affect the results? Finish the activity by filling the bottles with water and going to an area where there are several plants and invite the children to water the plants from various distances.

Want to Do More?

◆ Show the children how to draw water pictures on the sidewalk. Talk with them about evaporation as they draw.

◆ If it is a very warm day, invite the children to put on bathing suits and squirt each other.
    Note: Some children may not want to get wet, even in bathing suits.

◆ Set out larger and smaller bottles, and invite the children to try squirting with them. Ask the children to describe the designs the squirts make.

◆ Place a bucket a distance away and challenge the children fill the bucket by squirting water into it.

◆ Measure the distances the children squirt their water and help them chart the results.

Observing and Assessing the Children

Given two squirt bottles filled with water, can the child determine which will squirt water the farthest?

Learning in Other Curricular Areas

Language and literacy
◆ listening with understanding and responding to directions and conversations (receptive language)

Math
◆ determining the distance water squirts from the bottle (measurement)

Motor development
◆ using their hands to apply a squeezing pressure to the bottles (small motor)

Iron and Sand in a Bottle

Scientists use the word "mixture" to describe combined materials they can later separate by physical means. By making separation bottles in this activity, the children can experience separating the parts of a mixture.

Science Content Standard—begins to sort and characterize objects by physical characteristics (Physical Science)
Science Process Skills—observing; communicating

Words You Can Use

Measurement words
Attract
Mix
Mixture
Separate

Things You Can Use

Bottles (clear plastic, 1-liter)
Funnels
Magnets
Paper clips, washers, and other small objects attracted to magnets
Sand
Iron filings (optional, handled only by adults)

Before the Activity

Prepare a sample bottle to show the children. Set it out for the children to see as they fill their own plastic containers.

What to Do

1. Show the children the separation bottle you made earlier. Hold out a magnet and slowly drag it along the side of the bottle. The magnet will attract and hold the iron materials along the edge of the plastic bottle, separating them from the sand.

FUNNEL

MAGNETS

WASHERS & PAPER CLIPS

IRON FILINGS

SAND

SEPARATION BOTTLE (LITER BOTTLE)

① ADD IRON FILINGS

② FILL ½ FULL WITH SAND

③ ADD WASHERS and PAPER CLIPS

④ PUT CAP ON SECURELY

⑤ USE the MAGNET

2. Set out the bottles, sand, and other magnetic materials for the children to use to make their own separation bottles, asking the children to identify each item as you go. Explain to the children how to make a separation bottle.
    ◆ First, an adult must carefully add the iron filings, then give the children funnels and show them how to fill the bottles half-full with sand.
    ◆ Next, invite the children to add paper clips, staples, or other materials to their bottles. It may be easiest for children to work in pairs, taking turns holding and filling the bottle.
3. When the bottles are three-quarters full, help the children put the caps on securely, and then shake the bottles.
    Note: Make sure the children do not fill the bottles to the top, or the mixture in the bottles will be hard to mix.
4. Give the children magnets and challenge them to use the magnets to separate the magnetic materials from the sand.
5. Talk with the children about what they did when they mixed the materials together. Say, "You mixed the materials—the sand, iron filings, and the pieces of iron materials. Then you used the magnet to separate the materials in the mixture." This helps the children understand how to make a mixture, as well as how you can separate that mixture into its different parts.

Want to Do More?
◆ Set out some nonmetallic items, such as copper and aluminum, and invite the children to add them to their bottles. Discuss with the children why the metals are not attracted to the magnet. Next, set out plastic materials for the children to add, asking the children whether the think the magnet will attract the plastic materials.

Observing and Assessing the Children
Can the child use a magnet to separate out iron materials from the sand and describe how to separate the parts that make up this mixture?

Learning in Other Curricular Areas
Motor development
    ◆ adding sand, washers, and staples to the plastic containers; using a magnet to separate the iron objects from the sand (small motor)
    ◆ shaking the filled plastic containers (large motor)

Magnet Hunt

Children are fascinated with magnets. An outdoor exploration of magnets can add an extra element of fun.

Science Content Standard—matches like objects (Physical Science)
Science Process Skills—observing; classifying

Words You Can Use

Attract
Magnet
Magnetic

Things You Can Use

Collection of
    nonmagnetic objects
Small magnets for each
    child
Clipboard, paper, and
    pen

What to Do

1. Set out several magnets in the classroom, and invite the children to explore with them, experimenting to determine which objects in the classroom are magnetic and which are not.

2. Explain to the children that the magnets are attracted to the iron in objects. Once the children are comfortable experimenting with magnets in the classroom, bring everyone outside and go on a Magnet Hunt, where the children hunt for objects that are attracted to their magnets.

3. Explain that they will place their magnets on different objects, then pull them away, and feel whether the object tries to stick to the magnet. Encourage the children to share their magnetic discoveries by calling the other children over and inviting them to put their magnets on the object as well.

4. Keep a record of all the different magnetic objects the children find, as well as who found them.

5. When the children finish searching the area, review the places and objects where the children found magnetic objects. Encourage the children to discuss how the iron may not be seen easily because it is hidden in some way, by paint, wood, rubber, or plastic.
Note: Bar and horseshoe magnets will lose their magnetism if dropped. Ceramic and rubber-based magnets are more durable.

Want to Do More

◆ Make a map of the school or nearby outdoor area where the children went on their magnetic hunt, and invite them to indicate on the map where they found different magnetic objects.

◆ Collect different types of magnets and invite the children to use them in exploring for iron and magnetic objects outdoors. After the children are familiar with the various types of magnets, talk to them about comparing how effective certain magnets are at finding other magnetic objects.

Observing and Assessing the Children

Can the child go outside and use a magnet to find other magnetic materials?

Learning in Other Curricular Areas

Language and literacy

◆ understanding and responding to directions (receptive and expressive language)

Math

◆ counting (number operations)

Motor development

◆ walking to hunt items that are attracted to magnets (large motor)

◆ holding the magnets and placing them on items to learn if they are attracted to the magnet (small motor)

Rainbow Sprinkler

Rainbows form when sunlight shines through air that contains water vapor. Ask any scientist what makes a rainbow, and she or he will say light and a prism. When water is in the air, it functions as a prism, dispersing the sunlight in such a way to make a rainbow visible. It is easy to make a rainbow: spray a fine mist into the air and you will soon see a mist of red, orange, yellow, green, blue, indigo, and violet.

Science Content Standard—observes and interacts with physical science tools (Physical Science)
Science Process Skills—observing; classifying (ordering); communicating

Words You Can Use

Create
Mist
Names of colors
Rainbow
Spray
Sun
Sunshine
Water

Things You Can Use

Garden hose with mister
Outside water faucet
A sunny day!

What to Do

1. Turn on the garden hose and adjust its nozzle so that the water comes out in a fine spray.
2. Hold the hose nozzle so it shoots straight up in the air. If possible, find a way to attach the hose to a chair or some other stationary object, so you do not need to hold it.
3. Tell the children that they might be able to observe a rainbow as the sun's rays strike the water droplets in the spray. Suggest that the children move around the spray and look for a rainbow. You will have to experiment to find the best angle to form a rainbow.

Note: To see a rainbow, you have to stand between the airborne moisture and the light source. For example, a rainbow forms when the sun is behind you and the rain or mist is in front of you.

4. If the children do not see a rainbow, bring the children out at some other time in the day and try again. Good hot days will be all the incentive that the children will need to experiment again. To help them understand the role of the sun, choose a cloudy day to conduct this experiment again. Turn on the water, and then ask the children if they can see a rainbow. Unless the sun breaks through the clouds, there should be no rainbow visible. Encourage this kind of experimental attitude by explaining that the children can learn something even when the experiment does not work as expected.

5. After the children spend some time observing the rainbow, talk with them about ROY G. BIV, the mnemonic device for remembering the rainbow color order.

6. Next, put out a set of crayons or chalk and challenge the children to identify the crayons whose colors appear in rainbows, and put them in the rainbow order. Once the children do this, invite them to draw a rainbow with the crayons or chalk, or to make a picture that uses all the colors of the rainbow.

Want to Do More?

◆ Use a prism and light source to show the children all the colors of a rainbow.
◆ Talk with the children about the folklore of the rainbow or find a rainbow story to read to the children. Suggestions include *A Rainbow of My Own* by Don Freeman, *The Boy Who Swallowed a Rainbow* by Trevor Romain, and *How the First Rainbow Was Made: An American Indian Tale* by Ruth Robbins.
◆ Provide finger paints and paper with which the children can make individual rainbow pictures.
◆ Find a photograph of a rainbow to show the children. Encourage them to compare the colors seen in their water-hose rainbows to those in the picture. Ask, "Are the colors the same? (Because the colors blend into each other, often we can see only four or five colors clearly.) Are some missing or are they hidden by the other colors?"

Observing and Assessing the Children
Can the child see and identify the different colors in a rainbow?

Learning in Other Curricular Areas
Arts
◆ learning the names of colors (visual art/creativity)
Language and literacy
◆ communicating observations verbally as they observe and discover the colors of the rainbow (expressive language)
Math
◆ recognizing patterns (algebra)
◆ counting the colors in the rainbow (number operations)
Motor development
◆ moving the hose back and forth (large motor)

Slushy in a Bag

Use melting or new-fallen snow to add a "slushy" to the menu. This activity uses snow (or crushed ice) to freeze juice into a tasty slush.

Note: The children do not consume the snow. The children will be happy to follow directions and practice reading temperatures with this new treat as the reward.

Science Content Standard—observes and interacts with physical science tools (Physical Science)
Science Process Skill—observing

Words You Can Use

Descriptive words for
    temperature
Degrees Celsius (°C)
Degrees Fahrenheit (°F)
Measure
Mix
Melt
Recipe
Temperature
Temperature numbers

Things You Can Use

Heavy resealable freezer
    bags, 1-gallon (4-liter)
    and 1-quart (1-liter)
    for each child (These
    are reusable only if
    each child removes his
    slushy and puts it in a
    cup before eating it.)
Measuring cups and
    spoons
Salt
Snow or crushed ice
Juice of your choice,
    such as apple,
    orange, cranberry,
    grapefruit, and so on
Small paper cups
Plastic spoons

What to Do

1. Collect a tub of snow or crushed or chipped ice. Fill a gallon-size, resealable plastic bag about half full of the snow or ice.
2. Add 6–8 tablespoons of salt to the snow or ice. If it does not freeze, add more salt, as salt will not hurt the process, regardless of how much you add. It may actually aid with the freezing.
3. In a small, 1-quart resealable freezer bag, pour ½ cup (125 ml) of whatever juice the children enjoy the most, such as apple, orange, cranberry, grapefruit, and so on. Seal the bag tightly with duct tape.
4. Place the small bag inside the big bag, then seal the large bag securely. Show the children how to hold the top edge of the large bag and take turns gently shaking the bag. As they do so, the juice will turn to slush.

1. ½ FULL
GALLON-SIZE BAG

2. 6-8 TABLESPOONS of SALT

3. ADD JUICE
DUCT TAPE SHUT
QUART FREEZER BAG

4. ADD SMALLER BAG TO LARGER BAG & SHAKE

5. Because the bag will get cold, consider setting out several potholders or mittens the children can use to keep their hands warm.

6. When the juice starts to turn slushy, help the child take the small bag of now-slushy juice out of the larger bag. Show the child how to rinse and dry the outside of the small bag.

    Note: The mixture in the small bag changes from a juice to a "slushy" at about $-3°$ C ($27°$ F) with the exact temperature depending on the type of juice and the amount of sugar in the juice. Snow or chipped ice has a temperature of about $0°$ C ($32°$ F). The salt and snow mixture will drop to below $-5°$ C ($27°$ F). The salt/snow mixture lowers the temperature of the juice, causing it to freeze or to form slush. If the juice stays in the snow and salt mixture long enough, it will freeze solid.

7. Serve the slushy in individual small paper cups and give the children plastic spoons to eat their slushies.

8. If desired, immediately add a new bag of juice to the old bag of salty snow and give it to a child to start shaking it again. If the snow has melted too much, pour out the excess water, add more snow and salt, then begin the process again.

9. Discard the snow, wash the ice bags and place out to dry and save it for later use.

Want to Do More?

◆ Give the children a thermometer and encourage them to keep track of the ice's temperature as it changes through each stage of the activity. Help them make a chart of the temperatures.

◆ Make ice cream using the same method. Arrange a visit to a creamery where the children can watch as the employees pour in the mix and wait for the ice cream or slushy to form.

Observing and Assessing the Children

Can the child follow the steps needed to make a slushy?

Learning in Other Curricular Areas

Language and literacy

◆ communicating information to others (expressive language)

◆ listening with understanding and responding to directions (receptive language)

Math

◆ taking temperature readings using a thermometer (measurement)

◆ recording the temperature readings (data analysis and probability)

Motor development

◆ gently shaking the plastic bag (small motor)

Sounds All Around Us

The outdoors offers a great opportunity for children to use one of their most precious senses—the sense of hearing. Whether in an urban, suburban, or rural setting, if a child takes the time to listen carefully, he can hear wind blowing, birds singing, and leaves rustling in the trees. This activity emphasizes the value of listening as a means of learning about the world.

Science Content Standard—uses descriptive language when making observations (Physical Science)
Science Process Skill—observing

Words You Can Use

Ear
Hear
Listen
Loud
Noise
Soft
Sounds
Sound
Source names
Quiet

Things You Can Use

Tape recorder

Before the Activity

Find a natural, undeveloped outdoor location where all the children can gather and sit comfortably.

What to Do

1. Bring the children to the natural listening location you selected. On the way there, as preparation for the activity, encourage the children to listen quietly to whatever sounds they hear.
2. When the children come to the natural listening location, ask them each to find a spot on the ground, sit, and listen carefully to the sounds of nature.

plane
bird
baby birds
truck
bee
squirrel
dog

3. Set out a tape recorder to capture the sounds the children hear. This can be helpful when you return to the classroom and discuss the experience with the children.

4. After a minute or two of quiet listening, ask the children to describe the different sounds they hear. Ask them to count all the different sounds, challenging them to name the source of each sound as they go.

Want to Do More?

◆ Repeat the activity, challenging the children to count the sounds they hear quietly, and then compare their results with each other.

◆ Take the children on a walk in a rural area. If your school is in the city, a park or the zoo are great sites for listening.

◆ Invite the children to compare natural to man-made sounds. Talk with the children about how the sounds make them feel.

Observing and Assessing the Children

Can the child identify some of the sounds that he hears when you play back the recording of the sounds later in the classroom? Can the child identify and count the sounds that he heard?

Learning in Other Curricular Areas

Language and literacy

◆ identifying and communicating the sounds heard (descriptive and expressive language)

◆ listening with understanding and responding to directions (receptive language)

◆ discriminating sounds (reading readiness)

Math

◆ counting (number operations)

◆ classifying sounds into different categories (algebra)

INCORPORATING TECHNOLOGY

Use a tape recorder as a sound-collecting tool. Use a digital recorder to transfer the sound to MP3 players for later listening and storage. Use these tools to send sound collections home for the children's families to hear.

Sunglasses

Modern sunglasses come in a variety of colors. They diminish glare, sunlight, and ultraviolet light, and in doing so alter the wearer's view. Choose a bright, sunny day to give children a chance to compare the ways different sunglasses affect their views. They will be gathering information, just like any scientist.

Science Content Standard—observes and interacts with physical science tools (Physical Science)
Science Process Skills—observing; classifying

Words You Can Use

Change
Color words
Sunglass words, such as brand names and style names

Things You Can Use

A variety of sunglasses with a variety of lenses
Basket
Crayons
Drawing paper

Before the Activity

Contact the children's families and ask them to help you gather sets of old sunglasses. Place the sunglasses in a basket.
Safety note: Be sure that the children do not look directly at the sun, even with sunglasses on.

What to Do

1. Bring a basket of sunglasses outdoors. Place the basket on the ground. Ask the children to look around and describe what they see without wearing sunglasses. For example, they might comment on the green trees, plants with colorful blooms, road and street signs nearby, and any other colorful objects outside.

2. Ask the children to select pairs of sunglasses and look at the same objects they looked at in the previous step. Invite them to describe the changes they see. The children may focus on the way the sunglasses change the color of everything. If appropriate, draw the children's attention to how sunglasses reduce glare and make their eyes more safe and comfortable on a bright sunny day.

BASKET of SUNGLASSES

3. Suggest that the children try on several different pairs of sunglasses to compare how each pair differently affects their views.
4. Challenge the children to search for the object whose appearance they think changes the most when they look at it while wearing sunglasses. Hand out some crayons and drawing materials, and invite the children to create pictures of the object.
5. Talk with the children about how sunglasses alter their views because the lenses change how light comes into their eyes.

Want to Do More?

◆ Set out various differently colored objects for the children to look at through different sets of sunglasses, and invite the children to comment on the differences.

Observing and Assessing the Children

Can the child articulate the differences in what he sees while wearing sunglasses as opposed to wearing no sunglasses?

Learning in Other Curricular Areas

Arts

◆ learning or reinforcing recognition of various colors and their names (visual arts/creativity)
◆ drawing and creating their own perceptions of what they see through the glasses (visual arts/creativity)

CONNECTING TO CHILDREN WITH SPECIAL NEEDS

Children who have visual impairments may be sensitive to sunlight. Check with families and medical records to see if this activity is safe to do.

USING MUSEUMS AND OTHER COMMUNITY RESOURCES

Ask a local optometrist to come for a classroom visit and talk with the children about sunglasses and glasses in general.

Which Will Melt First?

When you see children noticing that the ice cubes in their drinks are melting or that the ice or snow outside is melting, take the opportunity to illustrate for the children how temperature affects the rate at which ice melts. This activity works best with small groups in which you can encourage conversation about their observations.

Science Content Standard—observes and interacts with physical science tools (Physical Science)
Science Process Skills—observing; measuring (temperature); communicating

Words You Can Use

Cold
Degrees Celsius (°C)
Degrees Fahrenheit (°F)
Hot
Melting
Temperature

Things You Can Use

4 unbreakable pitchers
Marker
Icicles from an outside roof or ice cubes
Clear plastic drinking cups, all the same size
Water of different temperatures

Before the Activity

Label the pitchers A, B, C, and D. Fill the pitchers (see directions below) with cold, hot, warm, and cool water.

◆ Pitcher A—Add a cup or two of ice to the pitcher, and then fill it with tap water.
◆ Pitcher B—Fill with hot tap water. (This is a good time to talk with the children about the safe use of hot water.)
◆ Pitcher C—Fill with warm water.
◆ Pitcher D—Fill with cool water.

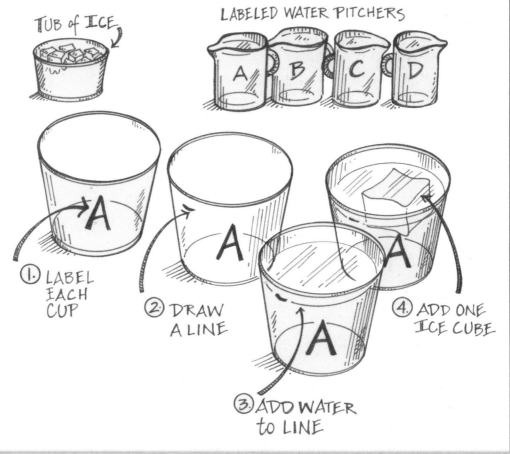

TUB of ICE

LABELED WATER PITCHERS
A B C D

① LABEL EACH CUP
② DRAW A LINE
③ ADD WATER to LINE
④ ADD ONE ICE CUBE

What to Do

1. Start a discussion with the children about ice. Ask them to describe what happens to ice over time, and what they think causes ice to melt.
2. Divide the class into several small groups. Set out four cups, labeled A, B, C, and D in front of each group of children. Each cup should have a line drawn about ½" below its lip. Explain to the children that they should fill each cup to the line, so the materials will be consistent for each part of the experiment.
3. Help the children fill each cup with water from the corresponding pitcher.
4. When the cups are ready, set out a tub of ice cubes and invite the children to place one ice cube in each cup, and invite them to observe what happens. Tell the children to watch until one cube melts completely, and then compare that cup to the other cups.
5. After the children see the ice cubes melt, encourage them to revisit their earlier discussion and see if their hypotheses were correct.

INCORPORATING TECHNOLOGY

A digital thermometer can give a clear reading without removing the instrument from the water solution. Some can even provide a printable record of the temperature changes over time.

Want to Do More?

◆ Set out a thermometer for each group and encourage them to take the temperature of the water before they add an ice cube, and then take the water's temperature again once the ice melts. Talk with the children about the results. Help them begin to see that the ice will melt more quickly in hotter water.

◆ Set out containers of various liquids, such as vinegar, salt water, or colored water. Invite the children to put ice cubes in the liquids and compare how quickly the ice melts in each liquid.

Observing and Assessing the Children

Can the child put one ice cube into each of four cups holding the same amount of water in different temperatures and predict which cube will melt first?

Learning in Other Curricular Areas

Math

◆ measuring and recording temperature data (measurement)

The Nose Knows

This activity gives the children an opportunity to "turn on" their noses to find out just how many different odors they can detect both indoors and out, from the waxy smell of crayons to the metallic odor of a fence or metal climber.

Science Content Standard—begins to sort and categorize objects by physical characteristics (Physical Science)

Science Process Skills—observing; classifying

Words You Can Use

Alike
Different
Identify
Indoor
Inside
Odor
Outdoor
Outside
Scent
Smell

Things You Can Use

Items that have
    detectible odors
Writing materials

Before the Activity

Identify and set out materials in the classroom that have detectible odors. These may include foods for snack, potted plants, pet cages, or art materials, such as playdough, markers, paint, or crayons. Be sure to add a few items with distinctive odors.

What to Do

1. Talk with the children about their sense of smell. Encourage them to identify smells they like and dislike. Discuss ways their noses help them know more about the world. For instance, their noses can let the children know what they will have for snack even before they see it. Encourage them to name some snacks that smelled particularly good, such as oranges or peanut butter and celery.

2. Invite the children to search the classroom for interesting smells. Ask them to announce each smell they discover. Make a list of all the odors the children find on their search. Challenge the children by encouraging them to describe the smells they find.

    Safety note: Prepare the children for both the indoor and outdoor activities by telling them about how to smell things safely: Warn them not to get too close to the objects they smell. Instead, get only close enough that the smell can come to them. Demonstrate how they should use their hands to waft smells to their noses. Warn them not to touch poison ivy, poison oak, or nettles.

3. After the children find several smells in the classroom, bring them back together to discuss the list of smells they found. Ask them to categorize the different smells. Ask, "Was the smell of crayons pleasant or unpleasant?" The children may discover that not everyone agrees about what smells good.

4. At another time, bring the children outside and repeat the activity. Before sending the children out to find new smells, explain to them that outdoor smells can be hard to find sometimes, as they often reside in the bark or leaves of a plant or tree. Show them how to crush a leaf, needle, or twig to release the odor.

    Note: Watch carefully to ensure they do not rip many leaves, twigs, and flowers from bushes and trees, particularly if there is not abundant plant life available nearby. Remind the children to be respectful of the environment and only to take one or two objects from a particular location.

5. After the children finish their outside smell search, bring the children back into the classroom and ask them to compare the lists from the indoor and

ACORN   DIRT   SPRUCE BRANCH   GRASS

WORM   BIRD EGG   SNAIL SHELL   ROSE

LEAF

outdoor smell searches. Encourage the children to discuss their findings. Ask, "In which location did most of the odors come from manufactured items?" Ask them which odors they prefer, and compare the popularity of the different odors.

Want to Do More?

- Let the children make a picture of something they enjoyed smelling. Challenge them to think of other objects the smells remind them of, and ask whether any of the smells serve as warnings of some kind.
- Set out several magazines and encourage the children to make collages with images they find that remind them of various odors.
- Show the children how odors of some items change when they mix with water. Give each child a small cup of water and an unbreakable eyedropper. Invite the children to observe the differences in the way the items like rocks or wood blocks smell before and after they squeeze drops of water on them.

Observing and Assessing the Children

Can the child identify various odors? Can he differentiate between indoor and outdoor odors?

Learning in Other Curricular Areas

Language and literacy
- observing the teacher writing lists (print awareness)
- describing smells (vocabulary development)

ADDRESSING THE NEEDS OF ENGLISH LANGUAGE LEARNERS
Say the name of each item the child handles and smells.

Acorns That Sink or Float

Acorns come in two groups—heavy and light. An acorn is light because a worm hollowed out the inside. If you see a hole in an acorn, it means the worm has already left. Those acorns that do not have holes in them may or may not be hollow, and may or may not have a worm in them waiting to burrow out. This activity helps the children determine which acorns are hollow and which are not.

Science Content Standard—begins to sort and categorize objects by physical characteristics (Physical Science)

Science Process Skills—classifying; inferring

Words You Can Use

Acorn
Classify
Float
Hole
Inside
Larva
Sink
Worm

Things You Can Use

Bags for collecting acorns
Large container filled with water
Hammer or rock
Clear jar for collecting larvae

Before the Activity

Find an oak tree near school that is dropping acorns. If you cannot find a nearby location where acorns are readily available, consider gathering several yourself elsewhere prior to the activity, or ask the children to gather them with their families and bring them in to class for the activity.

What to Do

1. Bring the children out to a nearby oak tree and ask them to collect acorns, or set out those brought to class earlier. Challenge the children to find the acorns with holes in them. Explain that these acorns once held the larvae of an insect called the acorn beetle. The beetles chewed their ways out of the acorns, leaving behind these holes. Explain that because we can see the hole it left, we know a worm was inside. Break some of these acorns open and show the children the hollow insides, then set them aside.

2. Explain to the children that some acorns still have larvae (worms) in them. Ask the children how they might try to determine if there are worms inside any of the other acorns. Explain that one way to determine which acorns have worms in them is by placing the acorns in water.
   Note: It is normal to find the larvae of acorn beetles in most oak acorns. This worm is in the second stage of the acorn beetle's metamorphosis. A larva enters an acorn when an adult beetle feeds on the acorn, then lays an egg inside it. The hole the adult made to insert the egg heals over before the larva hatches from its egg. The worm then spends much of the summer growing and feeding inside the acorn. In the fall, the larva eats its way to the surface and breaks through the acorn's hull, then falls to the ground and burrows into the soil. At this point, the worm enters the pupa or resting stage of its metamorphosis. The following spring, the adult acorn beetle will emerge.

3. Set out a container of water and encourage the children to put the acorns in the water one at a time. The acorns that sink are heavier because no little worms have hollowed them out. The ones floating near the top are likely to

have worms still growing inside them. To confirm this, help the children use hammers to break open one or two acorns and look for the larvae.

Safety note: Observe closely and be sure the children wear safety goggles and work on a stable surface when they break open the acorns.

4. When the children finish sorting the acorns by placing them in water, set out a clear jar and invite the children to gather all the acorns into it. As time goes by, the worms in the acorns will drill holes through the acorns' surfaces and then fall to the bottom of the jar for the children to observe.

5. When the children finish sorting the acorns, set the acorns out and ask the children to return them to the area where they found them so the squirrels can eat them.

Want to Do More?

◆ Gather various different species of acorns and invite the children to repeat the experiment with the new acorns.

◆ Bring the children outside to observe how squirrels and other animals use acorns.

◆ Set out several other types of nuts and encourage the children to see if the same system works for classifying them.

◆ Bring the children outside and invite them to plant some of the acorns.

Observing and Assessing the Children

Given a set of acorns, can the child sort them into three groups: those that had larvae, those that might have larvae, and those that do not have larvae?

Learning in Other Curricular Areas

Language and literacy

◆ listening with understanding and following directions (receptive language)

Math

◆ classifying, recognizing patterns (algebra)

◆ collecting and organizing data (data analysis and probability)

Motor development

◆ bending, squatting as they collect the acorns (large motor)

◆ placing acorns in the container (small motor)

INVOLVING FAMILIES

Ask families to help collect the acorns of different species of oak trees. Each type of oak tree produces acorns of different shapes and sizes.

USING MUSEUMS AND OTHER COMMUNITY RESOURCES

With the children, visit a park where many types of acorns grow and encourage the children to search the acorns for holes.

I Feel the Heat

This activity helps children understand how the kinds of clothes they wear affect their body temperatures. It also introduces children to the way the lines on thermometers illustrate various temperatures.

Science Content Standard—observes and interacts with physical science tools (Physical Science)
Science Process Skills—classifying (charting); measuring (temperature)

Words You Can Use

Color names
Cold
Degrees Celsius (°C)
Degrees Fahrenheit (°F)
Different
Hot
Temperature
Temperature values

Things You Can Use

Clothes, such as pants
 and T-shirts, in
 different colors
Paper
Markers or crayons
Masking tape
Thermometers—one for
 each color tested
Timer

Before the Activity

Gather several
thermometers and run a
piece of masking tape
along the entire length
of each.

What to Do

1. When the children come inside after they have been playing outdoors on a particularly hot day, talk with them about the different colors of clothing they are all wearing. Ask them if they think certain colors of clothing make them feel hotter than others.
2. Set out several articles of clothing, each in a light, medium, or dark color.
3. Invite the children to help you fold each item of clothing until each is a square of about the same size. Set the articles of clothing out and invite the children to feel each of them. Ask the children whether they notice a difference in each piece's temperature. At this point, because each piece of clothing was inside, they should all feel the same.
4. Set out several thermometers for the children to explore. Show them the lines on the thermometer and explain that they indicate different temperatures. Also, point out the red line that indicates the actual temperature. Pass the thermometers around so everyone gets a chance to see them. Ask the children whether the red lines on the thermometers all indicate the same temperature. If they do not, check to see whether a thermometer is broken, or the glass tube came loose. Adjust or change the thermometers as necessary.
5. Go outside, separate the children into groups, and give each group an article of clothing, asking them to place it in a separate, sunny area, then place one thermometer under a fold of each article of clothing. (This way the children can measure the temperature of the cloth, not what it is resting on.)
6. Bring the children back

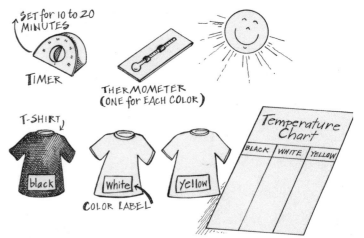

Language and literacy

◆ understanding
that symbols and
written words
have meaning
(early literacy)

◆ listening with
understanding
and responding
to directions
(receptive and
expressive
language)

Math

◆ using the tools
of measurement
to obtain
temperature
reading
(measurement)

◆ collecting and
organizing data
(data analysis
and probability)

inside and set a timer for 10–20 minutes, depending on the heat of the day. When the timer goes off, invite the children to come back outside and look at the thermometers.

7. Invite the children to touch each article of clothing. Ask them what they notice. For instance, ask "Does the black clothing feel hotter than the white clothing? What about the yellow clothing?" Can the children feel any differences? Ask which one feels hottest.

8. Next, ask the children to look at the three thermometers and make a line on each length of tape along their sides, marking the indicated temperatures. Talk with the children about the differences they notice between the various thermometers. Ask why the children think the thermometer in the black shirt has a higher line than the one in the white shirt, for instance. Explain that scientists indicate the different levels of warmth and temperature by quantities called degrees, and that scientists usually gauge temperatures in degrees Fahrenheit and Celsius. While young children may not read the temperatures accurately, many enjoy hearing these scientific words and trying to use them.

9. Ask the children to line up the three thermometers next to each other and compare the heights of the lines. Ask the children questions, such as "Does the thermometer with the highest line belong to the clothes that felt the hottest? Which color of clothes stayed the coolest? What does its thermometer indicate?"

Want to Do More?

◆ Help the children create a chart with lines the length of those marked on the tape attached to the thermometers and then record the temperature results, ranking the temperatures from hottest to coolest.

◆ Make a clothing-temperature chart like the one below and help the children record the different temperature results on it.

Temperature							
Clothing color	Black	White	Red	Green	Blue	Pink	Purple

◆ Set out in the sun articles of clothing that represent various shades of a single color and invite the children to gauge if the temperature varies from shade to shade of the color.

◆ Invite the children to set matching articles of clothing in the sun and shade, and compare the differences in the temperatures the articles reach.

Observing and Assessing the Children

Can the child describe how darker colors become hotter than lighter colors when both sit in the sun?

4+ Moving Air Moves Things

Air can move objects. With the help of a strong fan, the children can float objects across the schoolyard and measure the distance each object flies.

Science Content Standard—observes and interacts with physical science tools (Physical Science)
Science Process Skills—observing; inferring

Words You Can Use

Air
Measure
Move
Push

Things You Can Use

Fan
Tape measure
Tissue paper

Before the Activity

Find an open area where the wind will not interfere with the distance the tissue paper carries.

What to Do

1. Place a fan outside in a sheltered area.
2. Give each child a small piece of tissue paper. Invite the children to take turns putting their pieces of tissue paper in the fan's stream to see how far it will carry them.
   Safety note: Have an adult supervise throughout this activity. Consider having the adult put each child's tissue in front of the fan. Remind children to keep their distance from the fan and not to put their hands near the blades.
3. Suggest that the children tear their paper into strips, small pieces, or other shapes to find which design will float the farthest or highest.

4. Measure the distance each paper shape travels and record the results.
5. Pick up all the blown paper before returning to the building.
6. Come back into the classroom. Give each child a sheet of paper and invite him to paste his piece of tissue paper to it. Copy down the distance each piece of tissue paper traveled, then invite the children to rank the paper based on the distance each flew.

Want to Do More?

◆ When there is adequate wind outside, bring the children outside and invite them to release the sheets of tissue paper into the wind.
◆ Help the children make paper airplanes, then bring them outside to throw through the air.

Observing and Assessing the Children

Can the child tear a sheet of tissue paper into a shape that will float on a fan's current?

Learning in Other Curricular Areas

Language and literacy
◆ listening with understanding and following directions (receptive language)
◆ communicating information gathered with others (expressive language)

Math
◆ measuring distance objects fly (measurement)
◆ classifying and recognizing patterns (algebra)

4+ Pulley on a Limb

A pulley is a simple machine that children can learn to master as they play and have fun with it.

Science Content Standard—observes and interacts with physical science tools (Physical Science)
Science Process Skill—observing

Words You Can Use

Down   Up
Higher   Pull
Lower   Pulley
Lift

Things You Can Use

A bucket attached to a
    rope
A large eyebolt (also
    called an I-bolt)
A pulley (available at
    hardware stores)
Rope
Various objects for the
    children to lift, such as
    rocks, boards, dirt,
    and so on
Table or bench to lift
    items onto

Before the Activity

Before the children arrive, set up the pulley apparatus outside by screwing a large eye-bolt into the low limb of a tree or the wooden support of a wooden playground apparatus or a fence. Attach a pulley to the bolt, and ensure that it is stable and secure. Attach a bucket to one end of a piece of rope. For safety reasons, do not thread the rope into the pulley until later, when you come outside with the children. Put a table near the pulley, or some other raised flat surface to which the children can raise the bucket from the ground. Set out several objects that the children can lift with the pulley, such as rocks, boards, and so on.

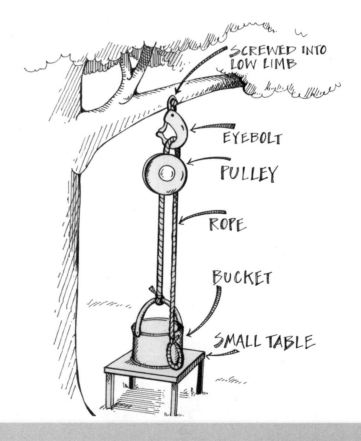

SCREWED INTO
LOW LIMB

EYEBOLT

PULLEY

ROPE

BUCKET

SMALL TABLE

What to Do

1. Bring the children outside and show them the pulley.
2. Thread the loose end of the rope through the pulley, and model for the children how to use the pulley to raise the bucket. Tell the children how the pulley is a simple machine created many hundreds of years ago.
3. Review some simple pulley safety rules with the children:
    ◆ Do not stand or sit under the pulley.
    ◆ Do not let go of the rope.
    ◆ Do not put too many items or too much weight in the bucket.
4. One at a time, invite the children to lift with their hands some of the objects you set out, and put them on the tabletop. Next, have the children put the objects in the bucket and use the pulley to lift them to the tabletop. After the children have a chance to lift the objects both ways, ask them about each experience. Ask which was easier, and which was more fun.
5. Encourage the children to experiment with using the pulley to lift various items onto the table.

Want to Do More?

◆ Set out a scale and invite the children to weigh the items they lift with the pulley.
◆ Help the children build a structure from blocks on the ground, and then lift everything up to another level (a card table) and rebuild the structure on top of the table.

Observing and Assessing the Children

Can the child use the pulley to lift materials?

Learning in Other Curricular Areas

Language and literacy
    ◆ listening with understanding and following directions (receptive language)
    ◆ communicating ideas and thoughts (expressive language)
Motor development
    ◆ picking up and lifting items with the pulley (large motor)

USING MUSEUMS AND OTHER COMMUNITY RESOURCES

Visit a construction site to see examples of pulleys in use.
A local contractor may have a pulley apparatus that you can borrow. Also, a university or high school physics teacher may be able to lend you a variety of pulleys.

4+ Pendulum on a Limb

This simple device is just plain fun! The children will love discovering how any dangling rope or string can become a pendulum.

Science Content Standard—observes and interacts with physical science tools (Physical Science)
Science Process Skills—predicting, inferring

Words You Can Use

Move
Pendulum
Rope
Swing

Things You Can Use

Eyebolt (as the center point to tie the rope or string)
String, yarn, or rope
Variety of small weights to tie to the rope or yarn

Before the Activity

Use the eyebolt from the "Pulley on a Limb" activity (on page 108) as the center point for the pendulum in this activity; simply tie a rope or string to the eye and let it hang. Also, consider making the pendulum by attaching a stick-on hook in a doorway or from a piece of playground equipment, or tying a string to a yardstick and placing it between two chairs.

What to Do

1. Before setting up the pendulum, show the children the eyebolt you will use as its center point. Pass it among the children and invite them to describe it, or set up the pendulum and pass a similar eyebolt or stick-on hook among the children. As the children investigate the object you are using as the center point of the pendulum, introduce them to the idea of a pendulum. Explain that a pendulum is a simple machine that people have used for hundreds of

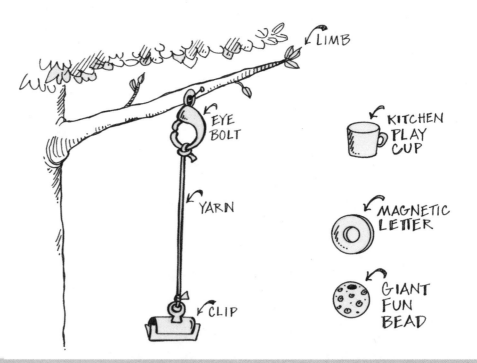

years, and as the children will today, these people experimented with the pendulum to get a better understanding of how it works.

2. Set up the pendulum by attaching a string to the eyebolt, without adding any weight to it yet. Draw the end of the pendulum back, and encourage the children to look for changes in the way it swings once you let it go. Challenge the children to describe the different speeds at which it moves, or ask leading questions about whether the pendulum is moving faster, slower, or at the same speed on each swing.

3. Once the string slows down and eventually stops, ask the children what they think they can do to make the rope move faster or slower the next time it swings. Suggestions include weighing down the rope, swinging it harder, making the rope longer or shorter, getting a bigger rope. Encourage the children to come up with these ideas on their own, or suggest these ideas to them. Let them make the changes to the rope themselves, then swing the pendulum to see what happens.

4. Record the results of each altered swing and discuss them with the children. The core lesson in this activity is that the only way to alter the speed at which the pendulum swings is by changing the length of the rope. With a bit of experimentation, the children should come to this conclusion.

   Note: A pendulum can be a very exact instrument for keeping time. Some children may have seen a grandfather clock. Invite those children familiar with grandfather clocks to discuss what they remember about how the clocks worked.

USING MUSEUMS AND OTHER COMMUNITY RESOURCES
Find a museum in your area with a large pendulum. Invite a clock-repair shop owner to visit the classroom to show and demonstrate a variety of clocks that have pendulums.

Want to Do More?

◆ Bring the children onto the playground and discuss with the children how a swing is like a pendulum.

◆ Bring in a clock with a pendulum for the children to observe.

◆ Set out a metronome and invite the children to compare it with their pendulums.

Observing and Assessing the Children

Can the child describe the motion of a pendulum?

Learning in Other Curricular Areas

Language and literacy

◆ listening with understanding and responding to directions and conversations (receptive language)

◆ communicating information to others (expressive language)

Math

◆ recognizing patterns that affect the pendulum swing, determining variables that affect the pendulum (algebra)

4+ Pusher or Roller

The ramp is another simple machine. The ramp does work for us by making some forms of motion easier. Some objects roll down a ramp; some do not. This activity helps the children determine which objects are rollers and which objects are pushers.

Science Content Standard—observes and interacts with physical science tools (Physical Science)
Science Process Skills—observing; classifying

Words You Can Use

Push
Pusher
Ramp
Roll
Roller

Things You Can Use

Paper and marker
Common natural and manmade objects that do and do not roll
A ramp made from a piece of plywood or board
Wooden blocks or bricks to set the ramp on

Before the Activity

Write "roller" on one piece of paper and "pusher" on another. Collect several objects that will fall into each category.

What to Do

1. With the children, bring the board, the blocks, and the collection of various objects outside. Ask the children to help you set up the ramp by propping up one end of the board on a stack of blocks.
2. Give a few children one roller object each and invite them to take turns placing the rollers on the ramp and letting go of them, as an example to the children. Encourage the other children to discuss why the objects rolled down the ramp.

Learning in Other Curricular Areas

Language and literacy
- listening with understanding and responding to directions (receptive language)
- understanding that print carries a message (reading readiness)

Math
- recognizing patterns and classifying (algebra)

Motor development
- collecting and placing objects in appropriately labeled piles (small motor)

3. Next, give a few different children one pusher object each and invite them to take turns letting go of the pushers at the top of the ramp. Encourage the children to compare what happens with the pusher objects to what happened to the roller objects.

4. After the children finish comparing the rollers and pushers you brought outside, ask them to search the playground, collecting items they think belong in both categories and bring them back to the ramp.

5. When each child has a few items, gather the children together and encourage them to look at one another's objects and predict the category in which each belongs by placing them on one of the two pieces of paper with labels on them.

6. Once the children finish sorting all the objects based on whether they think they are rollers or pushers, help them count the total number in each category and record the numbers.

7. With the children, test each object by putting it at the top of the ramp and letting go, then putting each object in the correct category. After the children finish testing and sorting all the objects, count the results and compare them to the children's predictions. Show the children the two sets of results and ask them to compare them. Were the predictions correct? What are the differences between the predictions and the results? Which predicted rollers turned out to be pushers?

8. Encourage the children to think about other categories they may have discovered. Some items will roll if given a slight push. Some items won't roll, but will slide without being pushed. Some items will be rollers in one position and pushers in another position. Challenge the children to identify these various subcategories.

Want to Do More?

- Show the children how to add more blocks below the ramp to increase its incline, then help them retest the various objects and see whether this change increases the number of rollers from the previous total.
- Rather than using a wooden ramp, show the children how to use the slide on the playground to conduct the same experiment.
- Provide the children with several larger objects to roll or push down the ramp and observe the difference size makes in the experiment.
- Show the children pictures of people using ramps to help the children get a sense of a ramp's productive value.

Observing and Assessing the Children

Can the child predict whether various objects will roll down a ramp?

4+ Riding Toys in the Yard

Almost every childcare center has access to a collection of tricycles. While the children ride around, help them use their tricycles to experiment with some of physics' basic laws of motion.

Science Content Standard—observes and interacts with physical science tools (Physical Science)
Science Process Skills—classifying; measuring (linear); identifying and controlling variables

Words You Can Use

Coast   Meters
Distance   Slow
Fast

Things You Can Use

Chalk
Wheeled toys that the
    children can ride
Linear measurement
    devices, such as
    measuring tapes,
    yardsticks, or meter
    sticks

Before the Activity

Find an out-of-the-way
location with a slight
incline where a vehicle
can roll a short distance
on its own.

What to Do

1. Bring the children out to the inclined riding area. Pick a couple of children to help you draw a chalk line along the ground part of the way down the incline. Tell the children this is the starting line, then, using the yardstick, help the children make additional marks going down the hill.

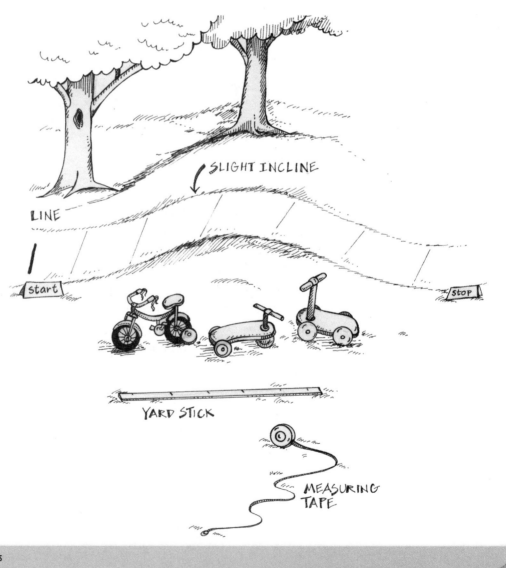

SLIGHT INCLINE

LINE

start   stop

YARD STICK

MEASURING TAPE

2. Talk with the children about momentum. Use the example of how a tricycle will continue to roll along after its rider stops pedaling. Tell the children the by experimenting with this idea, they can learn to determine which riding toys roll the farthest and how certain variables can affect the distances the objects roll.

3. Ask a child to pedal a tricycle up to the chalk starting line, then to stop pedaling and coast to a stop. Invite the other children to use the chalk marks the children made to measure how far the tricycle traveled.

4. Ask the children to think of ways they might increase the distance the tricycle coasted, such as having another child push the rider from behind, or having the rider pedal harder. Other suggestions include having a smaller or a larger child ride the tricycle or oiling the wheels. Record the children's suggestions, and then help them try each suggestion on the list one at a time, and compare the results.

5. If other riding toys are available, invite the children to compare them to the tricycles, then rate the various riding toys based on how far each coasted.

Want to Do More?

♦ Invite the children to bring in vehicles from home to expand the variety of objects they compare.

♦ Bring the children to a steeper slope, repeat the activity, and discuss with the children what differences they notice between the two inclines.

♦ Help the children build a simple racetrack, and invite them to measure the differences in time it takes the various vehicles to complete the track.

Observing and Assessing the Children

Can the child articulate how to measure the distance a tricycle coasts?

Learning in Other Curricular Areas

Language and literacy
♦ listening with understanding and responding to directions (receptive language)
♦ communicating ideas and thoughts with others (expressive language)

Math
♦ using yardsticks or meter sticks as tools (measurement)
♦ collecting and organizing data (data analysis and probability)

Motor development
♦ riding toys down the marked track (large motor)
♦ using a yardstick or meter stick to determine distances (small motor)

4+ Rusting Outside

Although rust is common everywhere, young children may not know how the process of rusting occurs, in part because rusting occurs over a long period of time. This activity speeds up the rusting process so the children can see what happens.

Science Content Standard—uses descriptive language when making observations of objects (Physical Science)
Science Process Skill—observing

Words You Can Use

Change
Rust
Rusting

Things You Can Use

Paper or cardboard
    pieces
Steel wool, cut into small
    pieces (adult-only
    step)
Glue
Marker

Before the Activity

Cut a sheet of inexpensive steel wool into 1" square pieces. Cut pieces of cardboard into 5" x 7" pieces. Use glue to attach one piece of steel wool to each cardboard piece. This way the children can hold the cardboard without actually touching the steel wool.

Safety note: This preparation is for adults to do. Be sure to make the steel wool cards when no children are present.

What to Do

1. Take the children on a "rust walk" around the school or immediate neighborhood, encouraging them to point out to everyone any rusted metal they see.

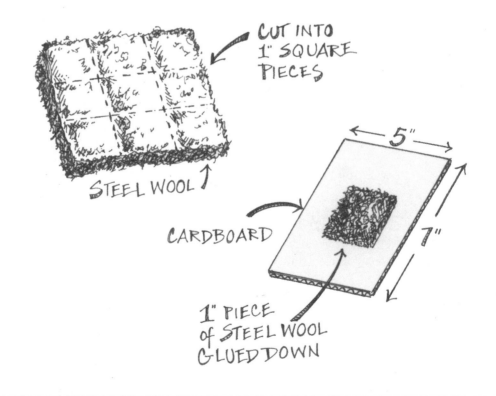

CUT INTO 1" SQUARE PIECES

STEEL WOOL

5"

7"

CARDBOARD

1" PIECE of STEEL WOOL GLUED DOWN

2. Either individually or in groups, give the children the steel-wool cards. Write the children's names on their cards.
   Safety note: Warn the children that steel wool is a hazardous material, and that they should not touch it or get any in their eyes. Explain to them that that is why you attached the steel wool to the cardboard.
3. Tell the children that the gray material on the card is iron. (Steel wool is made from iron.) Explain to the children that iron is a mineral that turns to rust over time.
4. Bring the children outside and ask them to find a place in the schoolyard to put their steel-wool cards. Remind the children to keep the steel-wool cards away from their faces and to handle the cards with caution.
5. Leave the cards outside overnight. The next morning, bring the children outside to check on their steel-wool cards. Encourage the children to describe any changes they see. Ask if they notice any rust starting to form.
   Note: Steel wool will rust more quickly if it is moist. If the weather forecast calls for clear skies the day the children put their steel-wool cards outside, have the children sprinkle some water on each card to accelerate the process.

Want to Do More?

◆ Set out different metals and materials overnight and invite the children to observe the differences in the amounts of rust on each the following day.

Observing and Assessing the Children

Can the child describe what will happen to steel wool left outside overnight? Can the child identify rust?

Learning in Other Curricular Areas

Language and literacy
◆ listening with understanding and responding to directions (receptive language)
◆ recognizing their names (letter recognition)
◆ learning that print carries a message (reading readiness)

Motor development
◆ placing cardboard pieces in the schoolyard (small motor)

Toss a Shape

In this activity, the children bounce various-shaped objects off a wall outside to observe and begin to predict the different ways the objects rebound.

Science Content Standard—begins to sort and characterize objects by physical characteristics (Physical Science)

Science Process Skills—classifying; inferring

Words You Can Use

Bounce
Carom
Direction words
Number words
Shape words
Trajectory

Things You Can Use

Rolled-up pairs of adult socks (different shapes will affect the path of the carom)

What to Do

1. Illustrate for the children how to throw a rolled-up sock at the wall at an angle and observe the way it bounces. Ask the children why the sock did not bounce straight back to you and how you might alter your throw to get it to bounce straight back.

2. Hand out several rolled-up socks to the children and invite them to bounce them off the walls to each other, exploring the different directions their rebounds take. Encourage them to talk about the different trajectories. Consider using a piece of chalk to copy the lines the socks rebound at, so the children can see the different trajectories simultaneously.

AT AN ANGLE

ONE to the OTHER

3. Once the children understand how to make the sock rolls bounce at an angle, draw or tape a 1'-square box about 1' away from the wall and challenge the children to toss the sock rolls against the wall and angle them so they rebound and land in the square.

4. As the children become more adept at controlling the way the socks rebound off the wall, encourage them to make their own targets to try to hit. Some of the children will become amazingly accurate!

Want to Do More?

◆ Set out several other objects, such as pennies and tennis balls, and encourage the children to throw and describe the differences in the ways they rebound.

◆ Use chalk to draw a line a foot or two away from the wall, give the children washers or pennies, and challenge the children to bounce them off the wall and onto the line.

Observing and Assessing the Children

Given an object to toss against a wall, can the child describe the possible ways that the object will rebound?

Learning in Other Curricular Areas

Language and literacy

◆ listening with understanding and responding to directions (receptive language)

◆ communicating ideas and thoughts to others (expressive language)

Math

◆ evaluating inferences and predictions (data analysis and probability)

Motor development

◆ tossing objects at various angles to affect their trajectory (large motor)

Moving Sunlight

Children are aware that the sun changes its position in the sky. They see it overhead during the day. They may know from experience that in winter that the sun comes later in the day and sets earlier in the evening. In most cases, however, children have not followed the trajectory of the sun during the day and noted that it moves through the sky in an orderly and predictable manner.

Science Content Standard—discusses predictions and explanations about experiences (Physical Science)
Science Process Skill—observing

Words You Can Use

15 minutes	Sunlight
30 minutes	Shadow
Light	Time
Moving	Timer
Pattern	

Things You Can Use

Commercially available
  timers—sand, liquid
  and/or mechanical
  varieties
Markers
Masking tape
Drawing of the outline of
  a person's arm with
  hand reaching out
  and pointing a finger
Yarn

Before the Activity

On tag board or paper, draw the figure of a person with an arm outstretched. Cut out the figure and tape it on the window so that the shadow of its fingertip falls on the wall opposite the window. Use a marker to put a dot on a piece of masking tape at the exact end of the fingertip shadow.

What to Do

1. Show the children the figure on the window, and the dot on the far wall that marks the end of the shadow of the figure's arm.
2. Ask the children what they think will happen to the shadow over the course of the day. Do they think it will stay in the same place all morning? Put a timer by the shadow and set it to go off every 30 minutes.

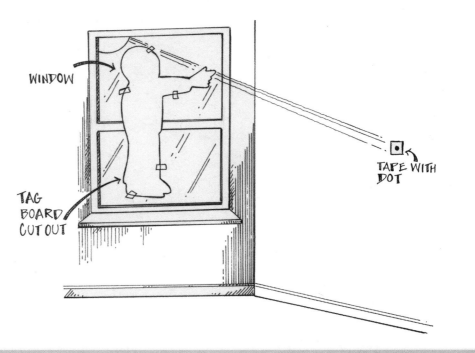

WINDOW

TAPE WITH
DOT

TAG
BOARD
CUT OUT

3. When the timer rings, call the children over to observe the shadow. Place a piece of masking tape at the end of the shadow of the figure's arm. Repeat this step every 30 minutes throughout the day.

3. When the timer rings, call the children over to observe the shadow. Place a piece of masking tape at the end of the shadow of the figure's arm. Repeat this step every 30 minutes throughout the day.

4. At the end of the day, before the children leave to go home, take out a length of yarn and help the children use it to connect the dots on the masking tape marks that indicate all the places where the figure's arm pointed throughout the day.

5. Encourage the children to describe the way the shadow moved across the room through the course of the day. Was the movement regular? Did it skip from place to place? Can the children see a pattern emerging?

Want to Do More?

◆ Leave the dots up on the wall, and in a month or during another season, repeat the activity. Ask the children if they think the shadow will move along a different line.

◆ As you add each dot to the wall, challenge the children to predict where the next dot will go, and mark that spot. In a half-hour, compare the actual location to the children's prediction.

Observing and Assessing the Children

Does the child understand the concept of time passing, for example, 15 or 30 minutes? Can he see a relationship between the movement of the shadow along the wall and the passage of time?

Learning in Other Curricular Areas

Language and literacy
◆ understanding and responding to directions (receptive language)

Math
◆ using tools of measurement to measure time passing (measurement)

INVOLVING FAMILIES

Ask a family with a sundial to bring it to school to show the children how it works —how the shadow moves to tell time.

USING MUSEUMS AND OTHER COMMUNITY RESOURCES

Arrange for the children to take a trip to the local planetarium and ask the personnel to talk with the children about the movement of the sun.

Mud Drops

This activity teaches the children how to read splash marks. What can we tell from a muddy splash mark? You'll be surprised. Let's experiment and find out.

Science Content Standard—uses descriptive language when making observations (Physical Science)
Science Process Skills—observing; inferring

Words You Can Use

Drop
Dropper
Baster
Pipette
Size and height words
Shape words

Things You Can Use

Containers to mix mud and water
Dirt from the schoolyard
Plastic turkey baster
Unbreakable pipettes or eyedroppers
Newspaper print or large sheets of paper

Before the Activity

Prepare some examples of splash marks by dropping muddy water onto separate sheets of paper. Drop one from a low height, and another from higher up. Squirt one splash directly on, and make another hit the paper at a slant.

What to Do

1. Set out several pipettes and eyedroppers, as well as a container of muddy water, and show the children how to squeeze the liquid into the eyedroppers and pipettes. Illustrate for the children how to hold a dropper above a sheet of paper and squeeze the liquid out.

2. Invite the children to pick an eyedropper or pipette and then experiment by dropping muddy water onto sheets of paper.

3. After the children explore various ways to splash water on paper, bring out the papers you prepared earlier. Show them to the children, and challenge them to think of how you dripped water to get the particular splash marks on each sheet. Write the children's suggestions on a separate sheet of paper.

4. After the children come up with several theories, challenge them to experiment with their theories to see which can replicate most closely the muddy splashes on your sheets of paper.

Want to Do More?

◆ Change the consistency of the mud the children drip onto the sheets of paper, repeat the experiment, and invite them to compare the results.
◆ Give the children specific heights from which to drop mud on the sheets of paper, and compare the effects of each.

Observing and Assessing the Children

Can the child predict what will occur when he squeezes muddy water from an eyedropper onto a sheet of paper from various heights and angles?

Learning in Other Curricular Areas

Language and literacy
◆ listening with understanding and responding to directions (receptive language)
◆ communicating ideas and thoughts (expressive language)

Math
◆ recognizing patterns (algebra)
◆ evaluating inferences and predictions (data analysis and probability)

Motor development
◆ squeezing pipettes or eyedroppers (small motor)

5+ The Wind Feels Cool

Children know the kinds of clothes that keep them warm on a cold day, and that even with warm clothes on, the wind can make it feel even colder than it is. In this blustery activity, the children bundle up, go outside, and learn about the difference between how thermometers and people react to the wind.

Science Content Standard—observes and interacts with physical science tools (Physical Science)
Science Process Skill—communicating

Words You Can Use

Compare
Degrees Celsius (°C)
Degrees Fahrenheit (°F)
Difference
Greater than
Less than
Temperature
Thermometer
Wind

Things You Can Use

Thermometers
Washcloths

Before the Activity

Prior to this activity, be sure the children have done several outdoor activities that teach about temperature.

What to Do

1. Bring the children outside on a windy day, and talk with them about how the weather feels. Ask, "Is it really colder on a windy day, or do you just feel that way? Let's find out."

2. Separate the children into pairs, and give each pair two thermometers. Ask the children to look at their thermometers and to read you the temperatures they indicate.

3. Next, give each child a wet washcloth and ask him to hold it across his hands. Ask one child in each pair to find a windy spot and stand in it with the washcloth across his hands, and for the other child in each pair to stand in a place where there is no wind. After a short period of time, ask the two children in each pair to switch positions. Once each child spends some time in each position, ask them to compare with one another which is the colder place, standing in the wind or out of the wind.

4. Explain to the children that the wind cools the body in two ways: One, by evaporating the water and cooling the skin, and two, by taking heat away from the body.

5. Repeat the activity using dry washcloths, and ask the children whether it is colder on their hands to stand in the wind or out of it. The children should find standing in the wind colder because the wind is taking away their body heat.

6. Occasionally throughout the activity, invite the children to check the temperature on the thermometer. Point out that the temperature on the thermometer is not changing, so the wind is what makes the children feel colder.

7. After this activity, talk with the children about the importance of dressing appropriately for all types of weather. Explain that it can be dangerous to go out on cold, windy days without wearing enough layers of clothes. Challenge the children to describe what is appropriate to wear in different weather.
   Note: Because cold wind takes heat away from the body more quickly than unmoving cold air—making windy days feel colder—scientists and meteorologists created the wind-chill index. This way, on days when the wind

is strong, people can gauge more accurately how they should dress to protect themselves from the cold.

Want to Do More?

◆ On a hot day, repeat the activity, substituting wet T-shirts for washcloths. Talk with the children about how in hot weather, dousing yourself with cool water can be refreshing.

◆ Set a thermometer outside and choose a different child every day to go outside, read the temperature, and report back to the class. Record the temperature this way for an entire month. At the end, invite the children to review the variations in temperature.

◆ Each day, go on the Internet and find information about the day's wind speeds and wind-chill factor. Record this information and share it with the children. Consider making a chart of this data, so the children can see the extent to which these things fluctuate over a given period of time. Ask, "Is there a relationship between the wind speeds and the difference in wind-chill factors for a given day?"

Observing and Assessing the Children

Can the child predict how and why the wind will affect his body temperature on a cold and windy day?

Learning in Other Curricular Areas

Math

◆ recording temperature findings (measurement)

INCORPORATING TECHNOLOGY
Before the children arrive, use the Internet to visit the local weather station website to get weather forecasts and rainfall statistics. Share this information with the children.

USING MUSEUMS AND OTHER COMMUNITY RESOURCES
Contact your local television or radio station to arrange the local weather forecaster to visit the classroom to talk about weather and wind chill.

5+ Nail It

This simple activity will provide hours of small and large motor development for active children. When you notice someone cutting down a tree, ask for a section of it with two flat ends. Bring it to the schoolyard, and, under close adult supervision, let the children pound nails into it.

Science Content Standard—observes and interacts with physical science tools (Physical Science)
Science Process Skill—communicating

Words You Can Use

Count
Force
Hammer
Nails
Number words
Pound
Weighs

Things You Can Use

Hammers of various weights
Large nails for hammering into the tree trunk
Piece of a tree trunk
Safety glasses for the children

Before the Activity

Find a log or stump at a height tall enough that the children can stand in front of it and comfortably pound on its top. A large board will also work. A tree with soft wood, such as a pine or poplar, makes the pounding easier.

What to Do

Safety note: Make sure all the children know how to use hammers safely. Before doing this activity, explain that nails and hammers can be very dangerous when used improperly. With the children, make a list of rules they must observe when hammering the nails. For instance: only one child hammers nails at a time, no swinging hammers at other children, and no pulling nails from wood. Make sure all the children understand the rules for using the hammer and nail site. With practice, and guidance and supervision from you, children can learn to start nails themselves.

1. Find an out-of-the-way place on the school grounds to put the log. Bring the children outside and show it to them, along with several hammers of various sizes.
2. Pound the nails 1" (a couple of centimeters) into the center of the log before the children finish nailing them. This way the nails are secure, and will not dislodge when the children hit them.

3. Challenge each child to drive a nail all the way into the log. Point out to the children that the bigger the nail is, the harder it is to drive into the log. Add math to the experience by inviting the children to count the number of times they hit their nails before they drive them all the way into the log.

4. Let each child pound a nail with a few different-sized hammers. As the children hammer with their second or third hammer, talk with them about how the experience differs when using the various hammers. Point out that a bigger hammer can help with the pounding because it does more work when it hits its target. In this way the child and the hammer work together to apply a greater force.

5. Discuss with the children how hammers are tools people use to build things like houses and tables.

Want to Do More?

◆ Bring lumber from a construction site on which the children can practice hammering. Invite them to compare the difficulty of hammering nails into this wood as opposed to hammering nails into the log.

◆ Start some screws in the log and give the children a screwdriver, encouraging them to twist the screws all the way into the log.

◆ Ask a carpenter to demonstrate how to drive in a nail in only a few blows. That will impress the children.

◆ Keep notes of how many times a child has to hit a nail with a hammer before he nails it all the way into the wood. When the child is more proficient with hammering, compare these records to his current skill level.

Observing and Assessing the Children

Can the child use a hammer to pound a nail into a log? Can the child keep count of how many hits it takes him to pound it all the way into the log?

Learning in Other Curricular Areas

Language and literacy
◆ listening with understanding and responding to directions and information (receptive and expressive language)

Math
◆ counting the number of hits needed to pound the nail into the wood (number operations)
◆ collecting and organizing data (data analysis and probability)

Motor development
◆ using a hammer to drive nails into the tree trunk (small motor)

Social/emotional development
◆ taking turns as the children hammer the nails into the tree trunk (social interaction)

Mirror Play Outside

Mirrors fascinate children. They can stand in front of the mirror for long periods of time, making faces and posing. In this activity, the children use a mirror to move light across space and to communicate, as people have throughout history.

Science Content Standard—observes and interacts with physical science tools (Physical Science)
Science Process Skill—observing

Words You Can Use

Angle	Mirror
Beam	Ray
Bright	Reflect
Light	Sun

Things You Can Use

Small and large plastic mirrors (Many glass shops will have leftover pieces of plastic mirror. Cover any sharp edges with duct tape.)
Light source

Before the Activity

Take a mirror outside to find the best location for using a mirror to reflect the sun onto the wall of the school. Remember that the sun's location changes with the day. Consider bringing a large movable object, such as a wastepaper basket, to be a light target, if you cannot find an angle at which to reflect sunlight onto the school's wall.

What to Do

1. On a sunny day, bring the children outside and give each of them a mirror. Give the children time to look at themselves in and play with their mirrors.
2. Illustrate for the children how to use a mirror to reflect sunlight at a particular location. Explain that they will need to hold their mirrors at just the right angle to best reflect the light.
3. When they are comfortable with controlling the reflected beams of light, challenge the children to reflect the light at the school wall or at a bucket or pail. Challenge all the children to reflect the light onto the same spot simultaneously.
   Safety note: Warn children not to direct the light into another person's eyes.

Want to Do More?

◆ Bring the children back outside at a different time of day and repeat the activity from the same spot, then discuss why it does not work this time.
◆ Bring a big mirror and a small mirror outside. Help the children use each to reflect spots of light on the wall near one another, and discuss the differences between the reflected spots.
◆ Set up a strong light source inside the classroom and challenge the children to use their mirrors to make reflections against the wall inside, and then compare the results with the reflections they made outdoors.

Observing and Assessing the Children

Given a mirror on a sunny day, can the child redirect the sun's rays onto a flat surface?

Learning in Other Curricular Areas

Motor development
◆ holding the mirror and moving it to look at themselves and to reflect light on various objects (small motor)

CHAPTER 3

Bugs, Birds, and Blossoms: Learning About Living Things (Life Science)

3+

Leaf Banners

This art activity gives children the opportunity to identify and learn the names of the plants that are common to their surroundings. It also encourages the children to use a number of natural, reusable, and renewable resources to produce art.

Science Content Standard—begins to understand the differences between living and nonliving things (Life Science)
Science Process Skill—observing

Words You Can Use

Blade   Spatter
Color names   Twig
Toothbrush   Banner
Leaf/tree names

Things You Can Use

Muslin or old white or
    pastel sheets cut into
    8" (20 cm) squares,
    one for each child
Masking tape
Art smocks or aprons
Old toothbrushes
Small twigs
Tempera paints diluted to
    a watery consistency
Small containers to hold
    the tempera paints
Sticks about 1' (30 cm)
    long
Yarn
Stapler

Before the Activity

Use a commercial plant press to collect and press leaves for the children to use, or place leaves between the pages of a thick phone directory with a heavy weight on top. The leaves will take about a week to dry. Do this with the children or prepare them yourself. Prepare diluted tempera paints and place in containers. Use a tree-identification book to find the name of the trees from which each leaf grew, and then attach a small label to each so you can identify them later.

What to Do

1. Set out the dried leaves, twigs, toothbrushes, tempera paints, and other materials in the art area. For each child, set a piece of cloth on the table in the art area, and then tape it to the table. Explain to the children that they will be painting the pieces of cloth to make leaf banners.

2. Ask each child to put on her art apron and select a leaf. As each child picks her leaf, mention the name of the leaf's tree and encourage the child to describe the leaf's appearance.

3. Invite the child to put her leaf down on the cloth-covered art table. Show her how to dip a toothbrush in the paint and tap off the excess paint. Then, show her how to hold the toothbrush over her leaf, run a twig along the bristles of the toothbrush, and sprinkle the paint onto the cloth in the area around the leaf so the silhouette of the leaf will form on the cloth.

4. Remind the children that if they want to have clear prints of the leaves, they should not move them as they sprinkle paint on them.

5. Once the children finish sprinkling their leaves, help them remove the leaves without smearing the paint, and then encourage the children to use their twigs to add designs to other portions of their banners.

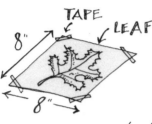

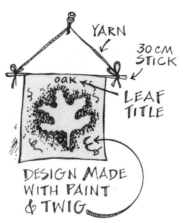

6. Once the children finish decorating their banners, set them aside in a place where they can dry without being disturbed. When the paint dries, help the children remember the names of the trees from which their leaves came, or match the labeled leaves to the silhouettes on the banners, and then help the children write the names of the trees along the bottom of the cloth. On the other edge of each cloth, help the children attach the foot-long twigs, and then tie the lengths of yarn to the exposed ends of the twigs and display them for everyone to enjoy.

Want to Do More?

◆ Challenge the children to make a patchwork banner by taping, gluing, or sewing all their individual squares together into one large banner.

Observing and Assessing the Children

Can the child make a spatter leaf print? Can the child identify and name the type of leaf she used in the print or match her banner to the leaf she used?

Learning in Other Curricular Areas

Arts

◆ Using spatter painting as a process to create an artistic leaf-shape banner (visual art/creativity)

Motor development

◆ dipping toothbrush into tempera paint; moving twig back and forth (fine motor)

A note about collecting items from the environment: Collecting from nature is always a dilemma because of the impact of collecting on the environment, especially the removal of flowers, which are how plants reproduce. Talk with the children about selective picking, meaning that it is okay to pick where there are many plants. When there is only one flower, teach the children to leave it there so the plant will continue to grow. For example, in the spring when the violets are growing in profusion, picking violets will not hurt the environment. Teaching children this rule now can help make them more conscientious about minimizing their affect on the environment for the rest of their lives.

Leaf Match

One way for children to make sense of the environment is to collect and classify items according to common attributes or traits. Couple this with children's natural tendency to pick up leaves when they are outside and you have a perfect match! Provide leaves that are common to your area and challenge the children to find leaves that match.

Science Content Standard—begins to use simple descriptive language about living things (Life Science)
Science Process Skills—observing; classifying

Words You Can Use

Blade
Characteristics
Classify
Collect
Leaf names
Match
Needle

Things You Can Use

Chart of leaves or other collectables (see chart)
Glue

Before the Activity

Prepare the chart (see sample on the next page) with all the children's names. Use glue to attach the leaves you want the children to find to the correct corresponding squares. Make sure the plants in the area have enough leaves for all the children to find at least one leaf without significantly diminishing their numbers.

What to Do

1. Show the children the chart you made. Engage the children in a discussion about the shapes and colors of the leaves.
2. Encourage the children to focus on the specific differences in shape and color. Ask them if they can remember any leaves outside that look similar to those on the chart. Depending on your locale and the time of year, the children may have noticed changing colors and many leaves on the ground.
3. Go outside with the children and encourage them to look for places where they might find leaves like those on the chart. For instance, they might notice a pile of leaves by the fence or many leaves under a tree.
4. Invite the children to search for leaf samples to match the leaves on the chart. Encourage them to run back to you with their finds.
   Note: Some children may need to take a sample leaf with them to find a match.
5. Encourage the children to help each other check the leaves they find against those on the chart.
6. As the children become more proficient at identifying plants, challenge them by asking them to find leaves that are similar to each other. With practice, and as memory improves, some children will be able to collect several leaves without needing to check your examples. What budding young botanists!

A Note About Leaves: There are several types of leaves that do not have the usual look or shape of leaves. For example, leaves on evergreen trees, such as pine or spruce, are atypical leaves. Explain to the children that the leaves from pine trees are called needles, and encourage them to talk about the differences between needles and other leaves. If you want to use grasses along with the leaves, show the children a blade of grass, and explain that blades of grass are like leaves. Also, if certain leaves or plants are rare in your area, do not pull them, and warn the children not to touch or damage them either. Instead, gather the children around the plant to look at and discuss the leaves.

	Oak	Bradford Pear	Pine	Maple	Grass	Sweet Gum
AMY						
JOHN						
ALETHIA						
RAMON						
RAJID						
SIMON						

Note: Chart should contain actual leaves in addition to labels.

OAK LEAF

SMALL PINECONE

CONNECTING TO CHILDREN WITH SPECIAL NEEDS

Provide a box filled with leaves for children with limited mobility to search through to find a match.

Want to Do More?

- Create similar charts using any set of natural objects such as seashells on the beach, rocks in a gravel pile or rock collections, insects, seeds, flowers, or other things common in your area.
- As the children become more adept at gathering leaves, challenge them by timing their searches, and invite the children to compare how long it takes them to find a leaf each time.

Observing and Assessing the Children

Can the child find a leaf in nature that matches her designated leaf on the chart?

Learning in Other Curricular Areas

Math
- collecting and organizing data (data analysis and probability)
- sorting and matching shapes (geometry)

Motor development
- running (large motor skills)

SWEET GUM

HICKORY NUT

MAPLE LEAF

3+

Little Sprouts

With the miniature greenhouses that the children make in this activity, they can watch the leaves, stems, and roots of plants grow. These usually mysterious underground phenomena are now visible. See what you can seed!

Science Content Standard—begins to understand the needs of living things (Life Science)
Science Process Skill—observing

Words You Can Use

Germinate   Seed
Grow   Sprout
Leaf   Root
Plant

Things You Can Use

Clothespins
Line for hanging the
    seed bags
Paper towels
Unbreakable measuring
    cups
Seeds such as radish,
    alfalfa, and grass
    (sprout quickly); beans
    and corn (take longer)
Resealable plastic bags
Permanent marker

Before the Activity

Set out several bags and label each one with a child's name. In a location where the children can see it easily, set up a clothesline across the room. The children will hang their seed bags here.

What to Do

1. Give each child a paper towel and baggie, and invite the children to fold the towels and place them inside the baggies.
2. Help the children pour just enough water into the bags to soak the folded paper towels. When the paper towel is soaked, help the children pour out excess water.
3. Set out several seeds, and invite each child to count out between four and six of them. Place the seeds about 1" (3 cm) from the bottom on the folded, water-soaked paper towel. This way the children will be able to see the roots grow down. Show the children how to flatten their bags and seal them.
4. Give the children clothespins and help them attach the bags to the clothesline hanging in the classroom.
5. Each day, invite the children to check on their seed bags to see how the sprouts are growing. The paper towels in the bags will stay moist without adding more water if the bags stay shut, and sprouts should form within three or four days.

6. As they observe the bags, ask the children to note which seeds sprout first in each bag. Encourage the children to measure the growth of the sprouts by marking the length of the sprouts on the bags.

Want to Do More?

- Encourage and help the children to make individual or class journals that document the growth of their seeds. Invite the children to make drawings of the seeds at various stages of growth, and include the drawings in their journals.
- Help the children gather seeds from outside and see how quickly (or slowly) they sprout. Typically, most seeds the children will find outside require either a period of freezing or drying before they will begin to grow.
- Set out various other types of seeds such as peas, beans, lettuce, or corn for the children to plant in baggies and compare to the original seeds they planted.
- Once the sprouts are large enough, help the children transplant them into the soil.
- Invite the children to create a second set of seed bags, helping the children water the second set occasionally, and compare them to the original set of seed bags.

Observing and Assessing the Children

Can the child follow the directions and plant the seeds in her bag? Can the child observe and describe the ways in which her seeds change and grow?

Learning in Other Curricular Areas

Language and literacy
- listening with understanding and responding to directions (receptive language)
- communicating information about observations with others (expressive language)

Math
- counting and folding paper towel in half (number operations)

Motor development
- folding paper towels (small motor); pouring water into the bags and then pouring it out (large motor)
- picking up and placing seeds into the plastic bags and using clothespins to attach the bags to strings (small motor)

CONNECTING TO CHILDREN WITH SPECIAL NEEDS

Support children with visual impairments by helping them pour water and place seeds in their plastic bags, describing the process to the children as you go.

INCORPORATING TECHNOLOGY

Use a tape recorder to document the children's comments and observations about the seeds, and set out the recordings for the children to listen to and enjoy.

Sticky-Tape Body Art

In this activity, the children will create an art piece that lives and moves with them by collecting things from nature and mounting them on their own bodies. An active youngster covered with things from outdoors is a delight to behold!

Science Content Standard—begins to use simple, descriptive language about living things (Life Science)
Science Process Skills—observing; classifying

Words You Can Use

Animal
Animal names
Plants
Plant names
Stick
Collect
Heavy

Things You Can Use

Two-sided sticky tape, masking tape, or duct tape

Before the Activity

Choose an outdoor location where the children will be able to find several different suitable objects to attach to themselves.

What to Do

1. Bring the children outside to the outdoor location you selected.
2. To illustrate how the activity will work, choose a child and help her attach a strip of two-sided tape to her chest. Explain to the child that this will be her collection strip, and invite her to look for things to stick to herself.
3. Help all the children attach strips of two-sided tape to themselves, and invite them to search for items they can stick to themselves. Explain that some objects will be too heavy to stay attached to the tape, and that the children should look for lightweight objects to stick to themselves.

4. As the children begin to gather various items, help each of them place an additional strip on their backs. Explain to the children that the tape on their backs will only hold a few things, so they must limit themselves to putting on their backs only those things they really like. Tell the children that when they

find something they really like, they should ask someone to help them add it to their special back strips.

Note: Before the children start collecting objects, caution them not to touch certain objects, such as poison ivy or sharp objects.

5. When the children finish walking and collecting objects, invite them to discuss with the rest of the children the various objects they collected. Ask them what drew them to the various objects.

6. When the children finish sharing with everyone the collections they have on their chests, ask them to turn around and you describe the objects they have on their backs. Challenge the children to see whether they can learn anything about one another based on what they attached to their special back strips. For instance, a child might have all flowers on her back, so the other children might say that she likes things that are pretty, bright, and smell nice.

INCORPORATING TECHNOLOGY

Use a digital camera to record the children's collections. Send photos to the children's homes, and urge the families to ask their children to explain the activity and why they chose the particular items they taped to themselves.

USING MUSEUMS AND OTHER COMMUNITY RESOURCES

Bring the children to a local museum, library, or college that has collections of some kind, and invite the children to look at and think about the different ways people sorted and grouped the objects.

Want to Do More?

◆ Take a picture of each child's sticky tape collection.

◆ Set out some art paper and invite the children to use the materials they attached to themselves to make sticky tape collections or collages.

◆ Wrap tape around the end of a yardstick with the sticky side out, and show the children how to use this as a collecting tool.

◆ Challenge the children to find the largest objects that will still stick to the tape.

◆ Set out a piece of cardboard and attach two-sided tape to it, inviting the children to gather heavier items on it.

YARD STICK

STICKY TAPE

Observing and Assessing the Children

Is the child able to collect the materials and describe why she put certain objects on her back?

Learning in Other Curricular Areas

Language and literacy

◆ communicating ideas and thoughts as the children explain the items collected and what they mean to them (expressive language)

Social/emotional development

◆ using appropriate communication skills while expressing feelings (social development)

3+ Time to Mime

Children enjoy pretending to jump like a kangaroo or flap their wings and waddle like a duck. However, because many children have not seen the animals whose movements they imitate, they usually mimic the ways adults act out the animals' movements. This activity gives children the opportunity to observe several different animals and see how they really move.

Science Content Standard—begins to use simple, descriptive language about living things (Life Science)
Science Process Skills—observing; communicating

Words You Can Use

Animal names
Examine   Observe
Explore   Search

Things You Can Use

Area to explore that has
    easily seen and
    identifiable animals
Chart paper
Markers

Before the Activity

Prior to doing this activity, find an area in the park, schoolyard, or local playground when the children can observe various animals such as squirrels, chipmunks, robins, pigeons, sparrows, starlings, lizards, grasshoppers, crickets, caterpillars, and earthworms. If you bring the children to a location where they can observe dogs or cats, be sure to point out the differences between wild and domesticated animals. Make a chart with three columns. Label the first column "animal," the second "where we found it," and the last "how it moves."

What to Do

1. Ask the children to think of different animals and describe how they move. When the children offer answers, ask them how people know how animals move. Explain to the children that people learn how animals move through observation and that learning to observe is an important science skill that helps everyone learn things about their environment.
2. Tell the children that this activity will familiarize them with local animals by giving the children the chance to observe how different animals move as they eat, play, and gather food.
3. Bring the children out to the location you selected earlier. Invite the children to look around for various animals of any kind.
4. Set up the three-column chart nearby, and ask the children to come to you and describe the animals they see and where they saw the animals. Record this information on the chart.
5. Once the children select several animals, invite them to choose one specific type of animal to observe in greater detail. Encourage the children to discuss how the animal moves around the area, and ask questions such as, "How does the butterfly move?," "Can you walk like a cat?," or "What is the difference between walking and flying?" Older children may notice additional details, such as what a squirrel has in its paws or the way a robin moves its tail when it hops.
6. Encourage the children to try mimicking some of the movements themselves while they are observing the animals.

7. Talk with the children about the various things an animal might need to do in its day. Perhaps a squirrel is hiding a nut, or a pigeon is looking for food. Lizards may lie in the sun to warm their cold-blooded bodies. A squirrel might scratch itself. Ask the children what they think these things mean. Does a squirrel get itchy like we do?

8. As the children describe the creatures' movements, record their descriptions in the third column on the chart.

9. Return to the classroom with the children, and encourage them to go through the list, trying to act out the different ways the various creatures moved.

Want to Do More?

◆ Encourage the children to compare and discuss the differences in animal and human movements.

◆ In the book area, set out books about the different animals the children observed.

◆ Set out paper, crayons, and markers, and invite the children to make drawings of their favorite animals. If the children are outside, set out clipboards so the children can draw while actually observing the animals. If the children are drawing a classroom pet, challenge them to make several drawings over a period of time, and look to see whether their drawings become more detailed over time.

Observing and Assessing the Children

Can the child identify and mimic the way the animal moves? Can the child add information about the location where she observed the animal?

Learning in Other Curricular Areas

Language and literacy
◆ expanding vocabulary by describing and talking about the movements made or the positions achieved (expressive language)
◆ observing and reading the three-column chart (symbols have meaning and print carries a message)

Math
◆ charting the animals (data analysis and probability)

Motor development
◆ moving like the animals (large motor)
◆ constructing the collage (small motor)

4+ Roly-Poly Roundup

Pill bugs, or roly-polies, are living creatures (isopods) that are common to many habitats. They prefer dark, moist places, and you can typically find them under rocks, boards, bricks, trash, decaying vegetation, or just beneath the soil surface. They venture out of their hiding places at night and eat decaying vegetation, such as leaf litter, rotting tree limbs, and grass clippings.

Science Content Standard—begins to understand the needs of living things (Life Science)
Science Process Skills—observing; classifying

Words You Can Use

Crawling	Look
Creatures	Moisture
Dark	Pill bugs
Dry	Roll
Find	Search
Hunt	Trap
Isopods	

Things You Can Use

Flashlight
Collecting jar or bag
Pictures of a pill bug
Potato
Knife (adults only)
Rubber band

Before the Activity

Check the area where the children will search for pill bugs to be sure they are plentiful and easy to find. Pill bugs live in abundance throughout most of the United States, except in very arid locations. In these arid areas, you can usually find them wherever constant moisture is available.

What to Do

1. Engage the children in a discussion about what they like about their homes. Point out to the children that animals also have homes, and there are specific things animals like about their homes, too. Tell the children that the animals that they will be looking for today, pill bugs, or roly-polies, prefer homes that are dark and moist. Explain that pill bugs stay in their homes during the daylight hours and only venture out when it is dark.

2. Bring the children outside and invite them to point out to you different places where they think pill bugs might live, such as under large rocks, bricks, boards, trash, piles of wet leaves or any decaying vegetation, or near damp and shady house foundations.

3. Encourage the children to search the locations where they think they might find pill bugs. Help them lift boards, small limbs, or brush aside piles of decaying vegetation.

4. Gather the children around a spot where someone finds some pill bugs, and encourage the children to count how many they see. Record their results.

5. Once the children find several pill bugs in different locations, invite them to talk about the similarities and differences between the various places where the bugs make their homes.

6. Ask the children to brainstorm ways to make a pill-bug trap. As the children discuss this, explain that pill bugs are attracted to potatoes. Then, while the children watch, cut a large potato in half.

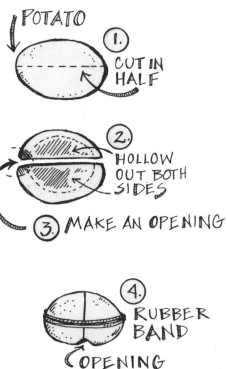

POTATO
1. CUT IN HALF
2. HOLLOW OUT BOTH SIDES
3. MAKE AN OPENING
4. RUBBER BAND
OPENING

Hollow out both sides, showing the children that you are leaving a small opening at one end. (See illustration.) Pull the two halves back together again, and place a rubber band around them to hold them together, and then set the potato outside in the yard.

Safety note: The preparation of the potato is an adult-only step. Consider hollowing out the potato halves before the children arrive at school that day.

7. Hollow out several additional potato halves, and invite the children to place them in the various locations where the children found pill bugs and where they did not find any bugs.

8. Let a few days pass, then invite the children to come outside and check on their pill-bug traps. Help the children uncover them, remove the rubber bands, and look inside. Invite the children to discuss what they see. If a trap did not catch any pill bugs, talk with the children about why they think this happened, then invite them to look for a better location and set the potatoes there.

Want to Do More?

◆ With the children, collect some of the pill bugs and place them in a dry, warm spot, and encourage the children to watch how long they stay.

Observing and Assessing the Children

Can the child identify a pill bug? Can the child tell you where pill bugs like to live or take you where they found pill bugs?

Learning in Other Curricular Areas

Language and literacy
◆ expanding vocabulary by describing and talking about the pill bugs and their preferred habitats (expressive and descriptive language)

Math
◆ counting and recording the number of pill bugs found in each discovered habitat (number operations)

Motor development
◆ walking around the building or yard to locate and identify various pill bug habitats (large motor)
◆ removing debris such as small boards, bricks, or leaves to expose the pill bugs (small motor)

INCORPORATING TECHNOLOGY

Take digital pictures of the pill bugs where the children found them, and then take pictures of them in the potatoes. Print the photographs and invite the children to dictate to you captions for the photos. Encourage the children to make books out of the images and captions. Consider inviting the children to assemble a collection of photographs of plants, insects, and other living things from the area to display in the classroom or use in class books.

4+   3-D Nature Collage

Making a nature collage provides an opportunity for children to interact with materials that are an integral part of the outdoor world. Children can collect materials from the playground, their own neighborhoods, from the ocean, a river, a creek, or a park. All it takes is a collecting bag and time to uncover a wealth of natural materials from which they can make three-dimensional collages.

Science Content Standard—begins to use simple, descriptive language about living things (Life Science)
Science Process Skill—observing

Words You Can Use

Collage   Press
Collect   Search
Feel   Shape
Find   Smell
Living   Touch
Names of items collected
Nonliving

Things You Can Use

Collecting bags, one per child
Objects collected outside, such as leaves, twigs, flowers, seeds, feathers, and rocks
Tag board or sturdy cardboard cut into squares (about 12" x 12" or 30 cm x 30 cm)
White glue

Before the Activity

Locate an area near your school that offers a variety of materials that the children can collect. If natural materials are limited in the immediate area, bring in additional materials.
Note: Fresh, green plant pieces wilt quickly. If the children want to use them, dry them using the instructions for making a plant press on page 172.

What to Do

1. Give each child a collecting bag. Bring the children outside to go on a collecting walk, gathering various natural materials. As the children collect materials, talk with them about how the different materials grow, or what brought them to the specific location. Wonder aloud about which tree grew a particular twig or leaf.

2. Encourage the children to name anything they know. Many young children can identify dandelions, grass, snail shells, and other similar items. If they find a manmade item such as a bottle cap, discuss it with them. Ask, "Did this grow here? How did it get here? I wonder how it was made." The difference between living and nonliving things can be a hard concept for young children to understand. Having repeated discussions with actual materials at hand helps children to learn the difference. As you talk about the materials the children collect, encourage them to describe the different things they see, feel, and smell.

   Safety note: Prepare for the collecting walk by using insect repellent and sunscreen. Remind the children not to taste anything they collect and not to touch poison ivy, poison oak, nettles, or any sharp objects. If the children collect near ponds, creeks, rivers, or the ocean, extra close supervision is mandatory.

3. After the children fill their collecting bags, return to the classroom and invite the children to make a collage using the materials they collected on their gathering walk.

4. Help the children place the various materials they collected on a table, and then give each child a piece of cardboard to use as the base for her collage.

INCORPORATING TECHNOLOGY

Take digital photos of the children's collages and share them with the children's families via email.

USING MUSEUMS AND OTHER COMMUNITY RESOURCES

Bring the children to an art gallery to view collages that are on display. Invite a local artist or a high school art student to share collage creations with the children.

As they begin, talk with the children about how gluing three-dimensional objects might be different from gluing flat objects. Remind the children that little dots of glue work better than big puddles!

Note: Making a 3-D collage is an art activity that can be either an individual or group project. As a group project, it can support social interaction and help the children learn how to work toward a common goal. Also, consider having the children work in pairs or small groups based on their different skills and abilities.

5. Encourage the children to try adding a variety of materials to their collages. Suggest that they try placing objects on top of each other or at different angles to create tall collages. Comment on the techniques children use. For instance, "You made the leaves stand up with their ends touching. It's like a little tent," or "It is interesting how you crisscrossed all the sticks." The more specific you make your comments, the better they will help the children discover new approaches to constructing their collages.

Want to Do More?

◆ Challenge the children to classify their natural collage materials by characteristics such as color, texture, size, and shape.

Observing and Assessing the Children

Can the child identify whether some of the objects she used in her collage are natural or manmade?

Learning in Other Curricular Areas

Arts

◆ creating collages (visual arts)

Language and literacy

◆ expanding vocabulary by describing and talking about the materials they collect (expressive language)

4+ Ant Restaurant

Just like people, ants like certain foods and dislike others. In this activity, the children make an ant "restaurant" and discover what foods ants like best. This is a good activity for warm weather when ants begin to become active.

Science Content Standard—begins to understand the needs of living things (Life Science)
Science Process Skills—observing; classifying

Words You Can Use

Ants   Sweet
Favorite   Lines
Salt   Time passing
Sugar

Things You Can Use

Bottle caps or margarine
    tub lids
Sugar
Salt
Crayons
Paper

Before the Activity

You may want to find anthills in your area and place your "restaurants" nearby. However, even if you cannot find evidence of ant activity, the sugar is likely to attract them.

What to Do

1. With the children, put a sugar cube or a teaspoon of sugar in a margarine lid, and invite the children to think of a name for the restaurant, "Sugar Land," for instance. Set out another lid, help the children put salt in it, and encourage them to think of a name for the restaurant, such as "The Salty Dog."

2. Bring the children outside, and invite them to find a quiet place away from active play areas where they can put the two ant "restaurants."

3. Gather the children around the two restaurants, so they can observe the activity that begins to occur. Initially, only a few ants will come, but the number of them should increase over time as they find the foods that they prefer.
4. Ask the children which restaurant the ants like best—"Sugar Land" or "The Salty Dog?"
5. Set out markers, crayons, and paper, and invite the children to make drawings of the lines of ants they observe coming to each restaurant.

Want to Do More?

◆ Try setting different food scraps in the lids, such as apple slices or breadcrumbs and invite the children to observe the results.
◆ Read *Hey, Little Ant* by Phillip and Hannah Hoose with the children to give them a look at life from an ant's point of view.

Observing and Assessing the Children

Is the child able to communicate that ants prefer sweet, sugary foods rather than salty ones?

Learning in Other Curricular Areas

Arts
◆ making drawings of the different ant lines and food preferences (visual art/creativity)

Language and literacy
◆ expanding vocabulary by describing and talking about the ants (expressive and descriptive language)

Math
◆ counting the number of ants that gather to collect the food (number operations)

4+ What Is Another Way to Sort?

"Sara Jane" is sorting shells into two piles. When asked to describe the two groups, "Sara Jane" cheerfully replied, "In these you can hear the ocean. In these you can't." Letting children come up with their own guidelines for sorting encourages creativity in problem solving, an approach to learning that is important to encourage in young children.

Science Content Standard—notes similarities and differences among living things and can describe them (Life Science)

Science Process Skill—classifying (sorting)

Words You Can Use

Characteristics, such as
    round, flat, and so on
Classify
Compare
Different
Group
Group names
Object names
Same
Sort

Things You Can Use

Sets of natural objects
    that you or the
    children collected
Two trays, shoebox lids,
    or box tops for the
    sorted objects

What to Do

1. Set out the collections of items and the sorting trays for the children to see.
2. As they look at the items you set out, ask the children to think of similarities and differences between the objects.
3. As the children discuss various differences and similarities between the objects, encourage them to focus on one general trait, and then separate the objects into two groups, putting each group on one tray, lid, or box.

4. Help the children as they sort the objects based on the characteristic they chose. Make sure that all the items fit into one of the two categories and that the children are separating them properly. If appropriate, ask the children to count the number of objects in each group.

5. After the children finish separating the items based on one characteristic, ask them to bring all the items back together and think about another specific characteristic they can use to sort the objects. Repeat the activity using the new characteristic.

Want to Do More?

◆ Set out a third tray and challenge the children to create three classification groups. They may discover that some items do not fit in any of the groups. If so, encourage the children to make a fourth group.

◆ As the children complete their sort of the items into two groups, introduce a new item, and ask the children whether it fits in one of the two groups they created or if they have to create a third group.

◆ Provide the children with a set of very similar items, such as acorns from the same tree, or a set of same species of shells, and challenge the children to find a way to separate them into two groups.

Observing and Assessing the Children

Given a set of natural objects, can the child sort them into two groups and explain which particular characteristic she used to separate the objects into groups?

Learning in Other Curricular Areas

Language and literacy
◆ listening with understanding and responding to directions (receptive language)
◆ communicating their ideas and thoughts (expressive language)

Math
◆ sorting and classifying objects by a variety of properties and making comparisons to other objects (algebra, geometry)
◆ counting with understanding and recognizing "how many" in sets of objects (number operations)

Motor development
◆ moving and sorting objects (small motor)

Counting Leaves

In this small-group activity, the children practice counting and classifying, and familiarize themselves with the trees in their area in the process.

Science Content Standard—notes similarities and differences among living things and can describe them (Life Science)
Science Process Skills—observing; classifying

Words You Can Use

Count
Color
Number names
Plant names
Total

Things You Can Use

Cards with numbers and
    number names written
    on them
Leaves
Tree identification book

Before the Activity

The children will need to collect large numbers of leaves in this activity, so be sure to choose a time of the year when leaves are plentiful. Remember that grasses have leaves, too.
Note: Adjust the number of leaves each child collects based on her counting abilities.

What to Do

1. Go outside with the children, and invite each child to collect a certain number of leaves. Ask younger children to collect one or two and older children to collect five or seven. Encourage the children to bring you the leaves they collect and count them with you, so you can be sure they collected the correct number of leaves.

2. After the children finish gathering their leaves, ask everyone to gather in a circle. Choose one child and ask her to put one of her leaves on the ground.

3. Show the children your leaf identification book, and encourage the children to describe the leaf to you as you identify it. Once you identify it as, for instance, an oak leaf, invite the other children to look through their leaves to see if they have the same kind of leaf. Ask those children who have matching leaves to put them next to the oak leaf. **Note:** If you are not able to identify the leaf, simply ask the children to describe it, and then invite them to look through their leaves to see if they have the same kind.

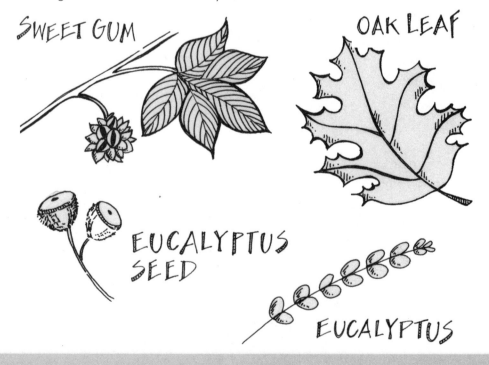

SWEET GUM

OAK LEAF

EUCALYPTUS SEED

EUCALYPTUS

4. Challenge the children to count these leaves to find the total number of oak leaves the group collected. Set out the numbered cards, and challenge one of the children to pick the card with the matching number on it and place it on the leaf collection. If the child is not sure which card has the correct number on it, invite the children to help her choose.
5. Challenge the children to classify and sort all the leaves they collected, match a number card to each group, and then count the total number of leaves.
6. Once the children understand the process, invite them to seek out more species of leaves and repeat the activity.

Want to Do More?

◆ Challenge the children to reclassify the leaves based on other properties, such as shape and color, and then count how many leaves are in each new group.
◆ Ask the children whether all the leaves in one species are the same size, and encourage them to measure the leaves and order them from smallest to largest within each species.

Observing and Assessing the Children

Can the child count her pile of leaves? Can she match two leaves from the same plant?

Learning in Other Curricular Areas

Language and literacy
◆ listening with understanding and responding to directions (receptive language)

Math
◆ exploring quantity and number (number operations)

Motor development
◆ walking and collecting leaves (large motor)

ASH

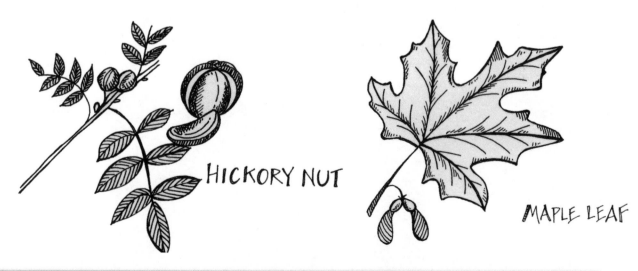

HICKORY NUT

MAPLE LEAF

4+ Everything Has to Eat

This activity illustrates for the children how they have something in common with several life forms. Children know that they eat to survive. If they have pets, the children may also know that pets eat to survive. But what about other creatures? Collecting and observing a few invertebrates gives the children a way to see how, like themselves, other creatures, even bugs, eat to live.

Science Content Standard—notes similarities and differences among living things and can describe them (Life Science)
Science Process Skill—observing

Words You Can Use

Animal names
Food names
Needs
Plant names

Things You Can Use

Small creatures such as
    crickets, grasshoppers,
    mealworms,
    caterpillars, ladybugs,
    ants, pill bugs,
    crawdads/crayfish, or
    hermit crabs
An aquarium, ant farm,
    or other large clear
    container

Before the Activity

Collect several of the animals listed above from outdoors, or obtain them from a pet store or bait shop. Keep the animals in separate containers.

What to Do

1. Invite the children to choose one or two animals to study. It is good if the children's interest in the animals develops naturally. For example, if in the fall the children notice large numbers of crickets outside, give the children containers and help them collect several crickets to study. Similarly, the children might want to catch several grasshoppers, caterpillars, or pill bugs.

2. Explain to the children that most insects and small creatures live on or near the plants they eat. This makes it easy to gather food. Encourage the children to bring a little of the plant with them when they catch a creature, and to remember where the plant is, in case they need to return for more.

    Note: Remind the children to be aware of the scarcity of the plants they collect. If a cricket is sitting on several kinds of plants, and one plant is more plentiful than another is, take a small amount of the more plentiful plant, and to leave the rarer plants alone.

3. Once the children catch enough creatures in containers, bring the creatures and plants back into the classroom. Back in the classroom, find a spot at the children's eye level where they

can see the containers from all sides, and designate this as the animal observation deck. Ask the children to put their containers there. **Note:** When the children bring the containers inside, explain to the children that they should not touch the containers, only observe them.

4. Engage the children in a discussion about the different animals' needs. Ask the children what the animals eat, and invite them to look closely to observe the creatures chewing on the various plants. If the insects do not eat the plants in their containers, ask the children why they think that might be so. Ask, "Could we have put the insect in with the wrong kinds of plants?," and help the children think of how to find the right food for the insect.
Note: Check in nature books or on the Internet to find information about what plants the various animals eat.

5. Ask the children to think of what else the animals might need. When doing this, ask the children to think of the basic things they need to survive, such as water, air, comfortable temperatures, and a safe environment in which to thrive. Ask the children to think about how they can provide their creatures with these things.

6. Next, explain to the children that the best method for giving the insects water is to put a jar lid with a moist paper towel or a piece of sponge in it in the creatures' containers. This way, the animals can climb on the towel or sponge and suck moisture from it. With an open container of water, the insects are likely to fall in and drown. Make sure the creatures have fresh air and a comfortable temperature by adding breathing holes in their containers.

7. Ask the children to describe the differences between the environment of the container and the outdoor environment.

8. Encourage the children to spend some time each day watching the creatures, and ask the children questions about what they see. Ask, "What do they do every day that we do every day as well?" After a few days of observation, help the children take the animals outside and set them free.

CONNECTING TO CHILDREN WITH SPECIAL NEEDS
Consult families regarding any allergic conditions children may have to outdoor plants and animals.

Want to Do More?

◆ Set out paper, markers, and crayons and invite the children to draw pictures of the animals and the plants they eat.

◆ Set out nature photographs and magazines with pictures of various animals eating and drinking.

Observing and Assessing the Children

Can the child describe the basic needs of the creatures under observation and explain what the class is doing to meet those needs?

Learning in Other Curricular Areas

Language and literacy

◆ communicating and sharing ideas and thoughts with others (expressive language)

4+ Fuzzy Seed Art

This is a great activity to do when there is an abundance of fuzzy plant seeds blowing in the wind or growing in the area. The children can use these fuzzy materials to add texture to and enhance their paintings.

Science Content Standard—begins to use simple, descriptive language about living things (Life Science)
Science Process Skills—observing; classifying

Words You Can Use

Blowing
Collect
Color names, such as
    white, green, brown,
    and so on
Feel   Seed
Fuzzy   Texture
Paint   Touch

Things You Can Use

Collecting bags
Art paper
Fluffy seed materials
Paintbrushes
Tempera paints

Before the Activity

Locate an area with an abundance of dandelions in seed, milkweed pods, cottonwood "cotton," or willow seeds growing on the tree or blowing in the wind.

What to Do

1. When you see fuzzy seeds growing in the area or blowing through the air, invite the children on a collecting walk and encourage them to gather several of the seeds.
2. Bring several different bags outside, and encourage the children to strip the seeds from their pods, then put each type of seed in a separate bag.
3. As the children collect the seeds, ask them where the seeds came from, why they think they are blowing around, and if they know which plants produced them.

DANDELION

4. Come back inside with the children, and go to the art area. Set out several sheets of paper, containers of tempera paint, and the bags of fuzzy seeds. Encourage the children to paint on the paper then place the fuzzy seeds on the wet paint to add texture to their paintings. Have them experiment with other ways to use the seeds to make art.

5. Discuss with the children different ways to experiment with the seeds, using them to make art. Make a list and share it with all the children, encouraging them to use some of their peers' ideas.

INCORPORATING TECHNOLOGY

Take pictures of the seeds with a digital camera and enlarge them as much as possible to help children see the detailed plant structures.

Want to Do More?

◆ Set up a magnifying glass and invite the children to examine the various seeds. Point out to the children that sometimes the fuzz contains tiny insects.

Observing and Assessing the Children

Can the child name the seed or seeds used in the fuzzy seed painting? Can the child demonstrate or list the steps she took to make her fuzzy seed paintings?

Learning in Other Curricular Areas

Arts

◆ create a visual art form (visual arts)

Language and literacy

◆ using painting to convey meaning and information (visual communication)

◆ describing art creations and other ways to use seeds (expressive language)

Motor development

◆ walking and running while collecting seeds (large motor)

◆ picking up seeds, placing them in the paint, and pressing materials onto paper (small motor)

Leaves in the Air, Grab a Pair

Children will want to do this activity over and over. It uses fun large and motor actions to reinforce memory and number skills

Science Content Standard—notes similarities and differences among living things and can describe them (Life Science)
Science Process Skills—observing; classifying

Words You Can Use

Big
Color names
Descriptive words
Fall
Little
Tree names, such as elm, maple, oak, and so on

Things You Can Use

A park or wooded area with a variety of tree species
A sheet or parachute
Tree identification books

Before the Activity

Locate an area near the school that has a variety of tree species whose leaves the children can gather. If the area near your school does not have many trees, collect the leaves from any site and bring them to your school.

What to Do

1. Bring the children out into the schoolyard or a nearby park and spread a sheet out on the ground. Ask the children to gather leaves and fill the center of the sheet with them. As the children bring leaves to the sheet, use a tree identification book to tell the children the names of the leaves they are carrying. While the children may not remember the names, hearing them will help the children be more attentive to the idea of differences among the leaves.

2. After the children make a large pile of leaves on the sheet, invite the children to gather around the edges of sheet, take hold of its edge with both hands, pick it up, and shake it lightly so the leaves toss into the air without falling out of the sheet.

3. Encourage the children to practice coordinating their movements. For instance, say, "Leaves in the air!" and have the children raise the sheet so the leaves fly up, then say, "Leaves on the ground!" and have the children bring the sheet down to the ground so the leaves fall down on the sheet. Practice this a few times.

4. When the children are can raise and lower the sheet of leaves easily, challenge them to follow additional steps. For instance, ask the children to raise and lower the sheet, and then say, "Now find two matching leaves," so that once the children put the sheet back on the ground, they search through the leaves on the sheet for a matching pair of leaves. Similarly, consider asking them to find a certain number of leaves, or a large leaf, or a particular species of leaf, such as oak.

OAK LEAF

SWEET GUM

MAPLE LEAF

5. As the activity continues, encourage the children to increase the speed with which they raise and lower the sheet of leaves, eventually going so fast that the children shake all the leaves off the sheet.

Want to Do More?

◆ Engage the children in a discussion about the different ways that leaves look and record the children's descriptions.

◆ Engage the children in a discussion about why leaves fall. Point out that some trees drop their leaves in the fall and others do not. Ask the children whether they think all leaves fall eventually.

◆ Find an elevated place, such as the top of a piece of playground equipment, where the children can stand safely and let go of a leaf to see what happens to it in the breeze.

Observing and Assessing the Children

Can the child raise and lower the sheet as directed? Can she select leaves from the sheet that match those you direct the children to pick?

Learning in Other Curricular Areas

Language and literacy
◆ communicating information about observations with others (expressive and descriptive language)

Math
◆ selecting the correct number of leaves (counting)

Motor development
◆ raising and lowering the sheet (large motor)
◆ selecting the leaves (small motor)

Underground Breakdown

The bacteria in soil are an important part of the breakdown of organic material. In this activity, the children compare what happens when organic and inorganic materials are exposed to bacteria in the soil. Put some organic material in touch with the soil and the little critters in it, and miracles happen. The organic material is decayed, broken down, and disappears as it becomes dirt.

Science Content Standard—begins to understand the needs of living things (Life Science)
Science Process Skills—observing; communicating

Words You Can Use

Bury   Change
Decay   Degradable
Litter
Materials names
No change
Non-degradable

Things You Can Use

Apple or orange peels
Cellophane wrapper
    pieces
Fast-food containers
Glass pieces
Grass leaves
Gum or gum wrapper
Permanent marker and
    plastic margarine—or
    yogurt—tub lids
Plant leaves
Plastic pieces
Shovel
Tin or aluminum cans
Tissue paper pieces
Tree leaves
Plastic netting bags, like
    those used for onions,
    or old nylon stocking
    socks
Child-safe scissors

What to Do

Safety Note: Be sure children do not handle any potentially dangerous items, such as pieces of glass.

1. Bring the children outside to collect a variety of natural materials and litter. Encourage the children to find a range of different materials, so they have at least one of each of the items listed in "Things You Can Use."

2. Once the children finish gathering various organic and inorganic materials, bring the children inside, give them child-safe scissors, and ask the children to cut the items into small pieces. Cutting the materials into small pieces will speed up the decomposition process.
    Note: Do not have the children cut up metal items, as that will create sharp edges.

3. Organize the children into six to eight small groups, give each group a plastic netting bag and ask the groups to fill the bags with a variety of the materials they found. Invite the children to record what they put in the bags by making drawings of the objects. If possible, photograph the items as the children put them in the bags. The photographs and drawings will help illustrate the changes that occur during decomposition.

4. Help the children label and date some of their drawings. Next, give each group a plastic lid, ask the children to come up with names for their groups, and help them write their group names on their lids. Place the lids at the tops of the bags. Keep some materials out of

ORANGE PEELS   CELLOPHANE   GRASS   LEAVES   STYROFOAM CUP

① CUT UP ITEMS and ADD to BAG
② ADD PLASTIC LID and CLOSE

grass   Wrapper
CUP
orange piece
leaf

DRAWING
NAME
DATE

Learning in Other Curricular Areas

Math

◆ looking at changes over time (measurement—time)

Motor development

◆ using shovel to dig hole, filling holes, and digging up the bags (large motor skills)

◆ drawing the bags and their contents (small motor)

the bags so the children can compare them to the other materials in the future.

5. Bring the children outside and help them bury their bags in a secluded spot. Choose a location large enough that the children can bury the bags at least 5" (10 cm) below the surface.

   Note: Moisture is key to decomposition. Decomposition also occurs more rapidly in rich, loose soil. Oxygen, worms, and insects are crucial parts of the process. Decomposition occurs more slowly in hard, packed soil, such as a worn pathway.

6. Bring the children back inside, and show them as you mark the calendar to indicate when they buried their bags. Also mark a date one or two months in the future, when the children will get to dig up the bags.

7. When one or two months pass, bring the children outside and invite them to dig up their bags and look at the decomposition of the materials they buried. Remind the children to bring their drawings and photographs of the materials, as well as the collection of materials they did not bury, so they can compare them with how the materials look after two months underground.

8. As the children discuss the changes, record some of their comments and add them to the photos or drawings of the items the children are talking about. Also, take photographs of the materials, and invite the children to make new drawings.

9. After the children look at and discuss all the different objects they buried, comparing the different levels of decomposition, ask them to put everything back in their bags and bury them in the same holes again. Encourage the children to compare the level of decomposition at each digging time. The idea that trash dropped on the ground does not just disappear is important even for young children to understand.

Want to Do More?

◆ Encourage the children to collect and separate the biodegradable portions of their lunch waste and add the materials to the compost pile.

   Note: Only include plant matter. Meat waste will attract unwanted pests and will stink.

◆ Bring the children on a field trip to the local composting area.

Observing and Assessing the Children

Can the child observe and describe the changes in materials buried in the ground over time?

4+ We're Going on a Bug Hunt

Collecting insects is an exciting activity. With practice, most children will quickly become adept at capturing insects. They may initially need help from adults to transfer insects from the net to an observation container so they don't squash any creatures in the process.

Science Content Standard—begins to understand the needs of living things (Life Science)
Science Process Skill—observing

Words You Can Use

Bug	Insect
Capture	Insect names
Collect	Magnifier
Container	Net
Gather	Release

Things You Can Use

Coat-hanger bug nets (see page 256 for assembly instructions) or commercial bug nets

Bug-holding devices, such as jars or plastic containers with lids, plastic collecting boxes with magnifier lids

Handheld magnifiers (optional)

Before the Activity

Invite the children's families to help build some of the nets the children will use to capture insects. Find a nearby field or grassy area where the children can search for insects.

What to Do

1. Set out the bug nets that you and the children made, and illustrate for them how, to capture insects, they should sweep the nets through high grass and weeds. When they have insects in their nets, the children should place the nets flat on the ground so the insects cannot escape.

2. Bring the children to a field or grassy area and invite them to try catching and releasing the various insects they see. Let the children enjoy practicing this for some time. It is great exercise and a way that the children can explore a space in a different way.

3. Once the children can capture insects easily, challenge them to look for and catch unusual-looking insects, and help the children transfer these insects into containers for closer viewing. When a child captures an interesting insect, bring the container, slip it under the netting, then guide the insect into the container and close the top.
   Safety note: Remind the children to avoid insects that sting, such as wasps or bees, and spiders that might bite.

4. Give the children plenty of time to observe and discuss the different insects they capture. Consider providing magnifiers for the children to use to observe the insects more closely.
   Note: Young children often have a hard time using handheld magnifiers effectively because most require focusing through one eye. With practice, the children can become more skilled in their use.

5. As the children observe the insects, encourage them to share their observations. Ask them questions, such as, "How many legs does the insect have?," or "What about wings or spots?" Set out paper, markers, and crayons, and invite the children to make drawings of the insects.
6. Once the children finish observing the insects, help the children release the insects into the field.

Want to Do More?

◆ Bring the children back inside and set out various books they can use to identify the insects they captured. Most libraries have very simple insect guides for young children, such as *The Ladybug and Other Insects* by Pascale de Bourgoing, Gallimard Jeunesse, and Sylvie Perols.

◆ Encourage the children to examine the insects very close, and discuss how many legs and body parts the insects have. Ask the children to compare this to their own bodies. If the children capture some spiders, encourage the children to compare the two different types of creature.

◆ Discuss the different types and numbers of wings on the various insects. Point out that flies have only two wings, while most others insects have four.

◆ Repeat the activity at different times of the school year, and in different locations, and encourage the children to compare the differences between the insects they catch.

Observing and Assessing the Children

Can the child use tools of science, such as insect nets and magnifiers, to observe insects? Can the child describe the individual characteristics of the different insects she observed?

Learning in Other Curricular Areas

Language and literacy
◆ listening and following directions (receptive language)

Motor development
◆ using bug nets to capture insects (large motor)
◆ placing and securing captured insects into bug-holding devices (small motor)

CONNECTING TO CHILDREN WITH SPECIAL NEEDS
Select a wheelchair-accessible area for the children to catch insects.

INCORPORATING TECHNOLOGY
Use a camera to take photographs of the insects the children find, and help them use the photographs to make display panels or posters for the classroom, or to make their own insect guidebooks. Before the children arrive, search the Internet for information about the insects captured, and discuss it with them later.

4+

What's Under That Board?

The habitats where animals live provide food, shelter, and safety. This activity helps young scientists understand this basic ecological concept, especially when they compare the animals' needs to their own.

Science Content Standard—begins to understand the needs of living things (Life Science)
Science Process Skills—observing; predicting

Words You Can Use

Animal
Animal names   Predict
Examine   Record
Explore   Safe
Habitat names   Search
Hide   Secure
Hiding places

Things You Can Use

Animal identification
   books
Outdoor area to explore
Writing materials

Before the Activity

Find an outdoor location where there are likely several small animals to observe. Check under rocks and boards to ensure there are various little creatures in the area, and bring identification books with you to familiarize yourself with the various creatures. You might see ants, pill bugs, earthworms, millipedes, spiders, wood roaches, centipedes, beetles, or termites. After checking for the creatures, replace the rocks, boards, and logs.

TREE STUMP
OLD LOGS
FLAT ROCKS
DIRT
FLAT BOARD
LEAVES

What to Do

1. Bring the children outside to the area you designated, and tell the children they will be looking for little creatures.
2. Challenge the children to think of the different creatures they might find under rocks, logs, and boards. Help the children by asking them how large the creatures must be to fit under the board or rock. Ask the children if they ever looked under a board or rock before and what creatures they found.
3. After the children make several predictions, show them the boards and rocks you looked beneath earlier. Explain to the children before you lift a board that the light will scare the animals, and that they will probably try to hide.
4. Lift the board and invite the children to look closely at the creatures scurrying around. Identify some of the creatures for the children, and encourage the children to describe the way they look and how they move.
5. Engage the children in a discussion about how animals need hiding places to stay safe. Living under a rock or board provides safety and shelter for these creatures. Ask the children if they see anything beneath the board that the creatures might eat, such as leaves, roots, seeds, or wood.
6. Ask the children if they see any similarities between what the board provides the insects and what the children get from their homes, classroom, or even an umbrella.

Want to Do More?

◆ Read Ruth Heller's *How to Hide a Butterfly* to the children. Set out paper and one color of paint or crayon and invite the children to draw or paint butterflies, then hide them the way the book hides its butterfly. Encourage the children to "hide" their butterflies by drawing them, then filling in the page with flowers, trees, clouds or anything else they want to create using the same color.

Observing and Assessing the Children

Can the child talk about where small animals live and what they need for food, safety, and shelter?

Learning in Other Curricular Areas

Language and literacy
◆ communicating information about animals and humans (expressive language)

Motor development
◆ walking to area where the animals are observed (large motor)

4+ What Am I?

In this activity, the children mimic the movements of the different creatures they observe, and even create their own animal costumes so they can frolic through the classroom as squirrels and robins.

Science Content Standard—begins to understand the needs of living things (Life Science)
Science Process Skills—observing; communicating observations

Words You Can Use

Animal names
Animal behavior words
Animal characteristic
  words

Things You Can Use

Pictures of a variety of animals easily observed in your area; for example, in an urban setting: squirrels, pigeons, sparrows, butterflies; in a suburban setting: rabbits, geese, caterpillars; in a rural setting: lizards, farm animals, dragonflies

What to Do

1. Over a period of a week or more, suggest that the children observe and imitate the movement and sounds of animals that are common to the local environment. Talk with the children about the animals they observe. Ask them what the names of the animals are and how the animals move. Encourage the children to try to imitate the animals' movements together. After the children try moving like several different animals, engage the children in a discussion about the similarities and differences between how the creatures move.

2. Choose one child, and ask her to think of an animal, then, without naming the animal, begin to imitate the way that animal moves. Challenge the rest of the children to guess which animal the child is pretending to be. Once the children guess the animal, choose another child and repeat the activity.

3. After the children pretend to be several animals, challenge them to think of other ways they might look even more like the animals. If the children do not mention it, suggest making costumes.

4. With the children, spend several days developing costumes and pretending to be animals. Occasionally take the children out to observe the real animals so the children can become more exact in their imitations.

5. As the children observe, encourage them to think about the differences between the creatures. For instance, how could the children tell the difference between a child imitating a sparrow and a child imitating a bee?

6. Continue repeating the activity from time to time as the children continue to develop their costumes and refine their imitations. Eventually, invite another class to come in and guess which creatures the children are imitating.

Want to Do More?

◆ Invite the children's families for a "family fun night" featuring the children's animal imitations. Challenge the audience to guess which creatures the children are imitating.

Observing and Assessing the Children

Can the child describe a special characteristic of the animal she chose to imitate, such as how it wiggles its tail?

Learning in Other Curricular Areas

Arts

◆ acting out behavior of animals (drama)

Language and literacy

◆ understanding that pictures have meaning (early literacy)
◆ retelling information about the animal they are portraying from what they hear and see in the classroom.

Motor development

◆ acting out animal behaviors (large and small motor)

Who Made It?

To adults, the difference between natural and manufactured objects is very apparent. For young children the differences may not be as obvious. This activity provides children the opportunity to handle and compare an array of natural and manufactured items.

Science Content Standard—begins to understand the difference between living and nonliving things (Life Science)
Science Process Skill—classifying

Words You Can Use

Human
Made by humans
Manufactured
Natural
Nature
People

Things You Can Use

Large index cards and marker
Collections of natural objects, such as leaves, rocks, shells, nuts, twigs, and bark
Collections of manufactured objects, such as glass, metal, and plastic containers or toys
Collections of manufactured objects obviously made using natural objects, such as bricks, stone carvings, and wooden blocks or wooden toys

What to Do

1. With the help of the children, over the course of a few days, collect several natural and manufactured objects. Once the collection is sufficiently large, set it out in front of the children.

2. Take out three index cards. On one card, write "natural." Write "made by humans" on another and "made using natural objects" on the third. Show the children the first two cards, set them out apart from one another, and set the third card aside until later.

3. Pick a leaf out of the collection and engage the children in a discussion about where leaves come from. Ask the children if the leaf is natural or manufactured. Explain to the children that because the leaves come from trees, and because trees are natural living things, the leaf is a natural object, and ask a child to place it beside the "natural" index card.

4. Pick up a plastic object and talk with the children about it. Ask them where it came from. Ask whether it grew naturally, or if someone made it. Once the children decide that it is a manufactured object, ask a child to put it beside the "made by humans" index card.

PLASTIC BUCKET

CUP

MARBLE

PENCIL

LEAF

SHELL

ROCK

PUSSY WILLOW

Natural

Made by humans

ADDRESSING
THE NEEDS OF
ENGLISH
LANGUAGE
LEARNERS

*Support children's
language development
by naming the objects
the children classify
and giving them
to the children
to handle.*

CONNECTING
TO CHILDREN
WITH SPECIAL
NEEDS

*For children who
have visual impairments,
use trays or paper
whose colors contrast
with the colors of
the materials the
children are classifying.*

5. Repeat the process of classifying the various objects with the children. Once the children become adept at identifying the natural from the manufactured, take out the "made using natural objects" index card and show it to the children. Explain this concept to the children, and then challenge them to look for objects that fit this category. Explain that objects like blocks fit into this category, because it is easy to see that they come from natural objects like trees. Explain to the children that manufactured objects are often made from natural materials. Sometimes you can easily see what natural material people used, but sometimes you cannot.

6. Once the children finish categorizing all the objects, invite them to count the number of objects in each category. If there are more objects in one particular category, ask the children what they think that might mean. For instance, if there are only two natural objects, one object manufactured using natural objects, and the rest are manufactured objects, does this mean that most of the objects came from a particular indoor location? Would the numbers of objects in the three categories differ if the children only sorted objects they collected from a location outdoors?

Want to Do More?

◆ Before the children arrive, search online for instructions on how to make paper by pressing other paper and leaves together. Help the children experiment with this so they can better understand the manufacturing process.

◆ Go on a fieldtrip to a woodcarver, pottery maker, or other artisan's studio so the children can see them make objects out of natural materials.

◆ Use Venn diagrams to illustrate for the children how the three classifications in the activity overlap.

Observing and Assessing the Children

Can the child classify objects based on whether they are "natural" or "manufactured"?

Learning in Other Curricular Areas

Language and literacy

◆ listening and responding to questions and directions (receptive language)

◆ communicating ideas and thoughts verbally to others (expressive language)

Math

◆ counting the objects in each category (number operations)

Motor development

◆ touching and handling collected objects (small motor)

5+ A Tree Through Time

In this activity, the children make a timeline that follows the "story" of one tree through the seasons and, in doing so, learn about how a single place and object changes over time.

Science Content Standard—begins to understand the needs of living things (Life Science)
Science Process Skills—observing; measuring (time)

Words You Can Use

Calendar
Fall
Spring
Summer
Tree name
Winter

Things You Can Use

Tree or other plant to observe (this can be a potted plant)
A notebook for holding pictures collected and made about the season
Digital camera
Drawing and writing paper

Before the Activity

Divide a notebook into four sections, and label each with a season. In an urban setting where trees are in short supply, find a plant nearby that the children can observe.

What to Do

1. Engage the children in a discussion about the seasons. As the discussion continues, make a list of things that the children think will happen during each season. Encourage the children to discuss the different clothes they wear each season, how the weather changes, how long the sun stays up, and anything else.
   Note: If you live in a hot climate, such as the South, children may have experienced snow during a vacation, or they may have watched movies or television that showed snow happening during the winter. Encourage the children to discuss both the weather in their immediate surroundings and in the world at large.

2. Show the children a calendar of the current year and show them the dates when each season begins. Explain that while the exact dates vary, summer in North America begins in June and ends in September, fall begins in September and ends in December, winter begins in December and ends in March, and spring begins in March and ends in June.

3. Show the children the current date on the calendar and name the season in which it falls. Ask the children to describe the current weather, and then explain to them that they will be studying the seasons observing what happens to one tree or bush as the seasons change.
   Note: It is best to begin this activity on the first day of a season.

4. Bring the children outside and show them the tree or bush they will observe. Use a digital camera to take a picture of the tree on this first day. Set out paper, markers, and crayons and suggest that the children make drawings of the tree and the ground or area around the tree.

5. Invite the children to pay special attention to the tree's leaves. Pull one from the tree and bring it back into the classroom to press (see "Press a Plant" on page 172).

6. Encourage the children to describe the tree and the area around it. Ask whether they see flowers, fruit, or seeds. Ask if they see any animals on or near the tree. Record this information in a notebook for the children.

Learning in Other Curricular Areas

Math

◆ collecting data over time (measurement—time)

Language and literacy

◆ dictating observational experiences (expressive language)

◆ drawing and writing to convey meaning and information (written communication)

7. Bring the children back inside and continue the discussion of the tree there, adding to your notes any additional comments the children make about what they observed.

8. Collect the children's drawings and observations, and then date and place them in the correct section of the seasonal notebook along with your notes of what the children said about the tree.

9. Ask the children to observe the tree periodically when they are near it, and to report to the class if they notice any changes. When someone notices something new happening to the tree, take the group out to observe the changes in the tree and the surrounding area. At least once each season, collect information about the tree. Each time the children make new observations about the tree, encourage them to compare these observations to those they made earlier.

10. Talk with the children about how the entire area around the tree is changing. In some areas, there may not be dramatic differences between the seasons. If so, encourage the children to discuss the ways the tree and surrounding area stay the same even as the seasons change.

Want to Do More?

◆ Include photographs of the children beside the tree in each section of the seasonal notebook so the children can see how they too change as time passes.

◆ Read books about the seasons, such as *The Seasons of Arnold's Apple Tree* by Gail Gibbons, *What Makes the Seasons* by Megan Cash, and *Four Seasons Make a Year* by Anne Rockwell.

◆ Help the children grow and observe potted plants, preferably outside, and encourage the children to discuss the ways the plants change throughout the year.

Observing and Assessing the Children

Can the child describe how the tree and surrounding area change over time?

Capture and Recapture

Do this activity in the fall, when grasshoppers, crickets, pill bugs, box-elder bugs, ladybugs, or other insects common to your location are out in large enough numbers that the children can catch several without great difficulty.

Science Content Standard—begins to understand the needs of living things (Life Science)
Science Process Skills—predicting; communicating

Words You Can Use

Capture
Insect names   Recapture
Less   Release
More   Same

Things You Can Use

Clipboard and paper
Colored nail polish, a metallic marker, or dark marker (Nail polish may be used for large insects, such as grasshoppers, but nail polish may harm the wings of small insects. Use a silver or gold marker instead to mark small, dark-colored insects and a dark marker for light-colored insects.)
Insect nets (see directions on page 256 for how to make your own)
Large container to hold animals for a short time—a clear plastic shoebox or jar works

What to Do

1. Bring the children outside and encourage them to observe and discuss the insects they see. Talk with the children about how insects are living things and are part of our world.

2. Show the children how to use the insect nets to capture an insect and transfer it to a container without hurting it. Encourage the children to catch as many insects as they can. Some children will understand right away and enthusiastically start catching insects, while other children may require help. Some may simply prefer to watch the other children catch insects.

3. After the children collect several specimens, ask the children to bring their collection jars inside, and help them use markers or nail polish to mark the insects by placing small dots between the shoulders on the top of the thorax region, then return the insects to their jars.

4. With the children, count and record the number of insects that they caught. This can be tricky with moving insects. You may encourage the children to transfer the insects from one jar to another, one at time, for easier counting.

5. Ask the children to bring their collection jars of insects back outside to the same area, and encourage the children to release the insects. Talk with the children about where they think the animals will go and what will happen to them.

6. A few days later, bring the children to the same area and ask them to collect several insects again.

7. After the children finish collecting several new insects, come inside with the children and ask them to look and see if any of the insects have the marks the children put on the first batch of insects they caught. Ask the children questions: How many insects did they find with a mark? How many new, unmarked insects did they collect? Did they collect more or fewer insects than on the previous expedition? Encourage the children to sort the insects by moving them into separate jars, as they had with the first batch of insects.

8. When the children finish sorting and counting the insects, have them bring the insects back outside and set them free again.

9. Later, engage the children in a discussion about possible reasons why the number of insects they captured varied or stayed the same. Possible explanations for a different count might be:
   ◆ Some were eaten by predators,
   ◆ Some died,
   ◆ Some flew or crawled out of the collection area, and
   ◆ Some were hiding in hard-to-find places.

Want to Do More?

◆ Divide the schoolyard into sections, and point them out to the children. When the children release then recapture several of the insects, challenge the children to remember the section of the schoolyard in which they found each of the insects. Later the children can determine which area most of the tagged insects moved into after their initial release. Discuss the results with the children, asking them which insects moved the longest and shortest distances from the point of release.

Observing and Assessing the Children

Can the child mark an insect with nail polish or a marker? Can the child provide some details about how she caught the insect, such as where she found the most insects or how many insects she recaptured on the second collection trip? Can the child share any ideas about why the number of insects she captured on the second collection trip might differ from the number she captured on the first trip?

Learning in Other Curricular Areas

Math
   ◆ counting (number operations)

Motor development
   ◆ chasing and capturing insects (large and small motor skills)

"Go Fish" for Plants

This activity uses the format of the card game "Go Fish" to teach the children about the various plants that are common in the local environment.

Science Content Standards—notes similarities and differences among living things and can describe them (Life Science)
Science Process Skills—observing; classifying

Words You Can Use

Collect	Grass
Bush	Identify
Flower	Plant

Plant part names, such as stem, trunk, leaf, bark, and root
Plant names, such as dandelion, maple tree, and so on
Tree

Things You Can Use

Card stock
Scissors
Collecting bags, such as small plastic bags
A big telephone book to press the plants
Clear tape
Marker
Laminating material

Before the Activity

Gather some tree and plant identification books, and walk the route the children will take when they go on their collecting walk so you will know the names of the plants and tress from which the children gather their leaves. You may wish to contact a local greenhouse, nursery, or family member to help you identify the various leaves. Cut pieces of card stock large enough so the children will be able to attach the largest leaves they collect. Copy the names of the trees and plants onto several sheets of paper and cut them out so the children will be able to paste them to the card stock when they attach their leaves.

What to Do

1. Engage the children in a discussion about plants. Tell them that scientists use leaves to identify plants.
2. Give the children bags for collecting leaves, and bring the children outside on a leaf-gathering walk. **Safety note:** Remind the children not to touch certain plants, such as poison ivy.
3. When the group comes to a plant, invite them to look carefully at the leaves and other plant parts. Help the children use words that describe the parts of

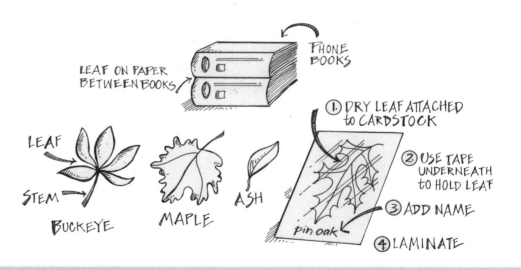

LEAF ON PAPER BETWEEN BOOKS / PHONE BOOKS

LEAF
STEM
BUCKEYE
MAPLE
ASH

① DRY LEAF ATTACHED to CARDSTOCK
② USE TAPE UNDERNEATH to HOLD LEAF
③ ADD NAME
④ LAMINATE
pin oak

Observing and Assessing the Children

Given a set of cards made from the leaves of plants that grow in the area, can the child form matching pairs of leaves?

Learning in Other Curricular Areas

Language and literacy
◆ understanding the rules and playing the game (receptive language)
◆ asking questions of each player (expressive language)

Math
◆ classifying the leaves (algebra)

Motor development
◆ picking leaves, taping leaves on card stock, dealing and playing the card game (small motor)

the plant, such as "leaf," "branch," or "stem." Encourage the children to notice the similarities and differences among trees, shrubs, and smaller plants. Ask the children to pick three or four leaves from each plant they observe.

4. When the children have several leaves, return to the classroom and help the children identify the leaves and match them to the sheets of paper on which you wrote the names. Show the children how to dry leaves by placing the leaves in a telephone book. Put the sheets with the leaves' names on them in the phone books with all the leaves, and give the leaves anywhere from a few days to more than a week to dry.

5. When the leaves are dry, help the children tape the leaves to the pieces of cardstock. Use one small piece of clear tape to hold the leaves for lamination, then add the names of the leaves to the cards.

6. Laminate the leaves and help the children cut off the extra laminate. Make two cards for each type of leaf. Hand the cards out to the children and help them read the names on each card. Encourage the children to describe the characteristics of each leaf. For example, some have many points, while others are more rounded.

7. Show the children how to play "Go Fish" using the cards.
   ◆ Deal 4–6 cards to each child, depending on the child's experience level.
   ◆ Place the remaining cards in the "Go Fish" pile. If the children have any pairs of matching leaves in their hands, ask them to place the pairs on the table.
   ◆ Ask the child to your left to start the round by asking any of the children whether they have a particular leaf card that matches one she is already holding. For example, the child might say, "Sam, do you have a dandelion leaf?"
   ◆ If Sam has one, then Sam gives the card to the child, and she places her pair down and then asks for another card from another child. If the next child she asks does not have the card, the child says "Go Fish."
   ◆ The child who asked for the card then pulls a card from the pile at the center of the table, and the child to her left repeats the process.
   ◆ The children continue playing until a child sets all her cards down on the table.

8. Save the cards for later use. If you or the children notice a new plant growing in your area, help the children identify the plant and add use its leaves to make new cards to add to the set.

Want to Do More?
◆ Take the cards outside and challenge the children to match the leaves on the cards to the plants in the area.
◆ Set out the cards and encourage the children to use them for matching, memory, or lotto games.

5+ Press a Plant

If you want to keep flowers and plants the children collect, a plant press is a handy thing to have. Involve the children as you construct and use a plant press to create an herbarium, or collection of the plants that are common to the local habitat.

Science Content Standard—describes and documents different environments (Life Science)
Science Process Skills—classifying (sorting); constructing models

Words You Can Use

Dry

Evaporate

Herbarium

Parts of a plant, such as flower, leaf, leaves, root, and stem

Plant names

Press

Things You Can Use

Two boards (¼" plywood)
Newspapers, full sheets
Rope or clothesline
   (4 ½', or 1.5 m)
Cardboard cut the size
   of the boards
Scissors
Dried plants
Plastic collecting bags
Laminating machine or
   clear plastic protectors

Before the Activity

Open each piece of newspaper. Fold one sheet of newspaper in half, and put it on a large piece of cardboard. Cut the cardboard so it is 16" x 12" (40 cm x 30 cm), or slightly larger than the newspaper half. Repeat the process 30 times with different pieces of cardboard. Set out two pieces of plywood, and cut them so they are the same size as the cardboard.

What to Do

1. Before the children arrive, dry a plant in the classroom. When the children come in, show them the dried plant, and explain to them that the first step scientists take to preserve plants for collections is drying them like this.
2. Tell the children that they will be making a collection of pressed plants out of the plants that grow in the area.
3. Bring the children outside and ask them to look for plants. When the children find a plant, ask them to call you to them.
4. Take out scissors or shears and cut the plants off just below the soil (adult-only step) or pull the plants out of the ground. Give the plants to the children to knock off all the dirt and then place the plants in plastic collecting bags until they return to the school.
   Note: You can press a small plant by placing it in a phone book for a few days.
5. Back inside, show the children the sheets of newspaper. Ask one child to pull a plant out of her bag and place it on one of the newspapers.
6. Take out two lengths of rope, place them on the ground parallel to each other, and then place a piece of plywood on top of the ropes.
7. Ask a child to place a piece of cardboard on the plywood, and then add three of the folded pieces of newspaper on the sheet of cardboard. Next, ask the child to place her plant on the folded newspaper. If you or the children know the name of the plant, help them write the name on the outside of the newspaper, along with the day's date.

Observing and Assessing the Children

Can the child follow directions and press plants or explain the steps in the drying process?

Learning in Other Curricular Areas

Language and literacy

◆ following directions (receptive language)

Motor development

◆ pulling up plants, shaking off soil, placing plants on newspaper, folding the newspaper in half, and placing between the two boards (small motor)

Social-emotional development

◆ engaging in cooperative group activities (social development)

8. Ask the child to lay several more sheets of folded newspaper on top of the plant, then add another piece of cardboard. Tell the children they are making a cardboard and newspaper sandwich, with the plant stuck in the middle. Explain that they will add an extra layer to the sandwich with each plant they want to press.

9. Help the children add layers of cardboard, newspaper, and plants in the same order on top of the first plant, until the children finish adding all their plants to the press. Then place the second piece of plywood on top of the stack.

10. Tightly pull the ropes around the press and tie them. To make the press more compact, ask a child to stand on top of the plywood as you knot the rope.

11. Set the press in a warm, dry place, and leave it for several days. The drying time will depend on the humidity in the air. The drier the climate, the faster the plants will dry. The newspapers help draw the moisture out of the plants. Depending on the humidity, a dandelion plant typically takes about a week to dry, whereas a single flower may need only a few days.

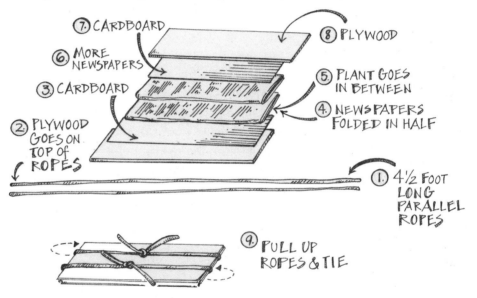

12. Once the plants are dry, remove them. Keep the plants in the labeled sheets of newspaper. Now the children are ready to make the herbarium. When botanists want to study particular plants, they gently bring out their dried plants and observe them.

13. To make the herbarium sturdy and accessible to the children, laminate the plants, or place them in clear plastic sleeve protectors. In either case, store the dried plants in a binder for the children to use. Label each plant with its common name, scientific name, the date and location where the children collected it, and the name of the child who found it. Help the children add new plants to the collection throughout the year.

Want to Do More?

◆ Set out extra dried plant parts for the children to use in collages or other artwork.

5+ How Old Is That Tree?

When you see someone cutting down a tree, ask the tree-cutter to slice off a piece of the trunk for you, and bring it back to the classroom. You now have a unique way to review counting and talk about the passage of time. Make sure the cross section is 1"–3" thick so it is easy to handle. With a little prep work, the tree trunk will be ready for the children to use.

Science Content Standard—begins to understand the needs of living things (Life Science)
Science Process Skills—observing; inferring

Words You Can Use

Count   Rings
Number words   Years

Things You Can Use

A cross section of a tree trunk
Finishing nails and hammer (adults only)
Sandpaper (optional)

Before the Activity

Obtain a cross section of a recently cut tree trunk. If you can, sand one side of the cross section to make the rings more obvious. Fast-growing trees, such as sycamores or pines, will have rings farther apart and that will make counting easier. When the surface is smooth, rub it with oil to make the rings stand out more clearly. Then, in a straight line from the outside to the center, pound a finishing nail into each growth ring.

What to Do

1. Bring the trunk piece into the room and show it to the children. Point out the rings and tell the children that each nail marks a year of the tree's growth. Point out that the youngest part of the tree is on the outside.
2. Invite the children to count the nails, starting with the outermost nail. When the children count in by four nails, explain to them that four years ago, that was the outermost section of the tree, so that was how large the tree was when all the four-year-old children in the class were born. Tell the children that if they go in by one more nail, they will see how large the tree was when all the five-year-olds in the class were born.
3. Find out when your school or center opened, and help the children count back to that year, or challenge the children to count back to the age of an older sibling.
4. Challenge the children to count all the nails and tell you how old the tree is.

Want to Do More?

◆ Bring in a cross section from another type of tree and help the children to compare the two.

Observing and Assessing the Children

Can the child count a given number of nails in the tree's cross section?

Learning in Other Curricular Areas

Language and literacy
   ◆ communicating ideas and thoughts (expressive language)
Math
   ◆ exploring quantity and number (number operations)
   ◆ constructing a sense of time passing (measurement)

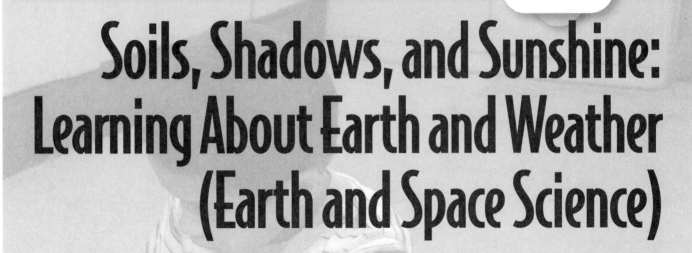

CHAPTER 4

Soils, Shadows, and Sunshine: Learning About Earth and Weather (Earth and Space Science)

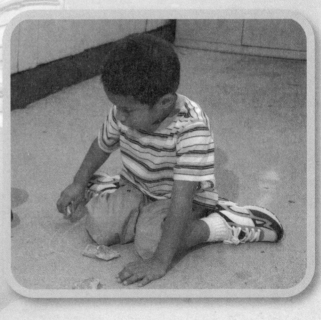

A Settling Experience—Mixing Soils with Water

Children can observe soil in many ways. By mixing large amounts of water and soil in plastic containers, and then shaking them vigorously, the children can see how soil separates into various types—from the heaviest rocks to the finest grains that come together to make clay. Give the children a chance to discover this for themselves—again and again.

Science Content Standard—explores the characteristics of soil, rocks, and water (Earth and Space Science)
Science Process Skill—observing

Words You Can Use

Different
Heavy
Light
Rocks
Same
Samples
Sand
Silt
Soil

Things You Can Use

Clear plastic jars with lids (plastic peanut butter or mayonnaise jars work well)
Samples of soil from various locations (collect new samples or use soil from other activities)
Water
Small pitchers for pouring water

Before the Activity

Collect several soil samples in resealable bags from various locations. Write the location on the bag.

What to Do

1. Engage the children in a discussion about various soil-based activities they may have done in the past. Challenge them to think about the differences between various kinds of soil they have used in activities. For example, can they describe the differences between mud, clay, and sand? How does each soil type smell and feel?

2. Set out several soil samples in clear plastic containers, and encourage the children to discuss the differences they see.
3. Separate the children into groups of two to four. Give each group an empty, clear container, and ask them to place a few scoops of soil in the container. Help the children fill the containers with water and close them. Remind the children to check that the lids are on tight.
4. Invite the children to take turns shaking their soil-water containers very well. **Note:** Because the containers of water and soil may be heavy, consider asking two children to shake the container together.
5. After they finish shaking the containers, ask the children to set the containers down on a table and observe how soil inside them settles. Ask the children to describe what they see and to describe the objects that settle to the bottom of the container first. Ask the children to look for plant parts settling in the mixture.
6. Encourage the children to compare the way the soil in their jars settles to the way the soil settles in their peers' containers. Introduce the children to the word "silt" to describe the very fine particles that make the water look cloudy.

CONNECTING TO CHILDREN WITH SPECIAL NEEDS

Involve children with physical challenges by having them shake the soil and water containers by rolling them across a table or the floor with their partners.

USING MUSEUMS AND OTHER COMMUNITY RESOURCES

Bring the children on a field trip to a garden where people have worked hard to make the soil good for growing plants. Encourage the children to compare that soil to the various samples they observed in the containers. Visit your county's Soil and Water Conservation District or invite a conservation office to talk about soil with the children.

7. Invite the children to talk about what makes the samples settle differently.
8. Help the children set the containers aside in a visible location, and encourage the children to visit them periodically throughout the day, to see if the soil continues to settle in the water. Leave the containers to settle overnight, and when the children come in the next morning, invite them to observe the extent to which the soil settled.
9. Leave the containers out for several days, giving the children many opportunities to shake them again and again. Point out to the children how the dirt settles in the same way every time.

Want to Do More?

◆ Gather soil from various sites, put it in containers with water, label the containers with the name of the location from which you took the soil, and then set them out for the children to compare to the other containers.

◆ Ask the children to bring soil samples from their homes in to the class so the children can study and compare them.

◆ Set out a container of sand, and challenge the children to predict what will happen when you mix it with water, then add it to a container and invite the children to watch the results.

◆ Help the children pour the mixture out of one of the containers and feel the different layers of soil. Show the children how to use the finest portion, the silt, as paint. The silt is kind of like watery mud. Invite the children to dip a brush in the silt and paint with it on paper. They may like what they see. Also, encourage the children to try finger painting with the silt.

Observing and Assessing the Children

Can the child describe how soil settles in water? For example, she might say, "First it's all mixed up, then the dirt goes to the bottom and the water stays on top."

Learning in Other Curricular Areas

Language and literacy
◆ describing the differences in soil (expressive language)
◆ listening with understanding and responding to directions (receptive language)

Math
◆ recognizing patterns (algebra)

Motor development
◆ shaking the jars of soil and water (large motor)
◆ placing scoops of soil into jars (small motor)

3+ Rocks That Write

This activity invites the children to experiment with ways to write on the sidewalk or blacktop using rocks. The children will find that some rocks are easier to write with than others are.

Science Content Standard—explores the characteristics of soil, rocks, and water (Earth and Space Science)
Science Process Skill—classifying

Words You Can Use
Hard
Rock names
Soft

Things You Can Use
A wide variety of rocks (Plant and tree nurseries and landscaping stores are good sources for finding a variety of rocks.)
A place to write, such as the sidewalk or blacktop
Sidewalk chalk

What to Do
1. Bring the children out to the sidewalk or blacktop area. Show them some pieces of sidewalk chalk, and invite them to draw or write with the chalk. Some children will make letters, numbers, or pictures, while others will scribble markings.
2. Set out the rock collection and explain to the children that the chalk they are using is like a rock (sidewalk chalk is, in fact, a manufactured rock). Tell the children that chalk works well as a drawing tool because it is a soft rock.
3. Say, "We can use rocks to draw and write too. We are going to figure out which rocks work well to write and draw with and which rocks do not."

4. Encourage the children to try drawing and writing with all of the different rocks in the collection.

5. After the children experiment with all the rocks, pick two spots on the ground, take a piece of sidewalk chalk, and write "writes well" on one spot and "does not write well" on the other spot. Ask the children to sort the rocks based on whether they can write well with them.

Want to Do More?

◆ Challenge the children to find different surfaces on which to draw and write.
◆ Challenge the children to find a rock with which they can write on paper.

Observing and Assessing the Children

Given a set of rocks, can the child determine which rocks she can use to write and draw?

Learning in Other Curricular Areas

Language and literacy
◆ listening with understanding and responding to directions (receptive and expressive language)
◆ using scribbles, and approximation of letters or known letters to represent written language (early literacy)

Math
◆ drawing representations of numbers (number operations)

Motor development
◆ grasping and drawing with chalk and rocks (small motor, large motor)

3+ | Weather Art

Children have their own visions of the world around them. It is fascinating to see how they depict visually the various stimuli that they encounter each day. This activity promotes the use of fantasy to stimulate children's visions of how they feel and think about various weather conditions, and it gives the children the chance to put their thoughts and feelings on paper.

Science Content Standard—uses weather vocabulary (Earth and Space Science)
Science Process Skill—observing

Words You Can Use

Breeze
Hail
Hurricane
Pretend
Rain
Sleet
Snow
Storm
Tornado
Wind

Things You Can Use

Recordings of weather sounds or music will remind children of weather images (for example, loud, crashing music like a thunderstorm); if not available, you or the children can make the sounds
Paper
Crayons or markers
Paint and paintbrushes

What to Do

1. Set out various art materials for the children.
2. Play a recording that depicts various weather conditions, or just talk with the children about the conditions that occur in your area. For example, invite the children to tell a story about a snowstorm, or some other weather event, and challenge them to describe it in vivid detail.
3. After the children finish describing the weather event, and while the weather sounds are still playing, encourage the children to draw scenes like those they described when telling the story.
4. After the children finish their drawings, laminate their pictures, and explain that the children can use the drawings as prompts to discuss the weather, and compare it to similar events from the past. Repeat this activity, encouraging the children to imagine, describe, and draw different kinds of weather events each time.

Want to Do More?

◆ Provide a variety of art materials for the children to use, giving them a chance to work with clay, finger paints, and so on.

Observing and Assessing the Children

Can the child describe her impressions of and make drawings of various weather conditions while listening to weather-based recordings?

Learning in Other Curricular Areas

Arts
   ◆ creating pictures of their weather interpretations (visual arts)
Language and literacy
   ◆ discussing sounds made by music (expressive and descriptive language)
Motor development
   ◆ drawing pictures (small motor)

Snowflakes

Capturing and making snowflakes are two exciting ways for the children to explore snow. Because the laws of nature control the formation of snowflakes, they are always six-sided figures. Help the children catch snowflake and observe them under the magnifier. Then, show the children how to fold and cut six-sided snowflakes similar to those they captured and observed.

Science Content Standard—explores the characteristics of soil, rocks, and water (Earth and Space Science)
Science Process Skills—observing; constructing models

Words You Can Use

Hexagon
Six-sided
Snow
Snowfall
Snowflake

Things You Can Use

White paper
Coffee can lid or other circular object
Scissors
Black construction paper cut in half or pieces of black felt cut to the same size as a half sheet of paper
Hand magnifiers or tripod magnifier (a microscope is optional)

Before the Activity

Make a sample snowflake from a circle of white paper. Also, search the Internet for images of snowflakes on websites such as www.snowcrystals.com and www.snowflake bentley.com.

What to Do

1. On a snowy day, give the children sheets of black paper or felt, bring the children outside, and invite them to try catching snowflakes.
2. After the children collect snowflakes, set out magnifiers and a microscope and invite the children to look at the snowflakes. Encourage the children to describe what they see. Explain to the children that objects with six sides, such as snowflakes, are called hexagons. Remind the children to look closely at their snowflakes in order to remember what they look like.
3. Bring the children inside. Show the children the images of snowflakes you downloaded before they arrived, as well as the snowflake you cut out. Ask the children to describe how they are similar, or what differences they see between the pictures, the cutout, and the snowflakes they caught outside.
4. Set out several sheets of white paper, and help the children make paper snowflakes.
   - Select paper that folds easily.
   - Trace a circle on the paper (use a 2-pound coffee can as a guide).
   - Cut out the circle using child-safe scissors.
   - Fold the circle shape in half. Fold the half-circle in thirds.
   - Use child-safe scissors to make cutouts anywhere on the sides of the paper.
   - Unfold the paper to see your six-sided snowflake.

Want to Do More?

- Read *Snowflake Bentley* by Jackelyn Briggs Martin to the children.

Observing and Assessing the Children

Can the child make a cutout snowflake and compare the way it looks to a real snowflake?

Learning in Other Curricular Areas

Language and literacy
   - listening with understanding and following directions (receptive language)

4+ All About Rain

Rain is a wonderful natural event. Of course, it can be inconvenient at times. It can be cold and make one uncomfortable, but rain keeps plants growing and the soil fertile. It replenishes, refreshes, and without it, life would not go on. Here are several ways the children can study rain.

Science Content Standard—describes changes in seasons and observable weather patterns (Earth and Space Science)

Science Process Skills—observing; communicating; measuring (standard and nonstandard); communicating

Words You Can Use

Degrees Celsius (°C)
Degrees Fahrenheit (°F)
Moisture
Rain
Sensory words that
    describe rain, such as
    wet, cold, warm
Temperature
Volume measurement,
    such as milliliter, cup,
    small cup

Things You Can Use

Books about rain, such as
    Umbrella by Taro
    Yashima; or *Flash,
    Crash, Rumble, and Roll*
    by Franklyn M. Branley
Clear plastic or glass
    cups
Coloring paper and
    crayons
Flat cake pans
Measuring containers
A "Rain Book," a book
    created by the children
    to record their
    observations of rain
Thermometers

Before the Activity

Check the weather forecast, looking for rainy days in the near future. When the forecast calls for rain, gather all the various materials listed above and have them ready for the children to use.

What to Do

1. On a day when you expect rain, engage the children in a discussion about what a rainy day is like. Record their comments, and make a list of the characteristics of a rainy day.
2. Read a book about rain to the children.
3. Set out several materials, and give the children the opportunity to choose from the various following rain-related activities.
    ◆ Encourage the children to sit by the window and watch the approaching rain clouds. Ask the children to describe the clouds, and record their descriptions in the "Rain Book." Set out paper, crayons, and markers, and invite the children to draw pictures of clouds for the "Rain Book."

- From under the shelter of a doorway or overhang, invite the children to take turns watching the rain hit the ground or sidewalk. Ask the children to describe what they see. What shapes do the raindrops make when they hit the ground? Encourage the children to comment on how through a storm, raindrops change in frequency, size, and speed. Ask the children to describe or draw the raindrops they see. Record their observations and place their drawings in the "Rain Book."
- When the rain begins, encourage the children to pay attention to how the air smells. Ask the children to describe how the air smells, and write their descriptions in the "Rain Book."
- Place a thermometer outside in a location where the children can observe it without getting wet, such as just outside a window or doorway. When the children arrive at school, if the rain has not started to fall, invite them to look at the temperature. Then, while it is raining, have the children look at the thermometer and discuss any changes in temperature, record their comments, and add them to the "Rain Book."
- If there is a location where the children can do this safely, invite them to place their hands or arms out into the rain. Ask, "What does rain feel like? Is it soft? Do the raindrops sting?" Record the children's observations in the "Rain Book."
- Just before the rain begins, suggest that the children put a cake pan outside so they can collect a sample of rainwater. After the rain stops, bring the cake pan inside and measure the rainfall in inches and centimeters. Record this information in the "Rain Book."
- Bring the children on an after-the-rain walk. Encourage the children to pay attention to how the water puddles and runs on the ground. Ask the children to describe the water. What colors do they see in it? Report the children's findings in the "Rain Book."

Want to Do More?
- Repeat this activity during different rain events, and record all the rain events in the "Rain Book."

Observing and Assessing the Children
Can the child describe and draw various characteristics of a rainy day?

Learning in Other Curricular Areas
Arts
- drawing observations (visual arts)

Language and literacy
- dictating and recording information in the "Rain Book" (expressive language)

Math
- measuring wind speed using non-standard tools of measurement (measurement)
- collecting and organizing date (data analysis and probability)

4+ All About Snow

Some parts of the country never experience snow, while others have more snow than they really want. Like rain, snow is a gift of nature that has its purpose in the scheme of life. Children can study snow by organizing their experiences and recording their observations. If the children have created a "Rain Book," then it is a natural extension to create a "Snow Book."

Science Content Standard—describes changes in seasons and observable weather patterns (Earth and Space Science)

Science Process Skills—observing; communicating; measuring (standard and nonstandard); communicating

Words You Can Use
Cold
Degrees Celsius (°C)
Degrees Fahrenheit (°F)
Moisture
Sensory words that
    describe snow on the
    fingers or face
Snow
Temperature

Things You Can Use
Black construction paper
    or black felt pieces
Books about snow
Clear plastic or glass
    cups
Coloring paper and
    crayons
Flat cake pans
A "Snow Book," a book
    created by the children
    to record their
    observations of snow
Thermometers
Yardstick or meter stick

Before the Activity
Gather all the materials listed above and have them ready for the children to use on a snowy day.

What to Do

1. Prepare this activity for a day when the weather forecast calls for snow. When the children arrive, engage them in a discussion about what a snowy day is like, and make a list of their descriptions of a snowy day.

2. With the children, watch the approach snow clouds through the window, and invite the children to describe the clouds, and record their descriptions in the "Snow Book."

3. Read the children books about snow. Some books discuss other cultures' perspectives on snow, such as *Snow* by Uri Shulevitz, *In the Snow* by Huy Vuon Lee, or *When This World Was New* by D. H. Figuerdeo. Other books describe the science of snow, such as *The Snowflake: A Water Cycle Story* by Neil Waldman and *Snow Is Falling* by Franklyn M. Branley.

4. Set out several materials, and give the children the opportunity to choose from the various following snow-related activities
   - Help the children find a place where a yardstick can stand for the duration of the snow, and stick it in the ground. When the snow stops, go outside and check how much snow fell. Record this information in the "Snow Book."
   - Gather a cupful of snow. Ask a child to place the cupful of snow in a warm place inside and let it melt. As the snow melts into slush, and

Learning in Other Curricular Areas

Language and literacy
- describing different characteristics of snow (expressive and descriptive language)

Math
- measuring volume, linear, and temperature (measurement)
- using the tools of measurement (measurement)
- collecting and organizing data (data analysis and probability)

eventually water, invite the children to take periodic measurements, and compare how much snow there was, as opposed to how much slush or water. Repeat, packing the cup with more or less snow each time, and compare the results. After each cup of snow melts to water, ask the child who brought it into the classroom to take it back outside to sit in the cold overnight. Ask, "What will happen to the water? Will it turn back into snow?" The next morning, note what happened to the water, and compare this to the child's predictions.

- From the shelter of doorway or overhang, watch the snowfall. Set out paper, crayons, and markers, and encourage the children to make drawings of the snow. Add the children's drawings and copy their observations about the snow into the "Snow Book."

- Set out several pieces of black felt or black paper, and let the children use them outside to catch snowflakes. Help the children observe and describe the shapes of the captured snowflakes.

- Before the children arrive, search the Internet for photographs of snowflakes. Gather the images and show them to the children. Point out to the children that snowflakes are six-sided, and then set out paper and help the children make their own cutout snowflakes.

- Find a location outside where the children can easily read a thermometer from inside. Each day, invite the children to observe and record the temperatures in their "Snow Book," and encourage the children to compare the temperatures on days when it does not snow to days when it does snow and discuss the differences.

- Help the children place their bare hands and arms in the falling snow for a brief time, and ask them to describe the sensation. Record the children's observations and include them in the "Snow Book."

- Ask the children, "What is in the snow? Is it just frozen water, or are there other particles and impurities?" Ask the children to collect some snow, melt the snow through a coffee filter, and then look at and describe the impurities caught in the filter.

- Go for an after-the-snow walk, and encourage the children to describe the drifts and other things they see. Copy their comments in the "Snow Book."

Want to Do More?
- Repeat this activity during different snow events, and record all the snow events in the "Snow Book."
- Suggest that the children make a collage to depict the various aspects of snow.

Observing and Assessing the Children
Can the child draw and describe various characteristics of snow?

4+ All About Wind

Like all parts of nature, the wind has its purpose in the scheme of life. Invite the children to study wind by helping them to organize their experiences and record their observations into a "Wind Book." If the children have created a "Rain Book" and a "Snow Book," then encourage them to compare the information in them to what they include in the "Wind Book."

Science Content Standard—describes changes in seasons and observable weather patterns (Earth and Space Science)
Science Process Skills—observing; communicating; measuring (standard and nonstandard); communicating

Words You Can Use

Blow
Breeze
Cold
Hard
Sensory words that
    describe wind
Soft
Warm
Wind

Things You Can Use

Books or poems about
    wind, such as *The
    Wind Blew* by Pat
    Hutchins and *Gilberto
    and the Wind* by
    Marie Hall Ets
Feathers
Kites
Thin thread
"Wind Book"
Tissue paper
Yardstick or meter stick

Before the Activity

Gather all the materials listed above and have them ready for the children to use on a windy day.

What to Do

1. On a day when the weather forecast calls for wind, engage the children in a discussion about what windy days are like, and make a list of some characteristics of a windy day.

2. Encourage the children to try several of the following activities.
    ◆ Help the children make a wind-detection machine by suspending a piece of thin thread from a low branch on a tree outside then observing how the thread moves. Encourage the children to make drawings of the string, showing how it moves on a windy day as opposed to a day with no wind, and add the children's drawings to the "Wind Book."
    ◆ Show the children how the wind carries soil particles by helping them wrap clear tape around a piece of cardboard, with the adhesive portion facing out, then set the cardboard outside in a location where the wind will hit the tape. After a time, ask the children to bring the cardboard and tape inside to look at the particles stuck to the tape.
    ◆ From the shelter of a doorway or overhang, invite the children to watch the wind blowing during a windstorm. Ask the children to describe the weather, and then set out paper, markers, and crayons, and invite the children to

Learning in Other Curricular Areas

Language and literacy

- using drawing and writing skills to convey meaning and information relative to the wind-detection machine results (early literacy)
- communicating ideas and thoughts about wind (expressive language)
- listening with understanding and responding to directions (receptive language)

Math

- measuring how far tissues blow on a windy day (measurement)
- collecting and organizing data (data analysis and probability)

Motor development

- drawing and recording information (small motor)

make drawings of what they see. Record their comments about the wind, and add them and their drawings to the "Wind Book."

- On very windy days, bring the children outside, give them paper, markers, and crayons, and invite them to draw the clouds. As the children draw, encourage them to compare the clouds they see to the clouds they remember from other windy days. Add the children's drawings to the "Wind Book."
- Bring the children outside and set out a container full of water where the children can dip their fingers. After the children wet their fingers, encourage them to hold their fingers up to the wind and describe the sensation. Record the children's observations in the "Wind Book."
- Read books that discuss wind from the perspective of various cultures, or books that examine the science of wind. An excellent resource is *Can You See the Wind?* by Allan Fowler. *Ping-Li's Kite* by Sanne Te Loo retells a Chinese folk tale of kite-flying adventures, while *Kite Flying* by Grace Lin is a story of modern-day Chinese kite-flying.
- Introduce the children to the concept of the wind-chill factor. Talk about how they dress on windy days. Discuss how the wind takes away body heat and makes it feel as though the temperature is much colder.
- Set out a fan and invite the children to experiment with putting various materials, such as papers and markers, in the wind stream to see how they respond. Talk with the children about their experiments. Ask, "Did the pencil blow away like the paper? Why not?"
- Engage the children in a discussion about various bad windstorms, such as tornadoes, hurricanes, and the winds that come with thunderstorms. Explain the safety procedures the children should follow during extreme wind conditions.
- Bring the children outside on a windy day and give them bubble mix to blow into the wind. Encourage them to describe what happens to the bubbles in the wind.

Want to Do More?

- Set out various materials and encourage the children to make a collage of the various aspects of wind.

Observing and Assessing the Children

Can the child describe and draw various characteristics of the wind?

4+ Dirt Detectives

Children enjoy collecting and analyzing samples of dirt. This activity gives them the opportunity to do so, and provides a model for formal and informal science experiences.

Science Content Standard—explores the characteristics of soil, rocks, and water (Earth and Space Science)
Science Process Skills—measuring (mass); communicating

Words You Can Use

Color words   Light
Different   Samples
Earth   Same
Heavy   Soil

Things You Can Use

Knife
Magnifying glass (a
    microscope is
    optional)
Permanent marker
Plastic sandwich bags
Spade
Scotch tape
Trowels, metal spoons
    and forks

Before the Activity

Look at various nearby locations outside to determine the best place to collect samples. Place all the necessary materials in a shopping bag. You can also use this bag for carrying the collections back to the classroom.

What to Do

1. Bring the children on a walk to two or three sites where the children will be able to collect soil, such as cracks in the sidewalk, a hard-packed playground, a local park, a wooded area, a lawn, a window box, a garden, or a plowed field. Engage the children in a discussion about the soil in each place.

2. Help the children use a garden trowel or metal spoon or fork to gather a soil sample from each site.

3. Show the children how to place the samples in sandwich

bags, seal them with tape and use permanent markers to write the names or descriptions of the sites where the children collected the soil.

4. Bring the children and soil samples back to the classroom.

5. Set out various magnifying glasses or microscopes and encourage the children to examine the samples from each site. Challenge the children to sort the samples by categories such as soil color, how moist they are, and

whether they contain rocks, worms, and vegetation. Keep the soil in the bags or remove it for examination.

Safety note: All soils contain bacteria and other microscopic organisms. While there will be little chance of soil transmitting any diseases to the children, caution them not to put their hands in their mouths or near their eyes after handling the soil. Children with hand cuts should be careful or not handle the soil. Be sure the children wash their hands after this activity, or any other time they handle soil.

6. Engage the children in a discussion about what makes the samples different. Ask, "What have humans done to it to make it the way it is?" For example, people may have trampled the footpath or plowed and fertilized the garden from which the children took the soil samples.

USING MUSEUMS AND OTHER COMMUNITY RESOURCES
Invite a gardener to discuss with the children how soil types affect growing conditions. Some nature centers have preserves that have never been farmed or developed.

Want to Do More?

◆ Encourage the children to draw or paint pictures of the sites they visited, and describe how the locations were different from each other.

◆ Set out a scale and encourage the children to compare the weights of equal quantities of the various soil samples, and encourage the children discuss their findings. Include weighted cubes the children can use to gauge the weights, and challenge the children to count how many cubes each different sample weighs. (See How to Measure—How Heavy? on page 230.)

◆ Ask, "What would the world be like if all the soil was like sand from the beach?"

Observing and Assessing the Children

Can the child compare and describe the differences between soil samples taken from different sites?

Learning in Other Curricular Areas

Language and literacy
◆ listening with understanding and responding to directions (receptive language)

Motor development
◆ walking to collection sites (large motor)
◆ digging with a trowel, collecting soil samples, and placing them in a plastic bag (large and small motor)

Dirt Holds Water

You can help children develop a sense of how scientists conduct an experiment. As the young scientists develop procedures for making mud, they form a foundation for scientific thinking.

Science Content Standard—explores the characteristics of soil, rocks, and water (Earth and Space Science)
Science Process Skill—measuring (volume)

Words You Can Use
Cupful
Dirt
Mix
Soil

Things You Can Use
Containers for mixing soil with water
1-cup measuring cups or several 8- or 10-ounce plastic drinking cups
Small medicine cups or paper cups
Spoons
Soil
Waste container
Water

Before the Activity
Find a place outside where the children can conduct the activity.

What to Do

1. Engage the children in a discussion about how to make mud. Some of the children will have made and played with mud and will want to talk about their experiences. Some of the children will have no experiences with mud.

2. Tell the children that they are going to experiment with finding the best procedure to make mud. Encourage the children to talk about their mud-making experiences, and encourage them to explain what they did when they made mud. For instance, was the mud that they made runny, or malleable like play dough?

3. After the children discuss the various ways they might make mud, ask them to choose a particular method and experiment with it. Help the children write their mud-making "recipe" on chart paper, or encourage the children to draw pictures that explain the steps in making mud.

4. Divide the class into small groups, pairs, or let them work individually. Set out several cups of soil, and tell each group or child to start working with one cup. Set out several smaller cups of water, and invite the children to continue adding cups of water to their soil until they think their mud is "just right." Challenge the children to keep track of how many cups of water they use. To help them keep track, consider giving the children a token each time they refill their cup of water, so they have a physical way to count the number of water refills they use.

5. Talk with the children about their mud, and encourage them to compare their mud with the other children's mud. Ask the children, "Is your mud the same as Jason's? Why? Why not?"

6. After the children finish making their mud, challenge them to collect all the mud and find an appropriate place to put all of it.

7. Help the children clean up the cups, the ground, and themselves, before coming back inside.

Want to Do More?

◆ Set out a large, flat container for the children to gather all the mud into, and invite the children to observe the mud as it dries.

◆ Set out cups of sand for the children to add to their mud, and encourage them to describe how it alters the mud's consistency.

Observing and Assessing Children

Can the child explain the process of making mud?

Learning in Other Curricular Areas

Language and literacy

◆ reading and following picture recipe (understanding that pictures and symbols have meaning and that print carries a message)

◆ communicating ideas and thoughts as to what mud is and how to make it (expressive language)

Math

◆ collecting and recording data, number recognition

◆ counting and one-to-one correspondence (number operations)

Motor development

◆ mixing water and soil (small and large motor)

4+ Coloring and Mixing Sand

Have fun showing the children how to paint sand, and then mix the sands to form new colors.

Science Content Standard—explores the characteristics of soil, rocks, and water (Earth and Space Science)
Science Process Skill—observing

Words You Can Use

Color words
Counting words
Mix
Mixture
Total
Pour

Things You Can Use

Containers for mixing
 sand and paint (one
 for each color)
Pans for drying sand
 (one for each color)
Resealable plastic bags,
 small
Sand (the whiter the
 sand, the easier the
 coloring process)
Spoons
Tempera paints
Mixing spoons
Permanent marker

Before the Activity

Collect several
containers of white sand,
various tempera paints,
and find a location
where the children can
set the painted sand out
to dry.

What to Do

1. Separate the children into groups. Explain that each group will make a color of sand, using separate containers to mix each of the primary colors—red, yellow, and blue.
2. Help each group of children measure and pour 1–2 cups of sand into each container, and then pour ¼ cup of wet or dry tempera paint into the containers. Explain to the children that they should add ½ cup of water for each cup of sand in their containers. Help the children add water and paint as needed to help make a good rich color and a runny mixture. Mix well.
3. Help the children pour the colored sand onto a tray to dry, and then place the tray in a warm, sunny place. When the sand is dry, encourage the children to crumble the sand back into granular form. At this point, each group should have one container each of red, yellow, and blue sand.

4. Next, talk with the children about the primary colors. Ask the children why they think we call the colors primary, and explain that these colors help to make all other colors.
5. Set out several mixing spoons and resealable plastic baggies. Invite the children to use the spoons to measure the colored sands carefully and combine spoonfuls of each in various plastic baggies. Tell the children to use no more than three spoonfuls of each color of sand. Be sure some children

mix one or two spoonfuls of one color with three spoonfuls of another color, so the children can see a variety of results.

6. Help the children record on the sides of the baggies the numbers of spoonfuls of each color of sand they add to each baggie, and then help the children seal the baggies.

7. Invite the children to shake the bags well to mix the colored sand and watch as a new, secondary color appears. Point out to the children how the grains of the primary colors are still visible in the secondary color.

Want to Do More?

◆ Challenge the children to organize the bags in order of color, based on the number of each color of sand they included. For instance, put baggies that contain one spoonful of red and three of yellow first, then baggies that contain two spoonfuls of red and three of yellow, then baggies that contain three spoonfuls of each color. This way, the children will be able to see a range of tints of the secondary colors.

◆ Create cards that illustrate the amount of each primary color to combine to get particular secondary colors, and set the cards out for the children to follow if they want to create specific colors.

◆ Set out sheets of paper, invite the children to draw the outlines of images on them, and then show the children how to glue the colored sand to their drawings to complete the images.

Observing and Assessing the Children

Can the child mix primary colors of sand to create secondary colors?

Learning in Other Curricular Areas

Math

◆ counting number of teaspoons (number operations)
◆ using measuring cups to place sand, paint, and water into plastic bags (measurement)

Motor development

◆ pouring cups of sand into plastic bags and mixing sand with colors (small motor)

Social-emotional development

◆ working together cooperatively in a small group (social interaction)

CONNECTING TO CHILDREN WITH SPECIAL NEEDS

Conduct this activity in a well-lighted area for children with visual impairments. Put the sand in small plastic containers and place them where they are easily accessible for children with motor challenges.

USING MUSEUMS AND OTHER COMMUNITY RESOURCES

Bring the children on a field trip to a museum that has Navaho sand art on display.

Watching Shadows Move

In this activity, the children look out the window to see how shadows move and change through the course of the day. Help them see the movement by marking the shadows' changes over time.

Science Content Standard—makes simple observations of the movement of sun and shadows (Earth and Space Science)
Science Process Skills—observing; measuring

Words You Can Use

Centimeters
Change
Inches
Measure
Move
Shadow
Sunlight

Things You Can Use

Chalk
Masking tape
String

Before the Activity

Make sure the window through which the children will observe the day's passing has at least one shadow that is plainly visible for a few hours.

What to Do

1. Select a window from which at least one shadow is visible during the morning, and ask the children to gather around the window and talk about the shadows they see.
2. Point out to the children the location of the sun, the object creating the shadow, and the shadow itself, and discuss with the children how the location of the sun in relation to the location of the object throwing the shadow determines not only where the shadow will fall but the shape and length of the shadow as well.
3. Explain to the children that shadows move through the course of the day, though they may move so slowly that the change is imperceptible over a short length of time. Challenge the children to think of ways that they can gauge how far a shadow moves through the day.

10:00 AM

2:00 PM

4. Help the children decide to use masking tape or chalk to mark the location of the shadow's edge on the ground. Every 30 minutes, choose an assistant to take masking tape or chalk outside and mark the new location of the shadow's edge in such a way that the children can see the mark from the classroom window. Continue doing this until the children cannot mark the movement of the shadow's edge any longer.
5. After the shadow's edge disappears, ask the children why they cannot see it anymore. Point out that this has to do with the position of the sun in relation to the position of the object casting the shadow.
6. At the end of the day, invite the children to look at all the marks indicating the movement of the shadow, and help the children use string to connect them all together.

Want to Do More?

◆ Show the children how to make shadow puppets, and encourage the children to put on a shadow play.

Observing and Assessing the Children

Can the child describe how shadows move over time?

Learning in Other Curriculum Areas

Language and literacy
◆ communicating the shadow movements with others (expressive language)
◆ listening with understanding and responding to directions (receptive language)

Math
◆ measuring movement of shadows using both linear and non-linear tools of measurement (measurement)

Seasonal Collage

This activity uses photographs from the children's pasts to help them explore their concepts of time. Time is made of the predictable cycle of the seasons, which contains the continuous, linear nature of the children's own growth. Consistent patterns organize all the cycles of life, but within these patterns are infinite varieties of experience that help to make life so interesting.

Science Content Standard—describes changes in seasons and observable weather patterns (Earth and Space Science)

Science Process Skills—observing; classifying

Words You Can Use

Change
Fall
Photograph
Season
Spring
Summer
Winter

Things You Can Use

Photographs of children outside during various seasons
Magazine pictures of seasonal activities
Child-safe scissors
Poster Board
Glue or tape

Before the Activity

Prior to doing this activity, send a note home with the children asking their families to send in photographs they took of their children playing outdoors during various seasons.

What to Do

1. Collect photographs of the children playing outside during the four seasons. If possible, the photographs should be of activities the children might engage in during the various seasons. For example, encourage the families to send in photographs of the children raking leaves in the fall, wearing warm clothes or playing in the snow in winter, running and swimming in the summer, and planting flowers in the spring. Also, set out several magazines

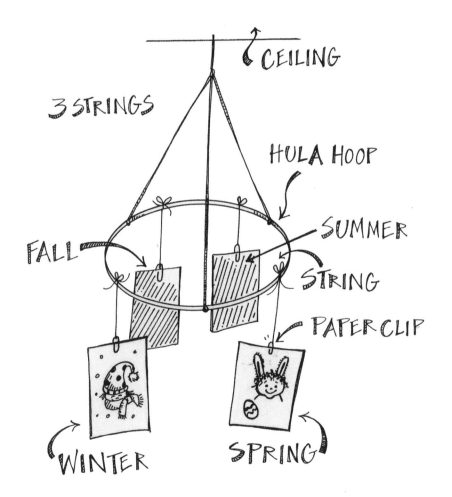

that contain images of people outside in various types of weather, and invite the children to cut images out of the magazines using child-safe scissors.

2. Set out four sheets of poster board, each with the name of one season on it, and invite the children to separate the photographs and magazine pictures onto each sheet of poster board, based on which seasons they depict.

3. After the children finish separating the images based on which seasons they depict, help them attach the images to the different pieces of poster board, making seasonal collages.

<table><tr><td></td></tr></table>

INCORPORATING TECHNOLOGY

Before the children arrive, search the Internet for images of children's clothes for various seasons. When the children arrive, show them the images.

Want to Do More?

◆ Help the children use their seasonal collages to make booklets of pictures for each season.

◆ Set out a hula-hoop, string, and paper clips. Help the children use the string and paper clips to attach photographs and magazine images of the seasons to the hula-hoop, in order from fall to winter to spring to summer. Hang the hula-hoop from the ceiling so it is at the children's eye-level, so they can observe the images of the seasons circling in order. (See illustration on previous page.)

Observing and Assessing the Children

Can the child properly identify and order pictures that depict each season?

Learning in Other Curricular Areas

Language and literacy
◆ understanding that pictures have meaning (early literacy)
◆ using pictures as guides to predict what will happen next (early literacy)
◆ communicating ideas and thoughts (expressive language)

Math
◆ recognizing and creating patterns, classifying (algebra)

4+ Icicles

Each winter, icicles form on the edges of roofs across the country. Icicles form when the sun melts the snow, and the melted snow, now water, trickles down the roof and refreezes in a different form. This process happens so slowly that people typically do not see it happen, but this activity gives the children the chance to see icicles form.

Science Content Standard—explores the characteristics of soil, rocks, and water (Earth and Space Science)
Science Process Skills—observing; measuring (volume, mass)

Words You Can Use

Ice
Icicle
Melt
Snow
Stalactite
Stalagmite
Sun
Water

Things You Can Use

Measuring tape or
    yardstick
Balance scale
Measuring cups
Water

Before the Activity

Check nearby roofs for icicles that the children can observe.

What to Do

1. On a cold clear, sunny winter day, icicles will begin to form a "curtain" along the roof's edge as the snow begins to melt. Bring the children outside and show them the icicles, and talk with the children about how icicles form.

2. If there are icicles within your reach, reach up and measure two icicles. Next, ask the children to move a safe distance away, and knock down one of the icicles.

    Safety note: Icicles can be very dangerous, and can dislodge easily under their own weight, particularly on sunny days when the snow is melting at an accelerated rate. Warn the children not to stand directly below the icicles at all times.

3. Set the icicle down and invite the children to study it. Set out paper, markers, and crayons, and invite the children to draw the icicle. Before the icicle melts, give each child a chance to hold the icicle in his hands, and ask him how much he thinks it weighs. Weigh the icicle and ask the children to compare their predictions. After weighing the icicle, place the icicle in a container.

4. When the icicle melts completely, ask the children how much they think the water will weigh, and then weigh the water. It should weigh the same as the frozen icicle. Is this what the children predicted?

    Safety note: Some children will be tempted to taste the icicles. Make it clear to the children that they are not to taste the icicles.

5. Invite the children to observe the water that melts off the icicle. Talk with the children about how the snow on the roof melted, trickled down to the edge, and then froze again, forming the icicle. Tell the children that these forms of water represent two parts of the water cycle. Explain that typically, the water from the icicles will drip to the ground and melt into the earth. If it is cold enough, though, the water may turn back into ice when it hits the ground. Challenge the children to look for little spots of ice below the icicles.

6. Help the children make an icicle of their own by dropping a small amount (a dropper full) of water onto a ledge outside. Challenge the children to watch the drop closely, and tell you when the first drop turns to ice. When the children see the drop turn to ice, add a second drop of water, and ask the children to tell you when that drop freezes. Repeat these steps until an icicle begins to form. Explain to the children that this is how nature makes icicles, except nature is much more patient and can take even longer to form icicles.

Want to Do More?

◆ Add drops of food coloring to the dropper you use to make the icicle with the children, and ask them to describe the difference between that icicle and the others hanging off the roofs.

◆ Show the children the icicles on multiple sides of one building and ask them to describe the differences they see.

Observing and Assessing the Children

Can the child describe how icicles form and explain that they are made of water?

Learning in Other Curricular Areas

Language and literacy

◆ communicating information with others (expressive language)

◆ listening with understanding and responding to directions and conversations (receptive language)

Math

◆ measuring and weighing the icicles (measurement—linear, volume, mass)

5+ Concrete

Concrete is part of our world. Homes have concrete foundations. We walk and drive on and over concrete. We enter our schools on concrete. Yet we never study concrete, until now! Your children can have fun with this hard subject, and so can you.

Science Content Standard—explores the characteristics of soil, rocks, and water (Earth and Space Science)
Science Process Skill—measuring (volume)

Words You Can Use
Concrete
Hard
Mix
Mixture
Names of things made from concrete, such as sidewalk, foundation, basement, walls, cinderblock, and so on

Things You Can Use
Concrete mix
Concrete pieces
Paper and marker
Measuring cups for water and concrete
Mixing bowls or cup, plastic, one for each child
Mixing spoons or sticks

Before the Activity
Take a quick survey of the nearby area for objects made from concrete that the children can visit. Collect a few pieces of broken concrete to bring in for the children to explore.

What to Do

1. Engage the children in a discussion about concrete. Ask them what they think concrete is. Explain that concrete is a manufactured rock people that use to build things like sidewalks. Next, bring the children outside and invite them to help you collect some small broken pieces of concrete, or take out the pieces of concrete you collected before the children arrived.
2. Pass the pieces of concrete around for the children to inspect them, and challenge the children to think of things in the world that are made of concrete. Make a list of the objects the children think are made of concrete.
3. Show the children a mixture of dry, unmixed concrete powder. Explain to the children that this is a mixture of ground-up rock, and that it hardens when you add water and mix up the compound and allow it to dry.
4. Give each child a disposable plastic bowl or cup, and carefully, spoon 1 cup of the dry concrete mixture into each cup.
5. Pour ½ cup of water into each bowl. Add more water as needed. Give the children plastic spoons or sticks and encourage them to mix the water into the concrete, and then ask the children to set the bowls aside and allow a couple of hours for the concrete to harden and dry.

   Safety note: Concrete is not a dangerous material to work with, but can burn the skin slightly if now washed off before it dries. Be sure to have water available so the children can wash off any concrete that they get on their hands or bodies. Be sure to remind the children to keep the powdered concrete from coming into contact with their eyes. Also, remember that concrete will set (harden) on any object or in any location if you leave it there long enough. Be sure to wash all tools and containers before completing this activity. Concrete will harden in a drain, so do not pour powdered or wet concrete down a drain.
6. When their concrete starts to harden, help the children scratch their names or initials into their sections, then set them aside and let the concrete harden overnight.
7. The following morning, when the concrete is set, invite the children to turn their containers over and hit them on the ground, to separate the concrete from the containers.

8. When the children's pieces of concrete break free, give the children some time to explore them. Encourage the children to compare them to the stray pieces you or the children collected earlier, and compare their similarities and differences, such as the difference in the size of the pebbles that make the concrete.

Want to Do More?

◆ Help the children make concrete blocks to use for simple construction. Ask the children's families to help making the casts the children will use to form the blocks.

◆ Repeat the process of making concrete stones, and help the children add their hand or footprints to them, rather than their names and initials.

◆ Make colored concrete by adding food coloring or tempera to the mixture as the children stir it.

◆ Repeat the process again, this time setting out rocks or other materials and inviting the children to add them to the mixtures, making designs as the concrete starts to dry.

◆ Set out a thermometer and invite the children to check the temperature of their concrete slabs. The temperature will increase as it hardens.

Observing and Assessing the Children

Can the child follow the instructions to make a concrete object? Can he name the materials he used and describes the steps in making concrete?

Learning in Other Curricular Areas

Language and literacy
◆ talking about items they think are made from concrete (expressive language)
◆ listening with understanding and responding to directions (receptive language)

Math
◆ measuring one cup of concrete mix with ½ cup of water (measurement)

Motor development
◆ mixing and stirring the concrete mixture (large and small motor)

CONNECTING TO CHILDREN WITH SPECIAL NEEDS

Place the activity's materials on low table so they are accessible for children who use wheelchairs.

INVOLVING FAMILIES

Invite family members who have experience with making and using concrete visit the children and help them make their concrete blocks.

USING MUSEUMS AND OTHER COMMUNITY RESOURCES

Bring the children on a field trip to a construction site so they can watch as the workers make and pour concrete.

I Love That Rock!

Rocks fascinate children. Place a collection of rocks out for the children to explore and they are sure to find special rocks for themselves.

Science Content Standard—explores the characteristics of soil, rocks, and water (Earth and Space Science)
Science Process Skills—observing; communicating

Words You Can Use

Color words
Descriptive words, such as sharp, rounded, layered, rough
Friend
Rock words, such as pebble, rock, boulder, stone
Shape words, such as round, triangular, oval
Size words, such as small, big

Things You Can Use

Everybody Needs a Rock by Byrd Baylor
A collection of rocks from previous field trips

Before the activity

Gather a good collection of rocks from which the children can select their rock friends. Be sure there is more than one rock per child, so each really has a choice when picking his rock.

What to Do

1. Read *Everybody Needs a Rock* by Byrd Baylor to the children.
2. Encourage the children to describe how they feel about their favorite toys. Remind the children that lots of things can be favorite toys. Point out, for instance, how the little boy in the story has a favorite rock.
3. Set out the collection of rocks you gathered before the children arrived, and invite each child to pick a rock he likes to be his friend.
4. Ask the children to take turns holding their rocks up to everyone and describing them to the other children. They can describe the rocks physically, or can offer imagined characteristics of their rocks as they share them with the other children
5. Set out paper, markers, and crayons, and ask the children make drawing of their rocks. As the children work on their drawings, circulate among them

Arts

◆ drawing and describing their own creative work (visual arts)

Math

◆ classifying (algebra)

One of the children's families may have a stone polisher they can bring in and demonstrate for the children.

Bring the children on a field trip to a museum's rock collection, or invite someone to bring a rock collection in to show the children.

and help them write their names on the rocks. Also, encourage the children to think of names for their rocks, and add a line below the children's drawings where they can add their rocks' names.

6. Invite the children to keep their rocks in their pockets or some other special place in the classroom, where they can visit it when they need a rock friend.

7. Call the children back together and continue with the day's activities. Later in the day, invite the children to bring their rocks back out and share with everyone the names they gave to their rocks. Help the children add these names to their drawings of the rocks.

Want to Do More?

◆ Challenge the children to use feeling words to describe how their rocks feel in various imaginary situations. How does the rock feel when it falls out of its house? How does the rock feel when you choose it to be your special friend? How does the rock feel when it falls out of the hole in your pocket? How does your rock feel when you hold it close?

◆ Set out various materials and encourage the children to make house for their rocks.

◆ Set out rock identification books and help the children find the scientific names for their rocks, such as lava, granite, limestone, marble, and so on.

◆ Encourage the children to share their rocks with one another, and use measurement terms to describe the rocks. For instance, ask, "Is his rock bigger than yours? Is it heavier or lighter?"

Observing and Assessing Children

Given a rock, can the child describe it using appropriate terms?

5+ My Twin Rocks

In this activity, the children collect, observe, and discuss their rock friends with one another, as well as make homes for their rock friends.

Science Content Standard—explores the characteristics of soil, rocks, and water (Earth and Space Science)
Science Process Skills—observing; classifying; communicating

Words You Can Use

Color words	Sharp
Hard	Shiny
Pair	Soft
Shape words	Twin

Things You Can Use

A collection of sets (2 each) of similar rocks or shells
Paper and markers
Measurement equipment, such as balance and ruler
Milk cartons for making the rock houses
Art materials for decorating the houses

Before the Activity

Collect several pairs of similar-looking rocks. There should be more than one pair of matching rocks per child, so each child has a variety of pairs to choose from when picking his pair.

What to Do

1. Set out the sets of rock pairs you collected before the children arrived. Invite the children to look through the sets of pairs and ask each child to pick one pair that they like best.
2. Using whatever materials are available, encourage the children to make comfortable homes for their pairs of rocks.
3. As the children work, ask them to talk about their pairs of rocks. In particular, ask the children to describe how they look. Help each child to make a list of his rocks' characteristics. Encourage the children to be specific enough that they can use these lists of characteristics to pick their rocks out from all the other children's rocks. Characteristics can include color, sheen, sharpness, shape, size, weight, hardness, as well as whether the rock can make marks on concrete. Point out to the children that certain qualities, such as size and weight, involve measurement. Consider discussing the different characteristics of various children in the classroom as a way to get the children thinking about how their rocks are unique.
4. After the children finish making homes for their rocks, ask the children to bring their rocks and rock homes to the circle area, and then put one of the rocks in their pairs in their pockets. Next, invite the children to pass their rocks around the circle until each child has someone else's rock.
5. Pick one child and ask him to cover the rock he is holding so the other children cannot see it, and then describe it to the group. Challenge the other children to listen carefully to how the child describes the rock, and to decide if the rock is theirs. If a child thinks the description the child gives is of her rock, have her take out her second rock and show it to the child describing the first rock to see if they match. Whenever a child finds the second rock in his pair, ask him to be the next child to describe the other child's rock he is holding, and repeat the process. Continue until all the children find their matching rocks.

USING
MUSEUMS
AND OTHER
COMMUNITY
RESOURCES
*Each state has
a branch of government
that focuses on rocks.
This geology section
may have rocks they
are willing to lend
to you to use
in the classroom.*

6. When all the children have their pairs of rocks back, ask them to put the rocks inside their rock houses to rest, explaining that it has been a very tiring and exhausting day for the rocks.

7. Next, set out paper, markers, crayons, and paints and brushes, and invite the children to make drawings or paintings of their rocks and rock houses. Encourage the children to remember the list of characteristics they used to describe their rocks, and challenge them to find ways to include the characteristics in their drawings and paintings.

8. As the children paint and draw, engage them in discussions about how they think their rocks might feel about having them as new friends, and how they feel about having rocks for friends.

Want to Do More?

◆ Invite the children to bring their rocks home for a visit. Give the children special instructions to take their rocks to visit other rocks and to remember the rocks' characteristics so they can describe them to the rest of the children when they bring their rocks and rock houses back to class.

◆ Encourage the children to find other matching pairs of rocks on their own, then to bring them in to share with the other children.

Observing and Assessing Children

Can the child describe the characteristics of a rock so that other children can recognize it?

Learning in Other Curricular Areas

Language and literacy
◆ communicating ideas and thoughts to others (expressive language)
◆ listening with understanding and responding (receptive language)

Math
◆ measuring the rocks (measurement)

5+ Sifting Soil

To sort the different materials in soil, children must select different sizes of sieves and use them properly to separate the parts of soil into separate piles. The children will discover that soil contains particles of all sizes, from large boulders to tiny flecks of silt.

Science Content Standard—explores the characteristics of soil, rocks, and water (Earth and Space Science)
Science Process Skills—observing; classifying

Words You Can Use

Comparison phrases, such as bigger than, smaller than, same size
Sift
Size words, such as big, small, tiny
Soil part names, such as rocks, clay, sand, lumps
Sort

Things You Can Use

Containers to hold sorted materials (beach buckets work well)
Sieves with various-sized openings
Soil with rocks, sand, and other material

Before the Activity

Because this is a messy activity, find a nearby area outside where the children can spill and shake dirt without having to clean it up afterwards.

Note: To make sieves, use a hot-glue gun to attach pieces of screening with holes of various sizes to one of the open ends of lengths of Trim the excess screen off the edges of the pipe and duct tape the edges so they are smooth. Also, consider using kitchen sifters and strainers. Have several sieves for the children to use, and label each, A, B, C, and so on, in order from those with the largest holes to those with the smallest.

What to Do

1. Bring the children outside. Show the children the set of sieves, pointing out the different sizes of holes in the screens. Next, show the children several containers of soil, and explain to them that they will be separating the soil into several piles, based on the size of the filterable material. Remind the children to leave one container of soil unsorted, so they can remember what the soil looked like before they started sifting.

2. To demonstrate to the children how to separate the parts of the soil, take a scoop of soil from a container and put it into sieve with the largest holes. Explain to the children that by using this sieve first, you are catching only the largest parts of the soil. Put the materials that the sieve caught into a separate container.

3. Set out several more containers and invite the children to begin sifting and separating into the containers the various materials that make up the soil.

4. Point out to the children how the sieves are all labeled A, B, C, and so on, and that each next letter corresponds to smaller holes in the sieves' screens. Talk about the sizes of the soil particles they separate with each sieve, and point out to them that the materials that pass through the sieves are always smaller than those that catch inside the sieves. Encourage the children to sift through and sort all of the soil into separate containers.

5. After the children finish sifting the soil, help them add water to each container, and engage the children in a discussion about which size of soil particle is best for making mud pies.

6. Point out a location where the children can set their mud pies out to dry. After the mud pies dry, try to determine which is the strongest.

Want to Do More?

◆ Visit a local nursery or some other location where you can collect a wide variety of soil types, such as rocks, sand, and gravel, and use them to make various combinations of soils for the children to sift.

Observing and Assessing the Children

Can the child use sieves to sort a soil sample into piles of soil particles, arranged by size?

Learning in Other Curricular Areas

Language and literacy
◆ listening with understanding and responding to directions (receptive language)
◆ communicating information regarding types of soil (expressive language)

Math
◆ recognizing patterns (algebra)
◆ sorting soil into piles by size (geometry)

Motor development
◆ using their hands and fingers to grasp the sieves and to pour the soil (small motor)

5+ Drifting Snow

This activity encourages the children to observe how the amount of snow on the ground varies over time, and thereby helps the children recognize how cold and warm spells, wind, and additional storms affect the amount of snow on the ground throughout the winter.

Science Content Standard—describes changes in seasons and observable weather patterns (Earth and Space Science)
Science Process Skills—observing; measuring (linear)

Words You Can Use

Accumulation
Centimeters
Freezing
Melt
Snow
Weather words

Things You Can Use

Calendar
Long stick
Permanent marker
Ruler

Before the Activity

Find a few good places where the children can measure snow. Look for locations where people will not walk or alter the way the snow lays on the ground. If wind is an issue, then choose several places: one where drifting occurs, one where the snow blows away completely, and another out in the open.

What to Do

1. When the weather forecast begins to predict the first snowfall of the year, talk with the children about snow, and how they think snow will affect the area.
2. Point out to the children that when meteorologists predict snowstorms, they indicate how much snow is supposed to fall. Ask the children if they can think of ways to check to see if the meteorologists' predictions are correct. Guide the children toward the idea of putting sticks outside in places where they will not be disturbed.
3. After the snow (assuming school does not close), bring the children outside and help them find a few locations where they can measure the snowfall.
4. Give the children sticks to put in the snow to measure how much snow falls. Give the children markers to draw lines on the sticks indicating the depths of the snow they measure, and then help them write the day's date on the sticks.
5. After a few days, depending on the weather, bring the children outside to measure and mark on their sticks the snow's new depth. After each snowstorm or change in the temperature, bring the children outside to measure the snow's new depth, and help them mark and date it on their sticks.
6. After the winter ends and the snow all melts, invite the children to look at all the sticks together and compare them.

Want to Do More?

◆ Engage the children in a discussion about how snow forms.

Observing and Assessing the Children

Can the child measure and compare the depths of the snow at different points throughout the winter?

Learning in Other Curricular Areas

Math

◆ measuring using nonstandard units of measurement (measurement)

CHAPTER **5**

Weighing, Working, and Watching: The Tools of Science (Science and Technology)

3+

Can You Make a House?

While the houses people live in are usually made of wood, stone or brick, pretend houses can be made of cardboard, sheets, and even sticks and stones. Remember the story of "The Three Little Pigs"!

Science Content Standard—begins to explore with tools of science (Science and Technology)
Science Process Skills—observing; constructing models

Words You Can Use

Build
Built
Construct
Material names
Plan
Structure

Things You Can Use

Bricks
Cardboard pieces
Lumber pieces
Sheets or blankets
String or rope
Tarps or tents
Tent pegs

Before the Activity

Select a dry, covered spot for storing the building materials for several weeks. Also, collect several pictures of people building houses so the children can use them as prompts when they begin to build their homes.

What to Do

1. Engage the children in a discussion about construction. Encourage them to describe the designs of their own homes. Encourage the children's interest in building or constructing by bringing building materials to the construction area you have selected. Show children the various pictures of construction you collected and talk with them about the various ways of making a structure.
2. Next, bring the children outside, show them the construction materials you collected, and explain that in this activity they will be building play homes together over the next several days.
3. Before the children begin building their homes, work with them to develop a list of safety rules to follow in the construction area. The guidelines you set with the children will vary with the materials you provide for them to use.

4. Once the children understand the safety rules, invite them to begin building houses together. Move through the children's construction zones as they work, talking with them about the various problems they have to work through as they make sections of their homes. For example, some children might talk about the difficulty they had getting a wall to stay up and explain that they solved the problem by using pieces of tape. Record their observations. As they work, ask the children to describe what particular parts of their homes they are working on and what they plan to work on once they complete their current tasks.

5. If it is possible for the children to leave their partially built homes outside for a week or more, work with them to develop construction schedules, so they can set daily goals to complete certain parts of their homes.

Want to Do More?

◆ Invite a family member with construction skills to visit the children and help them during one of their construction periods.

◆ Add new building materials as the children master working with some of the items.

◆ Bring the children on a field trip to a local construction site so they can observe professionals as they erect new buildings.

Observing and Assessing the Children

Can the child describe how she is making her building and talk about the construction she completed?

Learning in Other Curricular Areas

Language and literacy

◆ describing the procedure used to construct their house (descriptive and expressive language)

Math

◆ identifying spatial relationships (geometry)

◆ constructing a pretend house and discovering problems involved in building a house that will stay together (problem solving)

Motor development

◆ constructing the pretend house (small and large motor)

Social-emotional development

◆ engaging in cooperative play, sharing materials and taking turns, exhibiting persistence and creativity in seeking solutions to problems encountered as the pretend house is constructed (social interaction)

CONNECTING TO CHILDREN WITH SPECIAL NEEDS
The following actions support the development of children with visual, perceptual, and motor impairments: building with cardboard, lumber pieces, and bricks and blocks, and placing these components in relation to one another as they build with them in various combinations.

3+ Elf House

This activity challenges the children to build houses that are proportionally appropriate for a doll, stuffed animal, or some other toy. Through trial and error, the children will be able to determine the sizes of the houses they build.

Science Content Standard—begins to explore with tools of science (Science and Technology)
Science Process Skills—observing; constructing models

Words You Can Use

Construct
Make
Size

Things You Can Use

Flat rocks (½"–3" [2–8 cm] in diameter), sticks, and other natural materials
Small dolls or other toys

Before the Activity

As in the previous activity, find a dry, covered area outside where you can leave the various building materials the children will use. Be sure the location protects the materials from the elements.

What to Do

1. Bring the children outside to the designated construction area, and show them the building materials.
2. Invite the children to tell a story about a group of elves who each night come out of the forest and need a place to sleep. Encourage the children to describe what the elves wear, what their personalities are like, how many of them there are, and why they need to leave the forest at night.
3. When they finish describing the elves, separate the children into groups and invite them to use the materials available to make houses where the elves can sleep at night. Show the children the dolls or stuffed animals, and explain to the children that the elves are a similar size, so the children should build houses large enough for creatures of that size to sleep comfortably in them.
4. As the children work, encourage them to use the doll or stuffed animal occasionally to check to see if the rooms they make are of appropriate size, and talk with them about ways to alter rooms that are too small for the elves.

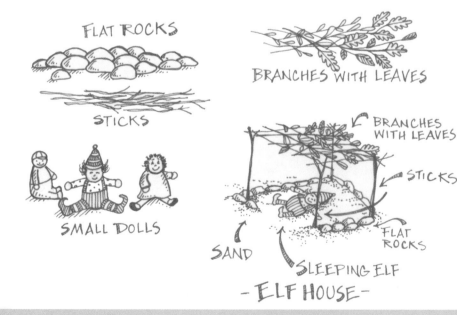

FLAT ROCKS

STICKS

BRANCHES WITH LEAVES

SMALL DOLLS

BRANCHES WITH LEAVES

STICKS

FLAT ROCKS

SAND

SLEEPING ELF

– ELF HOUSE –

Want to Do More?

- ◆ Show the children a toy farm or zoo animal and challenge them to make a home appropriate for an animal from either of those locations.
- ◆ Set out pieces of plywood or cardboard that the children can use as roofs.
- ◆ Challenge the children to arrange their houses so they form a small village with streets.
- ◆ Set out yardsticks and tape measures for the children so they can make more-accurate measurements as they build their houses.

Observing and Assessing the Children

Can the child build an appropriately sized house for the toy or stuffed animal you give her?

Learning in Other Curricular Areas

Language and literacy
- ◆ listening with understanding and responding to directions (receptive language)
- ◆ explaining how the house was built and any problems that were encountered (expressive language)

Math
- ◆ identifying spatial relationships (geometry)

Motor development
- ◆ picking up and building with small flat rocks (small motor)

INVOLVING FAMILIES

To collect a larger variety of building materials, ask each child's family to bring in a few different items with which the children can build.

USING MUSEUMS AND OTHER COMMUNITY RESOURCES

Ask a bricklayer or stonemason to come in to display some of his or her handiwork to the children. Bring the children on a field trip to a local landscaping business. Encourage the children to discuss the work they observe. Consider asking the company to donate several flat rocks for the children to use as building materials.

Area Construction

Construction typically involves the building of a three-dimensional structure. This activity shows the children how to build in two dimensions rather than three. Using rocks as their building materials, the children design the layout of imaginary communities. Here come city planners!

Science Content Standard—begins to explore with tools of science (Science and Technology)
Science Process Skills—observing; constructing models

Words You Can Use

Area
Block
Curved line
Straight line

Things You Can Use

Map of your community—enlarge as needed
Rocks (lots of them)—most should be about the size of a child's hand
A flat, out-of-the-way area of the schoolyard

Before the Activity

Go to a landscaping business to collect one or two 5-gallon buckets' worth of 2"–4" rocks. Find an out-of-the-way location outside where the children can build their city streets. A grassy area works well, but be sure to pick up the rocks before the lawn needs mowing.

What to Do

1. Set out a local street map for the children to discuss and explore with you. Point out any areas where the streets form a regular grid pattern. Encourage the children to trace other roadways that have curves and irregularities. Talk to the children about the differences between the grid and non-grid sections of the map.

2. Show the children the rocks you set out, and explain to them that they will be using the rocks to create the layout of a city. Explain to the children that the roads must connect if people are going to be able to get from one place to another.

3. Place several rocks on the ground to form the outline of the roads or streets for the children (see photo). Challenge the children to structure their city in a grid similar to the grid section of the local street map.

4. Observe as the children use the rocks to outline their streets. When the grid is complete, encourage the children to play with toy vehicles to roam the streets of their rock city. They can make rock houses and have friends live in those houses. It will be fun to pretend to drive to someone's house along the streets.

Want to Do More?

◆ Challenge the children to use the rocks to build more cities that follow different patterns.
◆ Invite the children to use the rocks to create their own houses or playgrounds on the grid.
◆ Add bricks, sticks, and pieces of wood to the rock sets for the children to use when building their neighborhoods.

Observing and Assessing the Children

Can the child help create a grid out of the rocks? Can the child show how to get from one location to another along the grid?

Learning in Other Curricular Areas

Language and literacy
◆ listening with understanding and responding to directions (receptive language)

Math
◆ creating grid-like patterns (algebra), identifying spatial relationships (geometry)

Motor development
◆ picking up and placing rocks on the ground to create a grid-like pattern, playing with toy cars (small motor)

INCORPORATING TECHNOLOGY
Around the world, people use rocks to make fences, streets, and buildings. Before the children arrive, search the Internet to find pictures of stone walls, streets, and buildings to show them to the children. Also, look for stone structures in the nearby area to photograph and show to the children.

INVOLVING FAMILIES
Ask the children's families to help collect rocks for the children to use in the construction area, and encourage them to find and bring in photographs of stone structures they find near their homes.

Balancing Collections

Learning to work with a balance—one of the main tools of science—is an important step for every child's educational development. In this activity, the children collect natural objects to weigh and balance, while reinforcing their naming and identifying skills. When the children say that 15 acorns weigh the same as "weight A," they are practicing skills crucial to both science and mathematics.

Science Content Standard—begins to explore with tools of science (Science and Technology)
Science Process Skills—classifying; measuring (mass)

Words You Can Use

Balance

Compare

Lighter and other comparative terms

Big

Heavier

Little

Scale

Weigh

Names of objects to weigh, such as acorns, pinecones, rocks, bark, sweet gum balls

Things You Can Use

Balance scale

Lots of objects to weigh, both small and large

Set of 3–4 containers, or rocks that are sequentially larger

Permanent marker

Before the Activity

Fill several plastic containers with different amounts of sand, and label each container A through D. Consider having duplicate containers with the same amount of sand, each marked with the same letter.

What to Do

1. Set the balance out for the children to explore. As they experiment with it, explain to them how it will tilt in different ways based on the weight of the objects they put on its two sides.

BALANCE SCALE

BUTTONS   MARBLES   ROCKS

2. When the children are comfortable with using the balance, show the children the containers of sand and the other various objects that you collected prior to the activity. Explain to the children that they will be comparing the weights of the containers of sand to the weights of the other objects.

INVOLVING FAMILIES
Send a note to families asking them to collect collections of pinecones, acorns, keys, plum pits, washers, or other things for the children to weigh.

3. Demonstrate for the children how to approximate a container of sand's weight by holding the container in your hand, then comparing its weight to the weight of one or several of the other objects. Encourage the children to practice this, and discuss with them the difference in weight between a container of sand and one acorn or pinecone.

4. Place the first container of sand on one side of the scale. Ask the children whether they think one of the other objects is lighter, heavier, or about the same as the container, and then challenge the children to estimate how many of that particular object they would need to put on the other side of the scale to balance it.

5. When the children make estimates of how many of an object they would need to use to balance the scale, invite them to collect the objects and take turns adding them to the balance to determine the accuracy of their estimates. You will find that some children become very accurate with practice, while other children continue to base their guess entirely on the size or volume of the objects.

Want to Do More?

◆ With children who can count, challenge them to make numerical comparisons. For example, three rocks balance nine pecans.

◆ With the children, compare the equal quantities of different objects, such as three peach seeds compared to three shells or a cottage cheese carton of foam packing pellets compared to a similar container filled with dried beans.

Observing and Assessing the Children

Can the child use the scale to balance objects of various weights?

Learning in Other Curricular Areas

Language and literacy

◆ listening with understanding and responding to directions (receptive language)

◆ communicating their ideas and thoughts as they compare various weights and their weight effects on the scale movement (comparative and expressive language)

Math

◆ using the tools of measurement to determine mass (measurement)

Big Step Measuring

Using nonstandard measurement tools is one of the basic steps in the mastery of the measurement process. Children can use their bodies to measure before they use the actual ruler. In this activity, the children use their own steps as a measurement tool, the way scientists do to determine a plot measurement. It is the first big step to a career in science.

Science Content Standard—begins to explore with tools of science (Science and Technology)
Science Process Skills—classifying; measuring (linear)

Words You Can Use

Big
Bigger
Biggest
Compare
Long
Measure
Other appropriate
    comparative terms

Things You Can Use

A collection of objects that have linear measuring capability, such as sticks, pieces of cardboard, blocks, pieces of plants, and so on

What to Do

1. Engage the children in a discussion in which they compare the sizes of various objects, people, and animals. Encourage them to compare things like sticks, leaves, toys, even their bodies or your own, by placing the objects side by side.

2. Next, use big steps to walk from one end of the room to the other, explaining to the children that you are counting off each big step so you can compare the size of the room to the sizes of other objects.

3. Ask the children to think of various nearby objects whose sizes they want to compare. For instance, ask the children, "I wonder which takes more steps to cross: the sidewalk in front of the school or the one behind the school?" Make a list of everything they mention.

4. With the children, visit the various items whose lengths they want to compare,

and invite the children to take turns using big steps to see which objects are longer. Encourage the children to count aloud the number of steps they take to measure each object.

5. Point out to the children that each of them may not take the same number of big steps when measuring the same objects. For instance, "John" and "Rachel" may take 10 big steps to measure the front sidewalk, while "Jamie" and "Montee" only take nine steps. Encourage the children to explore why they may take different numbers of steps to measure the same objects.

Want to Do More?

◆ Set out a ruler and a tape measure and invite the children to use them to measure objects, and then compare the results.

◆ Challenge the children to use big steps to measure the length of the block their school is on, and compare it to how many big steps it takes to measure the school itself.

Observing and Assessing the Children

Can the child use her steps to compare the sizes of objects, then use measurement terms such as longer or bigger to describe the differences between the objects?

Learning in Other Curricular Areas

Language and literacy

◆ listening with understanding and responding to directions and conversations (receptive language)

◆ communicating ideas and thoughts (expressive language)

Math

◆ measuring using nonstandard units of measurement (measurement)

Motor development

◆ using big steps as units of measurement (large motor)

Drawing with the Meter Stick

This activity introduces the children to meter sticks, and invites the children to see how they can use a meter stick to measure and draw shapes. If meter sticks are not available, use yardsticks for this activity.

Science Content Standard—begins to explore with tools of science (Science and Technology)
Science Process Skill—measuring (linear and area)

Words You Can Use

Area
Length
Measure
Meter
Meter stick
Number words

Things You Can Use

Meter sticks or yardsticks
Chalk (different colors so each group can use a color)
Cards with drawings on them (Sample cards would include a shape of 1 square meter, a rectangle 2 x 1 meters, a triangle with 1-meter sides, other shapes (label each side with the appropriate number of meters to be used)

Before the Activity

Make several cards that have various shapes on them for the children to draw.

What to Do

1. Bring the children outside. Set a meter stick (or yardstick) on the ground for the children to explore. Explain to the children how they can use the stick to measure objects, as well as draw lines and make shapes of specific lengths.

2. Demonstrate for the children how to use the meter stick to draw a line with sidewalk chalk, as well as how to draw squares and triangles of specific sizes. As you make the various shapes, ask the children to tell you how many sides you should draw.

3. Show the children the various shape cards you made before they arrived, and discuss with the children the number of sides on each shape.

4. Separate the children into groups, and give each group a meter stick and pieces of chalk. Be sure each group of children has a different color of chalk, so that later they can identify the shapes they drew together.

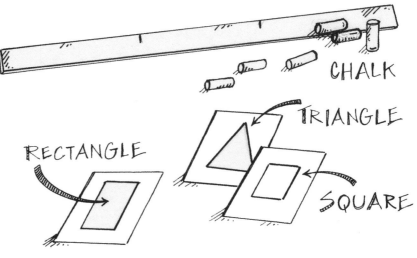

CHALK

TRIANGLE

RECTANGLE

SQUARE

CARDS

INCORPORATING TECHNOLOGY

Invite a carpenter to visit the children, and show them how to use a laser level. Bring the children outside, and show them how they can use a laser level to draw a line across the entire playground.

INVOLVING FAMILIES

Ask family members who use measurement tools in their work to visit the children and show them how to measure with the various tools.

5. Encourage the children in the groups to find ways to work together as they draw lines and shapes. For instance, have children in each group hold the meter stick down while the other children draw a line.
6. Challenge the children to make lines that are one, two, and several meters long. Then, as the children progress, challenge them to make large squares, rectangles, triangles, and other shapes.
7. When the children finish drawing their shapes, invite them to walk around and see the shapes the other groups drew. Challenge the children to identify the other shapes they see.

Want to Do More?

- With the children, put all the meter sticks in a row and make a long line.
- Challenge the children to use their meter sticks to measure sections of the schoolyard.
- Point out the centimeter measurements on the meter sticks, and explain how 100 centimeters equals 1 meter. Challenge the children to measure small objects in centimeters.
- Set out several pieces of cardboard and encourage the children to create three-dimensional shapes by standing the cardboard along the outlines of the shapes they drew.

Observing and Assessing the Children

Given a meter stick and a piece of chalk, can the child work with others to draw lines or shapes?

Learning in Other Curricular Areas

Language and literacy
- listening with understanding and following directions (receptive language)
- describing the different shapes they have drawn (expressive and descriptive language)

Math
- counting the lines needed to make various shapes (number operations)
- incorporating estimating and measuring activities into play using tools of measurement (measurement)
- recognizing and duplicating simple shape patterns (geometry)

Motor development
- holding and drawing geometric shapes using the meter stick (small motor)

4+ Forceps Forage

Forceps, or tweezers, are an important tool for many scientists. Forceps allow them to pick up small objects without having to touch them. Children will enjoy learning to use this scientific tool.

Science Content Standard—begins to explore with tools of science (Science and Technology)
Science Process Skill—observing

Words You Can Use

Forceps
Names of items
    collected
Size words

Things You Can Use

Containers for holding
    found objects or
    critters
Forceps (tweezers) for
    each child
Note: You can purchase
    plastic forceps from
    most science supply
    companies, or from
    early childhood stores
    and catalogs. They
    are inexpensive. Metal
    forceps may be too
    sharp to use.
Resealable bag for
    holding captured
    critters

Before the Activity

Go outside and find an area where the children will be able to find many small objects they can collect using forceps.

What to Do

1. Bring the children outside. Set out the sets of forceps and invite the children to pick up a set. Talk with the children about why scientists use forceps: Explain that scientists use forceps to pick up small objects they would not be able to hold in their fingers and to pick up objects that are not safe to touch, such as things that are hot or sharp. Tell the children that they are going to practice using forceps like scientists do.

2. Set out several containers for the children to hold the various objects they will collect. Demonstrate for the children how to use the forceps to pick up small objects, and then invite them to try collecting objects, such as leaves, grass, and anything else they find.

3. As the children become adept at working with forceps, challenge each child to use their forceps to find and collect objects that they find interesting or unusual, then put them in their container and bring them to you to identify.

4. Save the objects the children find. If the children bring you small insects or similar living creatures, help the children put them in separate plastic bags so the other children can see them.

5. After the children finish collecting various objects, invite them to gather to compare and discuss their discoveries. Encourage the children to discuss the techniques they used to collect the objects.

6. After they finish discussing how they collected their objects, help the children bring the living creatures they gathered back to the areas where they found them and release them there.

Want to Do More?

◆ Bring in ice-cube tongs, salad tongs, or cooking tongs, such as used for barbecues, and challenge the children to use them to pick up large items. Suggest that the children work together to pick up big objects.

◆ Set out collections of shells, nuts, or twigs for the children to move from one area to another, and encourage them to count the objects as they move them.

◆ Time the children to see how many small rocks they can collect in a certain period of time.

Observing and Assessing the Children

Can the child use forceps to collect various items?

Learning in Other Curricular Areas

Language and literacy

◆ listening with understanding and responding to directions (receptive language)

◆ communicating information as to what they found with others (expressive and descriptive language)

Motor development

◆ using forceps to pick up small items and placing them in collecting bags or containers (small motor)

CONNECTING TO CHILDREN WITH SPECIAL NEEDS

By doing this activity, children with fine motor challenges will repeat actions that support their wrist, hand, and finger manipulation and development.

Funnels Fill

Scientists use tools to make their work easier and more accurate. This activity introduces the children to ways they can use funnels.

Science Content Standard—begins to explore with tools of science (Science and Technology)
Science Process Skills—observing; communicating

Words You Can Use

Fill
Full
Funnel
Half

Things You Can Use

Containers (to hold large quantities of sand or water)
Containers (small and large plastic, opaque bottles to fill using the funnels)
Funnels of all different sizes
Sand or water

Before the Activity

Select an indoor or outdoor area where creating a mess is not a problem. Collect a variety of funnels and bottles. Fill and set out a large container with sand or water.

What to Do

1. Set out the funnels, bottles, and the container of sand or water. Engage the children in a discussion about the uses of funnels. Encourage the children to think of ways they might benefit from using them.

2. Demonstrate for the children how they can use a funnel by pouring a cup of water or sand through a funnel and into a plastic bottle without making a mess. Talk with the children about how scientists use funnels to be more accurate when they have to pour liquids into containers.

3. Invite the children to select funnels and practice pouring water or sand through them into bottles.

4. Once the children are adept at pouring through funnels, challenge them to experiment to determine which funnels best fit the various bottles. Ask the children questions. For instance, ask, "Does the opening of this funnel fit into the opening of this bottle?" It should soon become clear that the largest funnel that fits in the opening would allow them to fill a bottle faster than by using a funnel opening.

5. Encourage the children to explain to you why they pick certain funnels. If the children are not able to explain why, encourage them to demonstrate how the funnels they pick work best with the various bottles.

Want to Do More?

◆ Encourage the children to find jobs for the funnels, like mixing drinks for snack, or filling bottles of water for the children to drink when they go on a hike.

Observing and Assessing the Children

Can the child choose a funnel that will fill a bottle without spilling and explain or demonstrate why she chose that funnel over another?

Learning in Other Curricular Areas

Language and literacy
◆ listening with understanding and responding to directions and conversation (receptive language)
◆ questioning to seek answers to questions through active exploration, communicating ideas, thoughts and findings (expressive language)

Math
◆ collecting and organizing data (data analysis and probability)

Motor development
◆ filling a cup with sand or water and pouring contents into container through a funnel (small and large motor)

4+ Weigh a Big Rock

Give children a balance scale and a bucket of objects, and it will take no time at all for the children to be completely absorbed in measuring the items. This activity explores how children can use small objects, such as pebbles, to weigh larger objects, such as big rocks.

Science Content Standard—uses scientific tools for investigation (Science and Technology)
Science Process Skill—classifying, measuring

Words You Can Use

Balance
Big
Compare
Heavier
Lighter, and other
    comparative terms
Little
Scale
Weigh

Things You Can Use

Balance scale
Rocks sets (several big
    ones and many small
    ones)
Shell sets (several big
    ones and many small
    ones)

Before the Activity

Collect several sets of objects for the children to weigh. Each set should have a few large rocks and many small rocks.

What to Do

1. Talk with the children about how to compare the weights of objects. Explain that one large object can equal the combined weight of several small objects.
2. Show the children one of the big rocks from a set. Place it on one side of the balance. Next, pick up a small rock and place it on the other side, and ask the children to describe the effect. Explain to the children that you need to add more small rocks to the second side of the scale to balance it.
3. Help the children experiment with the numbers of small rocks they need to add to one side of the scale to balance it with the large rock on the other side. When a child balances the two sides, ask her to count the small rocks.
4. When a child tells you how many small rocks she used to balance a big rock, say, "Nadine balanced a big rock with 12 small rocks. Another way to say this is that 12 small rocks are equal to one big rock."

Want to Do More?

◆ When the children become adept at balancing small rocks with large rocks, challenge the children to place two big rocks in one side of the balance scale and estimate how many small rocks they will have to add to the other side of the scale for it to balance. Some children will be able to figure out that if they add the two sums from an earlier weighing process they will know how many rocks will balance the two big rocks. Others will keep weighing and counting the rocks and adding more and more until the two sides balance.

Observing and Assessing the Children

Can the child use the balance to weigh a large object?

Learning in Other Curricular Areas

Math

◆ using the tools of measurement to determine mass (measurement)

How to Measure: How Long?

4+

This is the first of four activities that introduce the children to methods of measuring. This activity introduces linear measurement, the concept of measurement most familiar to young children. When they begin to make long roads in the block area and to talk about how far they can jump, engage the children's interest in measuring distance by inviting them to compare the lengths of a collection of sticks.

Science Content Standard—uses scientific tools for investigation (Science and Technology)
Science Process Skills—classifying; measuring

Words You Can Use

Length
How long
How much
Measure
Same

Things You Can Use

Sticks of varying lengths
Small sticks of the same length
Grass stems (optional)

Before the Activity

Collect several sticks whose lengths the children can compare. Break some of the sticks so you have sets of sticks of various lengths.

What to Do

1. Engage the children in a discussion about measurement. Explain to the children that people measure things when they want to know how much there is of something. There are four ways people typically ask measurement questions: How long? How heavy? How full? How hot or cold?
2. Ask the children to tell the class about times when they have measured things or they have seen their family measure things. Tell the children that this activity focuses on measuring length. To do so, the children will compare the length of one object to another, such as the lengths of various sticks.
3. Invite each child to choose one stick from a group of sticks. Next, set out three sticks of various lengths. Ask the children to take turns comparing their sticks to each of the three sticks you set out, and encourage the children to describe similarities and differences.
4. After the children finish comparing their sticks to the three you set out, invite the children outside to gather various sticks and compare them with their sticks, looking for one of the same length.
5. When the children finish with this activity, collect all their sticks and put them together in a location in the classroom so you can use them with the children for later activities.

Want to Do More?

◆ Separate the children into pairs and encourage them to measure the lengths of their partners' bodies against other various objects.

Observing and Assessing the Children

Can the child find a stick that matches the length her stick?

Learning in Other Curricular Areas

Math

◆ incorporating estimating and measuring activities into play (number operations and measurement)

How to Measure: How Full?

When children see family members pour cups of milk, turn off the water before the pan overflows, measure cups of flour or sugar, and use teaspoons of vanilla, the children are observing people measuring volume. This activity introduces children to basic volume measurement.

Science Content Standard—uses scientific tools for investigation (Science and Technology)
Science Process Skill—measuring (volume)

Words You Can Use

How full
How much
Measure
Volume

Things You Can Use

Containers all the same size
Sand or water

Before the Activity

Fill several containers with sand. Fill one container completely full and one half full. Keep at least one container empty. Have more containers and sand available with which the children can fill their containers.

What to Do

1. Engage the children in a discussion about measurement. Review with the children the four ways people typically ask measurement questions: How long? How heavy? How full? How hot or cold? Tell them that this activity will explore how to measure fullness, or volume.

2. Encourage the children to think of times they or someone they know wondered about the volume of an object or container. Explain that volume is the word that describes how much a container holds. Ask the children questions about volume. For instance, "When you pour milk for snack, how do you know when to stop?," "Are there other times when you have to know when to stop?," and "What about when you take a bath?"

SAND

FULL   EMPTY   HALF FULL

Ask the families to collect a variety of containers for the children to use for this activity.

3. Show the children the sand and containers you collected. Point to a container full of sand, one that is empty, one that is half full, and ask the children to describe differences between the containers.

4. Encourage the children to fill the other containers with various amounts of sand, and ask them to compare their containers to the half full container you showed them. Ask them to determine if their containers have more or less sand than your half-full container. Encourage them to use phrases like more full or less full.

5. After the children are able to compare their containers to your own, challenge them to fill their containers so they have the same amount of sand as your container.

6. Finally, after the children are able to fill their containers with the same amount of sand as your own, select a new container, partially fill it with sand, hide it behind your back, then invite the children to fill their containers. After each child fills her container with a various amount of sand, hold out your container and ask the children to compare their containers to see whether they have more, less, or the same amount of sand.

Want to Do More?

◆ Separate the children into pairs and encourage the pairs of children to compare the amounts of sand they have in their containers.

◆ Introduce the children to standard units of measurement.

Observing and Assessing the Children

Can the child look at the amount of sand in one container and fill another container with the same amount of sand, or indicate that a second container has more, less, or the same amount of sand in it?

Learning in Other Curricular Areas

Language and literacy

◆ listening with understanding and responding to directions (receptive language)

◆ communicating their ideas and thoughts as they compare volume (comparative and expressive language)

Math

◆ using the tools of measurement to determine volume (measurement)

INVOLVING FAMILIES

How to Measure: How Heavy?

Children are familiar with the experience of weighing themselves, at doctors' offices or at home, and have seen family members weigh themselves, as well as other objects in the kitchen or other parts of the home. This activity introduces the children to the basics of measuring weight

Science Content Standard—uses scientific tools for investigation (Science and Technology)
Science Process Skill—classifying

Words You Can Use

Heavier
Heavy
How heavy
How much
Light
Lighter
Measure
Same
Weigh
Weight

Things You Can Use

Balance scale
Objects to weigh, such as rocks, shells, or pinecones
Index cards labeled "heavier" and "lighter"

Before the Activity

Make sure the balance scales are working properly. The day before you do this activity with the children, ask them to collect various objects to weigh and to bring them in to class the following day.

What to Do

1. Engage the children in a discussion about measurement. Review with the children the four ways people typically ask measurement questions: How long? How heavy? How full? How hot or cold? Explain that this activity will introduce the children to ways of measuring weight.
2. Ask the children if they can recall getting their weight measured in a doctor's office, or watching a family member weigh produce in the grocery store. Explain that this is the way people measure an object's weight, and that, in this activity, the children will use scales to compare the weights of the objects they brought in to class.
3. Put a rock out where all the children can see it. Ask the children to look at the objects they brought in to class, and ask them whether they think their objects are heavier, lighter, or the same weight as the rock. Next, invite each child to take turns holding the rock in one hand and the object she brought to class in the other hand. Encourage the children to describe the similarities or differences in the weights of the two objects.

4. Set out three cards, with the words "lighter," "heavier," and "equal" written on them. After the children use their hands to compare the weights of their objects to the weight of the rock, ask them to classify their objects and put them beside the corresponding card.

5. Once all the children choose a card to put their objects by, take out a scale and show it to the children. Next, set the rock on one side of the scale, and invite the children to take turns testing the weight of their objects against the rock. This will help them determine how accurate they were when they compared the weights in their hands. Help them put their objects in the correct category.

Want to Do More?

◆ Separate the children into pairs and invite them to compare the weights of each others' objects.
◆ Invite the children to use the balance to compare the weights of other various objects in the classroom.
◆ Introduce the children to the standard units of measurement.

Observing and Assessing the Children

Can the child estimate the weight of an object in comparison to a rock and then use a balance to verify the accuracy of her estimate?

Learning in Other Curricular Areas

Language and literacy
◆ listening with understanding and responding to directions (receptive language)
◆ communicating their ideas and thoughts as they compare various weights and their weight effects on the scale movement (comparative and expressive language)

Math
◆ using the tools of measurement to determine mass (measurement)

How to Measure: How Hot or Cold?

Children know that measurements are important, and they imitate measuring in their play, especially taking temperatures. This activity introduces children to how temperature is measured.

Science Content Standard—uses scientific tools for investigation (Science and Technology)
Science Process Skill—measuring

Words You Can Use

Degrees Celsius (°C)
Degrees Fahrenheit (°F)
How hot
How much
Measure
Same
Temperature

Things You Can Use

Thermometers
Containers of water with a variety of temperatures

Before the Activity

Collect several thermometers. Check them to be sure they work. Fill several containers with water, making sure some are hot, some are cold, and some are at room temperature.
Safety note: Make sure that the hot water is not hot enough to burn. Place your finger in the water to make sure it is not too hot.

What to Do

1. Engage the children in a discussion about measurement. Review with the children the four ways people typically ask measurement questions: How long? How heavy? How full? How hot or cold? Explain that this activity will introduce the children to ways of measuring temperature.

2. Talk with the children about times when they measured how hot something was, or when they saw a family member check the temperature of something. Younger children may not understand what you are asking until the discussion progresses and they hear a few examples. Tell the children that, in this activity, they will measure one container of water's temperature by comparing it (hotter or cooler than) to water in another container.

CUPS of WARM WATER

THERMOMETERS

CONTAINERS of WATER

THERMOMETERS ON the FLOOR

FAUCET

3. Place a cup of warm water where the children can touch it. Help the children take turns going to the water faucet and filling another cup with water. Ask, "Is your container of water warmer than my container of water?," and encourage the children to think of ways to compare the temperatures of the two containers of water. Set out several thermometers and explain to the children how thermometers indicate temperature by raising or lowering their red columns depending on the warmth of whatever they touch.

4. Invite the children to use the thermometers to compare the temperatures of the various containers of water. Encourage the children to touch the water with their hands as they put the thermometers in the water, so they can feel the varying temperatures. Discuss the results with the children.

5. Next, for each child, set out four containers of water, ranging in temperature from ice-cold to hot, and challenge the children to put the cups in order from coolest to warmest.

6. To finish, ask all the children to set their thermometers on the floor, or on a tabletop, and ask the children to describe what the red lines on all the thermometers do. Encourage the children to read the temperatures on their thermometers, and talk about why all the thermometers show the same temperature when they are out of the water.

Want to Do More?

◆ Introduce the children to standard units of heat measurement, such as Fahrenheit and Celsius.

◆ Suggest that the children find partners and compare the temperatures of various containers of water with their partners.

◆ If a refrigerator is available, invite the children to take the temperatures inside and outside of it and discuss the differences. Ask the children why it is so cold inside the refrigerator.

Observing and Assessing the Children

Does the child illustrate an understanding of varying temperatures when putting a thermometer into containers of warm and cool water?

Learning in Other Curricular Areas

Math

◆ measuring and recording temperature data (measurement)

Make It Bigger

The magnifier, or microscope, is an important tool for every scientist. These instruments allow researchers to enlarge their views of objects so they can observe them in detail. This activity introduces the children to ways to observe small things.

Science Content Standard—begins to explore with tools of science (Science and Technology)
Science Process Skill—observing

Words You Can Use

Enlarge   Microscope
Magnifier   Tool
Magnify

Things You Can Use

Magnifiers—hand
   lenses, large tripod
   magnifier (optional)
Microscope (optional)
Sets of small objects that
   might include some
   on microscope slides

Before the Activity

Prepare a set of outdoor objects that the children can place under the magnifiers. Some examples might be a dandelion flower or seed, a dead cicada, a butterfly wing, a dried leaf, a rock with something embedded in it, a pine needle, or a piece of snake skin. Collect a variety of magnifiers and, if possible, add a microscope.

What to Do

1. Show the children a magnifier. Ask the children if they have ever used one of these tools. If someone has, ask that child to demonstrate how to use the magnifier. Ask any others if they have used the magnifiers in a different way. Some may have scientist family members and can use it like a scientist. (Scientists generally hold the magnifier in place close to their eye and move the object they are looking at until it is in focus, while most people leave the object in place and move the magnifier, like Sherlock Holmes.) Other children may have simply had opportunities to play with magnifiers.

2. If the children are not able to demonstrate the proper way to use a magnifier, then show them how to hold the magnifier to the eye and bring the object they want to observe up to the magnifier until it is in focus. Most adults keep one eye closed, but children may not be able to master that. Just let them keep both eyes open.

3. Set out magnifiers for each child and natural objects they can observe through the magnifiers. Encourage the children to describe what they see when they look at a flower without the magnifier and then repeat the description using the magnifier. This may be as simple as, "It looks bigger," or it may be a description of some new things the children notice.

Want to Do More?

◆ Set out a microscope and encourage the children to describe how things look when they observe them in the microscope.

◆ Bring the children on a magnifier walk. Separate the children into pairs. Give each pair a magnifier, and challenge them to find interesting things to see through a magnifier.

◆ Set up a magnifying area in the classroom, and, at the start of each day, add more objects for the children to observe.

Observing and Assessing the Children

Can the child use a magnifier properly to observe small items?

INCORPORATING TECHNOLOGY

Collect a variety of magnifiers for the Science Center. Borrow or find at least one microscope. Give the children the opportunity to use these different tools.

Learning in Other Curricular Areas

Language and literacy

◆ listening with understanding and responding to directions (receptive language)

◆ describing the magnified images (expressive language)

Math

◆ recognizing patterns (algebra)

Motor development

◆ using the magnifiers to view objects (small motor)

Measuring with String

The more children practice measuring things, the better they become at this important scientific and mathematical skill. In this activity, the children use string or yarn to measure everything in the schoolyard. If possible, line up all the lengths of yarn the children used to measure various parts of the schoolyard to see which is the longest.

Science Content Standard—uses scientific tools for investigation (Science and Technology)
Science Process Skills—classifying (ordering); measuring (linear)

Words You Can Use

Big
Bigger
Circumference
Huge
Little
Object names
Same
Smaller
Wider

Things You Can Use

Yarn
Scissors
Masking tape

Before the Activity

Cut yarn into pieces about a yard in length so they are easy for the children to handle. Keep a full ball of yarn handy as well, in case some children want to measure very large objects.

What to Do

1. Take the children outside to the play area. Show them the pieces of yarn.

2. Demonstrate for the children how to measure an object using the lengths of yarn. For instance, go over to the swing and measure the distance across. Say to the children, "The width of the swing seat is from the end of the yarn that I am holding in my left hand to the end that I am holding in my right hand." Then take a pair of scissors and cut the yarn to that measurement. Take a piece of masking tape and label the yarn "swing seat width." Then, take another piece of yarn and measure the distance across the swing seat, labeling it "swing set across." Show them how to measure around something (circumference), such as a post or tree. Label the yarn "around a tree."

3. Give the children pieces of yarn and send them out to measure anything they want. When they measure something, ask them to come to you so you can cut and label the yarn.

STRING

4. Continue until the children measure a number of objects.
5. Bring all the labeled lengths of yarns to a flat place and invite the children to order them from the shortest to the longest. When the children finish putting the lengths of yarn in order, invite them to compare the measurements. For instance, the children might say that the width of the swing is longer than the length of the bench but shorter than the width of the sidewalk.

Want to Do More?

◆ Bring out a meter stick or yardstick and encourage the children to measure with it.

◆ Bring the children on a walk, and invite them to look at the trees and describe the differences in their heights. Challenge them to find the tallest tree and the shortest tree. Help the children use the ball of yarn to measure the circumferences of the trees, and ask which tree is biggest around.

Observing and Assessing the Children

Can the child use appropriate terms to compare two objects of different sizes?

Learning in Other Curricular Areas

Language and literacy

◆ listening with understanding and responding to directions and conversations (receptive language)

◆ communicating ideas and thoughts (expressive language)

Math

◆ measuring using nonstandard units (measurement)

Motor development

◆ picking up and using sticks and blocks to measure objects (small motor)

Planks and Logs

While nature provides many outdoor construction materials, adding a few materials from a building site really makes this activity fun. If possible, visit a local construction site, and ask if there is any scrap lumber available for you to take. Remove any nails, and set these materials out on the playground with a few inexpensive tarps, rope, and cardboard, and your building site is ready to go.

Science Content Standard—begins to explore the tools of science (Science and Technology)
Science Process Skills—observing; measuring

Words You Can Use

Build
Construct
Material names
Structure parts, such as
    wall, floor, ceiling,
    window, stairs, door,
    roof

Things You Can Use

Cardboard sheets
    Heavy plastic or tarp
    material
Rope pieces
Donated scrap lumber

What to Do

1. If possible, bring the children to the construction site to help you gather scrap wood. Encourage the children to ask the builders about what they are constructing. If the children cannot visit the site, show them the scrap wood you gathered from the site, and ask them to describe the photographs you took of the site.

2. Talk with the children about safe and responsible ways to use the scrap wood. Remind the children to be very careful whenever they lift or move the wood. Remind them that swinging a board is not safe.

3. Invite the children to work with the materials to build whatever they like. The children will discover that teamwork is necessary when working with large materials.

4. As the children work with the materials, ask them to describe to you what they are building.

Want to Do More?

◆ Set out paper, markers, and crayons, and invite the children to make drawings of their construction after completion.

◆ Challenge the children to plan the structure they want to make and then complete it.

Observing and Assessing the Children

Can the child use the materials in the construction center to make a structure? Can the child cooperate with others to make a structure?

Learning in Other Curricular Areas

Language and literacy

◆ describing what is being or has been constructed (expressive language)

Math

◆ identifying shapes and their properties, identifying spatial relationships (geometry; measurement—non-standard)

Motor development

◆ gathering, assembling, and constructing structures (small and large motor)

Social/emotional development

◆ showing initiative, independence, persistence, and creativity as they are seeking solutions to building a stable structure (social interaction)

INVOLVING FAMILIES

Ask the children's families to help collect wood for the children to use. It would be great to have volunteers from the families to supervise the children when they first begin building with the materials.

USING MUSEUMS AND OTHER COMMUNITY RESOURCES

Invite a construction site foreman to talk with the children about building projects and to share photos of buildings in a variety of construction stages from start to end.

String Water Movers

In this activity, the children observe the way water can use a string to travel from a cup to the ground. The water moves along some strings more quickly than it moves along others, and this provides the children with an opportunity to observe and discuss the impact that variables have on scientific inquiry. Also, in observing the variables, the children can learn about the impact of time on scientific inquiry.

Science Content Standard—uses scientific tools for investigation (Science and Technology)
Science Process Skills—observing; measuring (time)

Words You Can Use

Clock
String widths and types
Time
Timer
Variable

Things You Can Use

Plastic cups of the same
   size and shape
String or rope in a
   variety of materials
   and widths
Water
Pitcher of water or water
   from a tap to fill cups

Before the Activity

Measure several lengths of string or rope, and cut them so they are more than twice as long as the height of the cups the children will use in this activity. Find a location outside where it is okay to spill water and where the children can set the cups without their being disturbed.

What to Do

1. Invite each child to select a cup and length of rope or string. Help the children fill their cups with water. Next, demonstrate for the children how to dunk their rope or string into the cup of water so that the string or rope is completely soaked, and then hang it over the edge of the cup so it touches the bottom of the cup as well as the ground.

2. Invite the children to watch the water as it slowly moves through the string or rope and out of the cup.
3. Encourage the children to guess which cup will empty first and which one will empty last. Invite the children to talk about the reasons for their guesses.
4. Talk with the children about what they observed happening. Ask them which kind of string or rope worked the best.
   Note: Water has the tendency to stick to itself, which is why you use a wet string to begin the process. The water moves up and over the string by a process called capillary action.

5. Encourage the children to repeat the activity themselves with a different length of string or rope. Ask the children questions about the process. For instance, "If the string is too short on either end does it change the emptying time? Does all the water leave the cup?"

Want to Do More?

◆ Add different amounts of water to the same cups, and encourage the children to compare the results.

◆ Set out an actual clock and help the children calibrate their water clocks, noting how much water flows out in one, two, or three minutes.

◆ Help the children make a list of common activities that they can time using their string water clocks. Challenge the children to try to "beat the water clock" as they engage in one of the activities they choose.

Observing and Assessing the Children.

Given a container filled with water and a piece of string or rope, can the child describe whether the cup drains quickly or slowly?

Learning in Other Curricular Areas

Language and literacy

◆ listening with understanding and following directions (receptive language)

◆ guessing and communicating thoughts and ideas (expressive language)

Math

◆ developing a sense of time passing and exploring volume (measurement)

Motor development

◆ using fingers to place the string in the cups (small motor)

4+ Time to Time It

Young children like to run and move around. Give them an additional reason to move by introducing the concept of timed activities. This activity minimizes the competitive aspect inherent in recording time by keeping track of how long it takes for the group as a whole to complete various movements.

Science Content Standard—uses scientific tools for investigation (Science and Technology)
Science Process Skill—collecting and communicating

Words You Can Use

Begin
End
Measure
Minutes
Second
Stopwatch
Time

Things You Can Use

Stopwatch
Timer
Data table

Before the Activity

Prepare a table for recording data (see sample below).

What to Do

1. Show the children the stopwatch. Explain to the children that a stopwatch is a machine that measures time.
2. Engage the children in a discussion about tracking time. When someone times an action, it is because she wants to keep track of that information, usually to compare it to other recorded times. Explain that in this activity, you are going to track and record on a data table how long it takes the children to complete various activities.
3. Show the children the data table, and read off to them the various activities that you plan to time. Next, ask the whole group to run, walk, walk backwards, crawl, crabwalk, or any other action across an area of the playground. Time and record each activity.
4. Each time the children prepare to move in a new way, ask, "Do you think this time will be faster or slower than the time you just did?" After the children finish all the various activities, show them the data table and invite them to compare the various times. Ask the children questions about which activities took longer and which took less time.
5. Encourage the children to repeat some of the activities and see if they get the same results.

Task	Time
Run	
Roll	
Crawl	

Want to Do More?

◆ Add more timed activities that use different physical skills. One example is to time how long it takes a child to use a spoon to move ten marbles from one bowl to another.

◆ Time how long it takes the children to use a turkey baster to move water from one cup to another.
◆ Time how long it takes the children to blow a balloon across the floor.

Observing and Assessing the Children

Can the child talk about the differences in how long it takes to perform different tasks?

Learning in Other Curricular Areas

Math
◆ collecting and measuring time (measurement)
◆ collecting and organizing data (data analysis and probability)

Motor development
◆ walking, running, and crawling (large motor)

4+ Twig Teepees

Twigs and branches found on the ground under trees become the materials for construction in this activity. The pattern for the teepee house, the traditional home of the Plains American Indian, is a circle, and differs from the homes in which most children live.

Science Content Standard—begins to explore with tools of science (Science and Technology)
Science Process Skills—observing; constructing models

Words You Can Use

Circle
Circular
Construct
Count

Things You Can Use

String
Twigs and small
    branches

Before the Activity

Find a nearby location the children can walk to where there are several trees with fallen twigs that the children can gather.

What to Do

1. Bring the children outside to a location where there are several trees and invite the children to collect a number of twigs of various sizes. Separate the children into groups and show each group how to make the frame of a teepee by standing several twigs in a circle, then leaning their tips against one another above the center of the circle. Use string, as needed, to hold the tops of the twigs in place.
2. After illustrating for the children how to make the frame of a teepee, help them to make their own using three sticks. Next, encourage the children to add more sticks to see what happens to the form of the teepee.

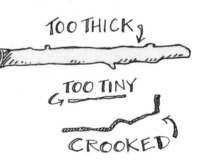

3. Ask the children if some sticks work better than others do to make the frames of teepees. Ask, "Which sticks do not work?" Encourage them to talk about why they do not work. Ask, "Are they too thick, too crooked, or too short? How many sticks are enough?"
4. Ask the children what they think will happen if they add too many sticks to the teepee. Encourage children to say what they think will happen and then try it.

5. When the children finish making their teepees, invite them to take a walk around to look at the other children's teepee frames.
6. Challenge the children to say which teepees took the most sticks or which used the longest sticks. Review with the children how they made their teepees. Ask them questions. For example, "What is the smallest number of sticks needed to make a teepee? What is the largest number you can use?"

Want to Do More?

◆ Depending on what is available in each season, encourage the children to use leaves or small pieces of cloth to cover the teepee frames and make teepees.
◆ Challenge the children to try making other structures from their twigs.
◆ Engage the children in a discussion about how American Indians used teepees.
◆ Set out various books that show different kinds of stick housing for the children to explore.

Observing and Assessing the Children

Can the child construct a teepee frame and indicate why some methods for making a teepee frame are better than other methods?

Learning in Other Curricular Areas

Language and literacy
◆ listening with understanding (receptive language)
◆ responding to directions and conversations and seeking answers (expressive language)

Math
◆ counting twigs (number operations)
◆ identifying shapes and their properties (geometry)

Motor development
◆ collecting twigs; constructing teepees (small and large motor)

5+ Balancing Cups

This activity gives the children another way to use the balance scale while introducing the concept of volume. A unique characteristic of the metric system is that the volume of water relates directly to the mass of water. This means that 100 milliliters of water has a mass of 100 grams. In the metric system, one can use a measuring cup to weigh something.

Science Content Standard—becomes increasingly accurate in the use of scientific tools (Science and Technology)
Science Process Skill—measuring

Words You Can Use

Equal
Heavier
Lighter
Measuring cup
Same

Things You Can Use

Index cards
Permanent marker
Balance
Clear plastic cups
Measuring cup sets
Pitcher filled with water

Before the Activity

This is a wet and messy activity so choose a warm day for the children to do the activity as well as a spot where the water will drain away easily without making a muddy mess. Create "recipe cards" for the activity. (See illustrations.) It is best to draw the cup as well as the value.

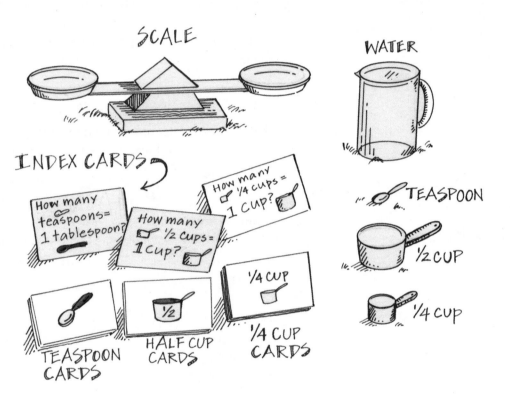

What to Do

1. Gather the materials and bring the children outdoors to the site of the activity.
2. Place a clear plastic cup on each side of the balance. Point out to the children that the balance is level (both sides have equal weight).
3. Select a 1-cup sized container, fill it with water, and then pour the water into one of the clear cups on the balance. The children should notice that the side of the scale with the water-filled cup goes down. Ask the children to explain what this means: The cup with the water in it is heavier than the empty cup.

4. Pour water into the other clear cup, using the ¼-cup measuring cup. Invite the children to help you count the number of times you have to fill the second cup using the smaller ¼-cup container before the two cups on the scale balance.

5. Set out a variety of measuring cups and spoons, from one teaspoon to one cup, and ask the children to compare the sizes of them visually. Explain to the children that each size is larger by a given amount.

6. Show the children the recipe cards you made. Depending on the age and abilities of the children, discuss the meaning of what you wrote on the cards. Challenge the children to look at the spoons and cups that you set out and find the ones that answer the questions on the recipe cards. Give the children hints to get them started.

Want to Do More?

◆ Make up recipe cards that call for larger measurements, and challenge the children to add various measuring cups and spoons together to get the answer.

◆ Set out a container that will not fit on the balance and challenge the children to work as a group to find out how much water it can hold and the weight of the water it can hold.

Observing and Assessing the Children

Can the child use a balance to compare the amounts of liquid that various measuring cups and spoons can hold?

Learning in Other Curricular Areas

Language and literacy

◆ listening with understanding and responding to directions (receptive language)

Math

◆ using a balance to find equal weight in measuring cups (measurement)

Meet the Meter Stick

The meter stick (or yardstick) is the basis for much measurement. Marking a few simple lines on the sidewalk with chalk helps familiarize the children with this standard measurement tool.

Science Content Standard—uses scientific tools for investigation (Science and Technology)
Science Process Skill—measuring

Words You Can Use

Length
Long
Longer
Measure
Meter
Meter stick
Number words

Things You Can Use

Meter sticks or yardsticks
Chalk
Answer sheet showing
    the lengths of the
    various chalk lines

Before the Activity

On the pavement or the sidewalk, draw several lines of varying lengths. Make one line exactly 1 meter (or 1 yard) long. Label this line "A." Draw additional lines, each 1 meter or 1 yard longer than the previous. Label each line with a different letter. Make an answer sheet that indicates the length of each line.

What to Do

1. Set out the meter stick for the children to explore. Explain to the children that people use meter sticks to measure things, including how tall they are. Tell the children that they will get to measure their heights soon, but that first, they can practice by measuring the chalk lines you drew on the ground outside.

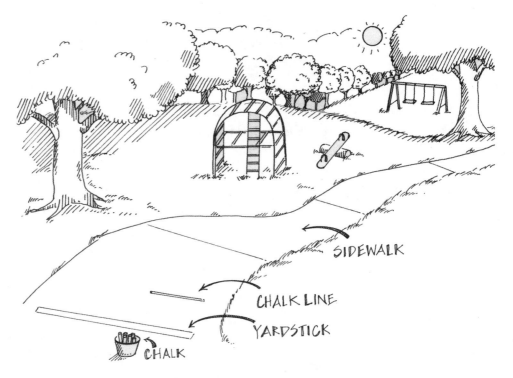

2. Show the children the set of lines, and demonstrate for the children how to measure the lines by setting the meter stick beside line A. Show the children that according to the stick, the line is 1 meter long. Next, show the children the answer on your answer-sheet card, so they know how to check their measurements.

3. Set the answer sheet somewhere where the children can refer to it, and invite them to measure the various lettered lines on the ground.
4. After the children finish measuring the various lines and checking their measurements on the answer sheet, invite them to measure one another's heights.
5. Set out chalk so the children can get on the ground and have someone draw a line beside them to indicate their heights, or separate the children into pairs and have each child in a pair measure the height of the other.

Want to Do More?
♦ Draw a round shape and challenge the children to measure it.
♦ On the ground, draw some very long lines or lines in the shapes of letters, such as "W," and challenge the children to measure them.

Observing and Assessing the Children
Can the child use a meter stick to measure (to the nearest meter) the length of a line drawn on the ground?

Learning in Other Curricular Areas
Math
♦ incorporating estimating and measuring activities into play; using basic standard measurement (measurement)

5+ Outdoor Temperatures

In this activity, the children use a thermometer to read the many temperatures of a selected outdoor location. It also gives them a chance to use a thermometer and to read temperatures repeatedly throughout the day.

Science Content Standard—uses scientific tools for investigation (Science and Technology)
Science Process Skill—measuring—temperature

Words You Can Use

Absorb
Cold
Colder
Cool
Cooler
Decrease
Degrees Celsius (°C)
Degrees Fahrenheit (°F)
Hot
Hotter
Increase
Temperature
Thermometer
Warm
Warmer

Things You Can Use

Thermometers (alcohol based), one for every 3–4 children
Safety note: Make sure that you do not have mercury-based thermometers.
Journal and pen

Before the Activity

Collect several thermometers, and use colored permanent markers on each to color-code different ranges on each thermometer. For instance, on each thermometer, color the area from 0°–10° C (32°–50° F) blue, 10°–20° C (51°–68° F) green, 20°–30° C (69°–86° F) orange, and 30°–40° C (87°–104° F) red. It is easier to color the thermometers if they are made of plastic. For metal thermometers, attach a strip of white tape along the side and color it.

What to Do

1. Pick a time when the children are aware of how warm it is getting outside. Bring the children outside and encourage them to walk around feeling the various surfaces of objects in the schoolyard. Ask the children to describe whether those surfaces are hot, warm, cool, or cold. Make a list of the children's observations. When the children return to the classroom, review these temperatures with the children and place the information on a chart.

2. Engage the children in a discussion about which locations feel hottest or coolest. Help the children understand that items that are hot will get hotter through the course of the day and remain hotter longer into the evening.

3. Explain to the children how they can read one of the thermometers. If the group is older, encourage them to read the actual temperature rather than the color-coated range in which the temperature falls.

4. Separate the children into groups of three or four, and ask each group to select a spot outside where they can follow the changes in the temperature throughout the day.

5. Every hour, bring the children outside and ask them to take the temperature at their particular location. Create a chart for each group, and help the children fill in the chart with the temperatures they take at their various locations throughout the day (see the sample on the next page).

6. After the children finish taking the temperatures of their various locations, invite them to compare their temperatures to those taken at earlier times in the day and those taken by other groups at other locations.

Want to Do More?

◆ Demonstrate for the children how to graph the temperature, and help them use this information to determine the highest and lowest temperatures they measured.

◆ Bring the children out to take temperatures when the day is rainy and cloudy or sunny and hot. Note the days on the calendar, and encourage the children to compare the day's results with other days.

Observing and Assessing the Children

Can the child use a thermometer to determine either the color-coated range of the temperature or the exact temperature?

Learning in Other Curricular Areas

Math

◆ measuring and recording temperature data using tools of measurement (measurement)

INCORPORATING TECHNOLOGY

Bring in digital thermometers and help the children use them to determine the temperatures of their outdoor locations.

Temperature (°C or °F) of a location over time
Location of temperature collection_____

Time	Temperature °C (or °F)
9.00 AM	
10:00 AM	
11:00 AM	
12:00 Noon	
1:00 PM	
2:00 PM	
3:00 PM	
4:00 PM	
5:00 PM	
6:00 PM	

Top It Off

Understanding how to use the tools of measurement is an important step in the mathematical and scientific development of any child. Because scientists gather data to support their studies, measuring is critical. This activity invites the children to explore ways to measure water.

Science Content Standard—becomes increasingly accurate in the use of scientific tools (Science and Technology)
Science Process Skill—measuring (volume)

Words You Can Use

Equal	More
Full	Same
Measuring cup	

Things You Can Use

Large containers
Permanent marker
Unbreakable 1-cup
   measuring cups

Before the Activity

Collect 5–10 big containers and use a permanent marker to label them alphabetically. Have several different measuring cups available; the cups may look different but all should hold 1 cup. Use a water table if available.
Note: This is a wet and messy activity that is easier to do outdoors in warm weather.

What to Do

1. Bring the children outside to a specific location where it is okay for the children to get wet and messy. Show the children the labeled containers and the measuring cups. Be sure you have access to water from either a nearby hose or from additional containers you bring outside.

2. Demonstrate for the children how to fill a measuring cup until it holds 1 cup of water, and then empty it into container "A," saying "1 cup" aloud.

3. Next, separate the children into groups of two to four children, and invite the groups to fill the various containers with water, counting the number of cups they pour into the containers until they are full.

4. When one group finishes filling their container, invite them to empty the container and then pass it on to another group of children, and then invite that group to repeat the process.

5. After several groups of children fill a specific container, invite the groups to compare their experiences. Ask the groups to say how many cups it took to fill the container. The children should all have poured the same number of cups into the container to fill it. Engage the children in a discussion about why they all poured the same number of cups to fill the specific container. Explain that scientists repeat their measurements to be sure their answers are correct.

6. Encourage the children to continue filling the various labeled containers, counting how many cups it takes to fill each, and discussing and comparing their numbers from group to group.

Want to Do More?

◆ Set out more containers that hold larger amounts of water, and challenge the groups of children to count how many cups of water it takes to fill them then compare the totals.

Observing and Assessing the Children

Can the child count how many cups of water her group must pour into a container to fill the container?

Learning in Other Curricular Areas

Language and literacy

◆ listening with understanding and responding to directions (receptive language)
◆ communicating their ideas and thoughts as they compare volume (comparative and expressive language)

Math

◆ using the tools of measurement to determine volume (measurement)

Which Weighs More?

This activity uses a balance scale to compare the weights of objects the children find outdoors. Once the children determine the weight of ten sycamore leaves, for example, they can begin to determine how much one sycamore leaf weighs.

Science Content Standard—becomes increasingly accurate in the use of scientific tools (Science and Technology)
Science Process Skill—measuring (mass)

Words You Can Use

Balance scale
Heavy
Heaviest
Light
Leaf names
Number words
Same
Weigh

Things You Can Use

Balance scale
Sets of leaves, shells, or gravel
Counters, such as bear counters or counting blocks

What to Do

1. Bring the children outside, and encourage them to collect various objects, such as leaves from particular trees.
2. Bring the children back inside and set out the balance scale as well as a set of counters, and explain to the children that they can use the counters to determine the weight of a set of 10 of the objects they gathered outside.
3. With the children, count out 10 leaves, pinecones, or acorns, for example, from the objects they gathered and place them on one side of the balance scale.
4. Next, help the children to begin setting counters on the other side of the balance. Count each counter as the children put them on the scale until it balances. If four counters balance 10 oak leaves, for instance, then help the children write this information on a sheet of paper and place that paper beside the pile of 10 oak leaves. For lightweight leaves, for instance, use smaller counters, such as buttons or chips, instead of teddy bear counters. Provide the options and point out the problem.
5. Invite the children to continue counting and weighing the rest of the sets of objects they gathered from outside, and challenge the children to compare the weights of each set of objects to determine which set is the heaviest.

Want to Do More?

◆ Place a constant weight on one side of the balance and invite the children to add the objects they gathered outdoors until the scale balances.

Observing and Assessing the Children

Can the child use a balance scale and set of counters to determine the weight of various sets of objects she gathered outdoors?

Learning in Other Curricular Areas

Math

◆ using the tools of measurement to determine mass (measurement)

A

Appendix

Coat Hanger Bug Net

Materials

coat hanger
roll of duct tape
gallon-size paint strainer, purchased from a paint
   store

What to do

1. Unwind the coat hanger and bend it into a circular shape with a handle. The circular shape's diameter should equal the size of the paint strainer.
2. Wrap the open ends of the paint strainer around the hanger's circular edge, and then use five or six 4" (10 cm) pieces of duct tape to tack the paint strainer to the rim of the coat hanger.
3. Wrap the handle in duct tape so that the children can hold the net more easily, and so that the tape covers the two ends of the unwound coat hanger for safety. This net is now ready for bug catching.

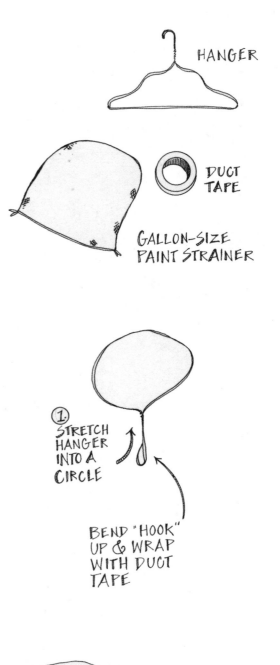

HANGER

DUCT TAPE

GALLON-SIZE PAINT STRAINER

① STRETCH HANGER INTO A CIRCLE

BEND "HOOK" UP & WRAP WITH DUCT TAPE

② SLIP STRAINER OVER HANGER

③ ATTACH WITH DUCT TAPE

DUCT TAPE

Outdoor Science Prop Boxes

Prop boxes provide a playful and interesting way to promote children's understanding of the many ways science is a part of our world. Create prop boxes by filling a cardboard box, a lidded plastic tub, or even a large plastic or cloth sack with materials related to a topic. Because the following prop boxes are for outside use, keep them separate from prop boxes used indoors. The contents may get dirty faster and may need to be frequently cleaned or replaced.

The materials listed for each of the following science topics can be expanded by adding more materials. Consider reading related books to the children, taking a related field trip, or inviting a family member or professional to speak with the children.

Archaeologist/Paleontologist

- Backpack
- Beads
- Bones
- Explorer hat
- Small notebook
- Toy dinosaurs or extinct animals
- Toy dishes or pottery
- Tub filled with sand in which to bury the items

Camper

- Backpack
- Bottles of sunscreen (empty or filled with water)
- Camping dishes
- Flashlight
- Hiker's hat
- Sleeping bags
- Tent

Farmer or Gardener

- Child-sized gardening tools
- Farm-equipment toys
- Farmer's hat
- Pretend food
- Toy farm animals
- Toy trucks

At the Beach

- Backpack
- Beach balls
- Beach towels
- Bottles of sunscreen (empty or filled with water)
- Seashells
- Sunglasses
- T-shirts

Going Fishing

- Bucket
- Fishing hat
- Pretend fishing license
- Rubber fishing boots
- Small notebook
- Toy fishing set
- Toy water animals and fish

Picnicking

- Bottles of sunscreen (empty or filled with water)
- Dishes
- Picnic basket
- Picnicking hats
- Play food
- Tablecloth
- Utensils

Hiker and Collector

- Backpack
- Binoculars
- Bird or butterfly ID book
- Bottles of sunscreen (empty or filled with water)
- Hiking boots
- Hiking hats
- Hiking shorts
- Insect net
- Toy animals to be observed

Teacher/Naturalist

- Books about plants and animals
- Construction paper
- Pencils
- Ranger hat
- Small notebook
- Slate and chalk

Park Ranger/Conservation Officer

- Backpack
- Badge
- Pencil
- Ranger hat
- Small notebook
- Toy whistle
- Toy wild animals

Zookeeper

- Brushes for cleaning animals
- Child-sized broom
- Pretend food for the animals
- Small buckets for water
- Toy zoo animals
- Zookeeper's rubber boots
- Zookeeper's hat
- Zookeeper's uniform

Family Meetings About Science

"Early childhood educators recognize the need for communication and collaboration with parents and families of children. The family meeting format has proven to be an excellent strategy for establishing a reciprocal relationship between home and school. This relationship, once established, enhances a program's positive impact on child development and develops and strengthens home-school connections" (Rockwell & Kniepkamp, 2003).

Hands-on meetings invite the entire family to be a part of the science learning by doing science activities and handling materials in the same way that the children do at school. After attending the meetings, families may be more adept at supporting, modeling, and discussing science with their children.

On the next pages you will find five sample family meetings—one for each of the following science content standard categories: Science as Inquiry; Physical Science; Life Science; Earth and Space Science; and Science and Technology.

The following organizational meeting format includes the information that you need to present a successful meeting. **Note:** Schedule meetings at a time that is convenient for most families. Consider changing the day of the week or time of day of meetings throughout the year to allow for maximum participation. For example, hold your first family meeting on a Thursday evening, the next on a Saturday afternoon, the next on a Tuesday evening, and so on.

- **Content Area(s):** All of the curricular areas that the meeting addresses.
- **Title:** A suggested title for the meeting that is catchy and upbeat and is certain to get the attention of the families.

- **Purpose:** The reason for the meeting and what it will try to accomplish.
- **Invitation:** Information sent to the home at least two weeks in advance to announce the meeting. Provides title, content, date, time (including when the family meeting will end), and location. Also gives a suggestion for the type of dress and contact name for additional information and for making a reservation to attend.
- **Reminder:** A friendly hint to help family members remember the forthcoming meeting, sent home one to three days before the meeting.
- **Nametag:** Used to identify participants and to facilitate station rotation.
- **Mixer:** An activity designed to make the participants feel welcome, get acquainted with each other, and set a fun, relaxing tone for the meeting.
- **Introduction:** Helpful information relating to meeting content and the procedures that will be followed regarding initial station assignment and rotation procedure.
- **Stations:** Areas that are set up where families participate in hands-on activities, following a time schedule. A signal (bell, whistle, and so on) is given when it is time to move to the next station. There are four stations for each of the meetings presented. Each station is titled, has a list of materials needed, advance preparation information, if needed, and step-by-step procedures to be followed by the participants. (The activities listed in each of the following family meetings reference activities in this book.)
- **Evaluation:** Forms that require a simple mark (circling or underlining a character) and also provide space for comments should participants wish to write reactions. The design of the evaluation forms is sensitive to individuals with limited English language proficiency and low literacy skills.
- **Refreshments:** Refreshments are always a hit. They need not be expensive or elaborate. Cookies or pretzels and coffee and juice contribute to the relaxed atmosphere that is conducive to families and teachers sharing and working together as science education partners.

Science as Inquiry Sample Family Meeting
(evening meeting)

Time	Activity	Technique	Resources and Materials
7:00–7:05	Greeting	Greet families as they arrive and distribute nametags.	Nametags, crayons, markers
7:05–7:10	Mixer	Introduce and begin the get-acquainted mixer.	Materials for activity, if needed
7:10–7:20	Briefly explain what Science as Inquiry means.	Explain each of the four activity stations and what the participants will do at each. The color of their nametags designates the station where they begin.	Detailed procedural instructions for each activity written or drawn on tag board and posted at each station
7:20–7:45	Family members go to their designated starting stations.	Family members interact with the materials at each station.	Four stations: Color Scramble, Following Written Directions: by Yourself, Hit the Bucket, and This Is the Longest! It is helpful to have a staff member or a volunteer at each station to answer questions and assist with the activities.
7:45–7:50	Reassemble into large group.	Distribute take-home copies of the activities at each station.	Detailed instructions of each of the four activities, which are in this book.
7:50–8:00	Closing, evaluation, and refreshments	Thank everyone for coming. Distribute evaluation forms and serve refreshments.	Evaluation forms, crayons, and pencils, refreshments

Physical Science Sample Family Meeting
(evening meeting)

Time	Activity	Technique	Resources and Materials
7:00–7:10	Greeting	Greet the families as they arrive. Distribute nametags.	Nametags, crayons, markers
7:10–7:20	Mixer	Welcome everyone. Introduce and begin the mixer.	Materials specific to the mixer chosen
7:20–7:25	Briefly explain what Physical Science is. Tell them that they will do four Physical Science activities tonight.	Explain each of the Physical Science stations and what families will do at those stations. The color on their nametags designates the station where they start.	Write and post step-by-step procedures to be followed by the participants at each station.
7:25–7:55	Family members proceed to their assigned station and begin the activity.	Families work at each station until a signal (bell, or flick of a light switch) signifies that it is time to move clockwise to the next station.	Four stations: Toss a Shape, The Nose Knows, Magnet Hunt, and Slushy in a Bag. Participants can use this latter activity as a snack station
7:55–8:05	Reassemble as a large group.	Distribute copies of the Physical Science activities that were at each station.	Copies of directions for the four activities taken from the book.
8:05–8:15	Closing, evaluation, and refreshments	Thank everyone for coming. Distribute evaluation forms and serve refreshments.	Evaluation forms, crayons, and pencils

Life Science Sample Family Meeting (afternoon meeting)

Time	Activity	Technique	Resources and Materials
1:00	Greeting	Greet families as they arrive. Hand out nametags	Nametags, pencils, pens, crayons
1:00–1:10	Mixer	Introduce and begin the mixer.	Materials for activity
1:10–1:20	Explain what Life Science is. Introduce the four Life Science hands-on activities that they will do this afternoon.	Explain each of the four Life Science work stations. Tell them that the color on their nametag designates the station where they will begin. Explain that detailed instructions are located at each table.	Write and post step-by-step procedures to be followed by the participants at each station. You may want to have a volunteer at each station to clarify the instructions should you feel it necessary.
1:20–1:50	Family members proceed to their assigned station. They work at each station until a signal (bell) is given to signify that it is time to move clockwise to the next station.	Family members interact with the materials at each work station.	Four stations: Time to Mime, Leaf Banners, Fuzzy Seed Art, and Leaf Match
1:50–2:00	Reassemble into a large group.	Wrap up the meeting. Distribute copies of the Life Science activities that were at each station.	Detailed instructions of the four activities that were taken from this book.
2:00–2:10	Closing, evaluation, and refreshments	Distribute evaluation forms; serve refreshments; thank everyone for coming and invite them to the next meeting.	Evaluation forms, pens, crayons or pencils

Earth and Space Science Sample Family Meeting (evening meeting)

Time	Activity	Technique	Resources and Materials
7:00–7:10	Greeting	As families arrive, greet them and distribute nametags.	Nametags, crayons, or other appropriate markers
7:10–7:15	Mixer	Introduce and begin a get-acquainted mixer.	Materials for activity
7:15–7:25	Briefly explain what Earth Science entails. Introduce the Earth Science activities.	Discuss each of the three Earth Science stations and what the families will do at them. Explain that the color of their nametags designates which station they will start at. They will work at each station for a designated amount of time. At the signal (a bell or music) they will move clockwise to the next station.	Write and post detailed step-by-step instructions at each station.
7:25–7:55	Family members proceed to their assigned station and begin the activity.	Families do the activities at each station.	Three stations: A Settling Experience, Coloring and Mixing Sand, and Concrete. Pie tins disposable cake pans for concrete forms.
7:55–8:00	Reassemble as a large group.	Distribute take-home copies of the Earth Science activities that the families completed.	Copies of the three activities, taken from this book.
8:00–8:10	Closing, evaluation, and refreshments	Thank everyone for coming. Distribute evaluation forms and serve refreshments.	Evaluation forms, crayons, pencils, refreshments

Science and Technology Sample Family Meeting (morning meeting)

Time	Activity	Technique	Resources and Materials
10:00–10:05	Greeting	Greet families as they arrive and distribute nametags.	Nametags, pens
10:05–10:15	Mixer	Explain procedure to be followed in the get-acquainted mixer.	Materials for activity
10:15–10:20	Briefly explain what Technology is and the objective of this family meeting.	Describe each of the four Technology stations and what they will do at each station. Tell them that the color on their nametags designates the station where they will start.	Write and post detailed step-by-step procedures to be followed by the participants at each station.
10:20–10:50	Family members proceed to their assigned stations and begin the activities.	Families work at each station until a signal is sounded to tell them that it is time to move clockwise to the next station.	Four outdoor stations: Balancing Collections, Big Step Measuring, Can You Make a House? and Forceps Forage.
10:50–10:55	Reassemble in a large group.	Distribute take-home copies of the activities from each station.	Copies of activities from the book
10:55–11:10	Closing, evaluation, and refreshments	Thank everyone for coming. Distribute evaluation forms and serve refreshments.	Evaluation forms, crayons, pencils, and refreshments

Index